Abraham Berinyuu

Healing Rituals as Theological Drama

Religionsethnologie

Band 1

LIT

Abraham Berinyuu

Healing Rituals as Theological Drama

Insights from Kaaba Healing Rituals Among the Frafra in Ghana

LIT

Cover Picture: Abraham Berinyuu

Bibliographic information published by the Deutsche Nationalbibliothek
The Deutsche Nationalbibliothek lists this publication in the Deutsche Nationalbibliografie; detailed bibliographic data are available in the Internet at http://dnb.d-nb.de.

ISBN 978-3-8258-9940-0
Zugl.: University of Edinburgh, Dept. of Practical Theology and Christian Ethics, Diss., 1995: *A Study of the Frafra Healing Rituals of Kaaga and their Implication for a Practical Theology of Healing in Ghana*

A catalogue record for this book is available from the British Library

Auslieferung/Verlagskontakt:
Fresnostr. 2 48159 Münster
Tel. +49 (0)251–62 03 20 Fax +49 (0)251–23 19 72
e-Mail: lit@lit-verlag.de http://www.lit-verlag.de

Distributed in the UK by: Global Book Marketing, 99B Wallis Rd, London, E9 5LN
Phone: +44 (0) 20 8533 5800 – Fax: +44 (0) 1600 775 663
http://www.centralbooks.co.uk/acatalog/search.html

Distributed in North America by:

Transaction Publishers
New Brunswick (U.S.A.) and London (U.K.)

Transaction Publishers
Rutgers University
35 Berrue Circle
Piscataway, NJ 08854

Phone: +1 (732) 445 - 2280
Fax: + 1 (732) 445 - 3138
for orders (U. S. only):
toll free (888) 999 - 6778
e-mail:
orders@transactionspub.com

TABLE CONTENTS

PREFACE

Before the Frafra become Christians, they use their mythic world as an interpretative mechanism in times of sickness through the symbolic representation of kaaba. When they become Christians and they fall sick, they are torn between returning to their old mythic world which they used to deal with their experiences of sickness represented in kaaba, or being faithful to Western Christian ministry of healing which does not use their mythic world. Indeed in many instances the Church practice of conversion seeks to wipe out the mythic world the came with to the Christian faith.

The use of Frafra mythic world as an interpretative mechanism in times of sickness through the symbolic representation of kaaba is of central significance to the Frafra of the Upper East Region of Ghana.

Therefore a Frafra Christian ministry of healing has to begin with the Frafra understanding of their experiences of sickness and healing represented in kaaba in their mythic world. This seeks to share some insights into how the Frafra use their mythic world in their understanding of their experiences of sickness in kaaba, before we can determine how a contextualised Frafra Christian ministry of healing will be like. In this project three objectives were set.

The first objective was to conduct among non Christian Frafra an empirical research into the nature of kaaba and how they use their mythic world as an interpretative mechanism represented in kaaba.

The second objective was to determine how their views of the traditional mythic worlds of their cultural background. In order to achieve these objectives, we developed an interdisciplinary qualitative research approach, utilizing perspectives from social and human sciences, studies in primal ‘ religions and Christian theology. The methods of data collection included participant observations, case studies, accounts of healings, interviews, and oral histories from village elders.

The third objective was to use a contextual critical theological reflection method to analyze our data. The method of contextual critical theological reflection was used because our overriding goal in this project is how to contextualise Christian ministry of healing to Frafra Christian who fall sick.

Our research found that in times of sickness the Frafra use their mythic world as an interpretative mechanism through kaaba to invoke their belief in the interconnectedness of the spiritual, social, psychological, and the cultural in which humans can mediate or transfer spiritual powers to heal. There is also a central role of confession in kaaba. For the Frafra, kaaba is a symbolic representation of their mythic world through which they achieve a sense of the equivalent of the modern concept of well being or the Judaeo-Christian concept of shalom.

Our over-all conclusion is that the area of sickness, ritual and healing is of central significance in the enculturation of Christianity among the Frafra. Therefore a Frafra Christian ministry of healing should seek to mobilize the Frafra mythic world, if such a theology of healing is to be genuinely a Christian Pastoral theology of healing of the Frafra, for the Frafra and by the Frafra Christians.

CHAPTER ONE

Introduction

In this introductory chapter we shall begin with a story, which serves as the background to the hypothesis of this project. A brief review of the present situation in Ghana in particular and Africa in general with respect to healing and theological education will be given.

We shall also briefly offer the Frafra understands of sickness, healing, and health in kaaba, which is the impetus and primary concept of this project. A detailed explanation of kaaba will be given later. In order to undertake the field research necessary for this project, we had to devise appropriate methods for data collection in the field for analysis. These are treated in the relevant sections of the chapter. These methods served to bridge what Panikkar calls the "epistemological distance".[1] The definition of this term will be given later. We are adapting it here to refer to the gap between the researcher and the researched. In this case we need to bridge the gap between the Frafra's understanding of sickness, kaaba, and health in their mythic world and that of mine. As a Frafra, I was raised in the Frafra mythic world. However, my current beliefs on sickness are a composite of the Frafra mythic world, Christianity, Western scientific medicine, and psychology.

We shall follow this section with the findings from our investigations as well as propose a method of doing contextualized pastoral theology. The last section of this chapter provides an overview of the remaining chapters of the thesis.

Pastoral cases leading to Hypothesis Buo is the first convert of the Presbyterian Church in Yela. She is the first wife of her husband and in Frafra culture she occupies a special role in the family. She has three grown up children. The first born is a son who farms with his father. By virtue of being the first son he also has a special role and authority. He is the first heir to the family property as we as custodian of the family tradition when his father dies. Her second child is a woman who has married in another village. The third child is now a teacher in the local primary school.

One day, Buo woke up at dawn with a severe headache. She sent for Peter, the local lay leader of the Church who also called me, as he was aware of my research. Peter's wife sells aspirin in the village, so he took some of the aspirin with him. On arrival it was obvious that Buo was in pain. Peter gave her the aspirin to take immediately.

Meanwhile, her son, who is a teacher, was busy dressing up to send Buo to the regional hospital about ten miles away. Her husband and her first son insisted that she was so seriously sick that unless they called the traditional specialists and also performed the ancestral kaaba immediately she would die before reaching the hospital. While these arguments were going on and tempers rising, Buo looked at Peter and me for a few seconds, bowed down and wept.

There are so many complex and varied issues in this story, which form the basis of the hypothesis and motivation of this research. We will only pick the most poignant issue to illustrate the importance of this project. Buo's look at peter and me, the bowing down and weeping are three different actions but carry one important message to the church to offer a contextualized pastoral response to predicaments. In these three actions Buo is asking the church questions of identity: Who am I, and where do I belong? At a theological level Buo's actions ask the question: who can deliver me? Indeed, Buo's is symbolically asking the church to justify its claims in the midst of conflicting claims in a life threatening situation. What we saw was typical of the everyday experiences of many Frafra Christians rather than an exception.

From the perspective of a contextual pastoral theologian, Buo's actions are asking the church to come forth with a pastoral hermeneutic that can help her bridge the gap between her mythic world and what the Church preaches in order that she can experience well-being or wholeness. In our view the situation among the Frafra Christians calls for the kind of hermeneutic defined by Panikkar. According to Panikkar, "Hermeneutic is the art and science of interpretation, of bringing forth significance, of conveying meaning, of restoring symbols to life and eventually of letting new symbols emerge."[2] This kind of hermeneutic Panikkar suggests, " … is the method of overcoming the distance between a knowing subject and an object to be known, once the two have been estranged".[3]

In this case, the knowing subject is the contextual pastor who is very knowledgeable in Western Theology, scientific medicine, and psychology. The object to be known is Buo's experience of sickness, kaaba and health according to her Frafra mythic world.

It is obvious from Frafra Christians like Buo that they do not come to the Christian faith as empty containers. Busia made an important observation worth quoting here:

> The converts come with such knowledge of, beliefs and assumptions about nature, society and God as their culture offers them. These go to the root of life as well as seeking to give meaning to the whole of life, in this world and hereafter.[4]

This "knowledge of, beliefs and assumptions about nature, society and God" which they use to achieve liberation, wholeness, sharing and caring in love is what we call the interpretative functions of the indigenous mythic world.

The mythic world relates symbols and experience in order to interpret their meaning. It is the basis for the formation of collective and personal value systems and the application of those value systems in different situation. It can use the old symbols to interpret new symbols and experiences. It can simultaneously also use new symbols and experiences to transform the old symbols and experience. In other words, it is collective as well as personal and dynamic. Its interpretative functions are interconnected. The mythic world is the conceptual basis of identification, association, and interpretation of symbolic images, and events and the raison d'etre of life in a given community sharing this mythic world. It enables persons to experience life in its totality.

Hypothesis

our hypothesis is that the interpretative functions of the Frafra mythic world symbolically represented in kaaba are central to the Frafra experiences of sickness, healing and wholeness. Therefore in order to offer the Frafra Christians a contextualized Christian holistic ministry of healing, one must firstly seek to understand the interpretative functions of their mythic world symbolically represented in kaaba, and, secondly, use those insights to mobilize the mythic world to construct a contextual Christian ministry of healing.

Throughout this book we shall use sickness to include disease, and illness. Our reason is that to apply Western scientific medical distinctions will not require only medical training which we do not have but also specialized knowledge of tropical categories of sickness, illness, and disease. We have also used mostly the Frafra categories without trying to translate them into their Western scientific medical equivalent categories for the reasons already stated.

We set three tasks, which we deemed imperative for a contextualized Frafra Christian pastoral theologian who hopes to offer the Frafra Christians a holistic contextualized ministry of healing. Theses are:

1. The theoretical and practical task of devising appropriate empirical methods of field research.
2. Understanding how the Frafra use their mythic world as a source and resource for dealing with their experience of sickness, ritual and healing.
3. Exploring ways in which the results of such a study help us to construct a contextualized Frafra Christian ministry of healing.Justification of Hypothesis

The Christian faith was exported to Frafraland with no respect for, or recognition of the Frafra traditions. The Christian Church also came with Western medical healing systems. The irony is that the Christian Church has not only refused to recognize Frafra ways of healing but also neglected to integrate the Christian rituals with the Western healing system that they brought to Frafraland. The aspirin represents Western scientific medical healing system. Peter and I represent the Church. Her husband and her first born represent kaaba. These threes roles have become confused and diffused. This confusion has been compounded by the fact that the Church hitherto has not taken seriously the Frafra mythic world, which the Frafra people bring with them to the Christian faith. The danger of not taking that world seriously is well expressed by Panikkar. He writes:

> To cross the boundaries of one's own culture without realizing that another culture may have a radically different approach to reality is today no longer admissible. If still consciously done, it would be philosophically naïve, politically outrageous and religiously sinful.[5]

These three offences have been committed in Ghana in general and in Frafraland in particular. However, recently there have been various attempts made by grass roots Christian and Western trained theologians to offer relevant contextualized pastoral responses.

Some of the most recent significant contextualized pastoral responses have led to the observation by Hollenweger that "Ghanaian Christians seem to be particularly interested in the contributions of traditional African healers to health and welfare and especially Christian pastoral."[6] He mentions kofi Appiah-Kubi and Emmanuel Yartekwei Lartey as two leading researchers who have drawn attention to this important Field.[7]

We seek in this thesis to join in this important search of the Church to offer a contextualized Christian pastoral hermeneutic to Ghanaian Christians with respect to the Christian ministry of healing. However, we realize that the Ghana context is both Ghanaian and African as well. So we shall also seek in this thesis to engage the general African Christian quest and questions of contextualized Christian ministry of healing of the Church in Africa.

The Evidence that Demands Verdict

We shall provide here the evidence for our claim that the three offences were committed and because of these offences Ghanaian Christian like Buo are calling upon the Church to justify its claims and existence.

Between April 12-16, 1967, a consultation on the healing ministry of the Church was held in Trinity College, Legon, Ghana. The medical workers of Church hospitals requested the consultation. The doctors and nurses who were working in these mission hospitals were frustrated by the lack of clear guidance by or the meaningful participation of pastors in the offering of holistic healing in Church clinics and hospitals. They were also frustrated because they realized that there was a gap between their Western medical healing systems and the kind of healing which grassroots Ghanaians were expecting from them. The proceedings of this consultation were published in the Ghana Bulletin of Theology (1967)[8] Huppenbauer, then a lecturer at Trinity College, and Verstraelen, a Roman Catholic Church missionary wrote:

> ... For many of the theologians it was the first time they were forced to think about the healing task of the Church. For them the consultation may have been aHealthy exercise in re-assessing their theological Outlook.[9]

This startling admission of these missionary theologians at the heart of missionary-founded Churches' theological education clearly shows how little the role of the indigenous mythic worlds seemed to played in the Churches' preparation of ministers for the ministry of healing.

In this consultation, two papers focused on how the ministry of healing could be integrated into both theological education and medical education respectively. We shall consider both here. They are evidence of the fact that the offences were committed because of the existence of the "epistemological distance". Hence, there is the need for a contextualized Christian pastoral hermeneutic.

Gastel's article on the healing ministry in theological centers rightly suggests that a theological education without an emphasis on healing is incomplete. [10] One of his reasons is that the inclusion of healing in theological education enables students to co-operate with medical personnel in their hospitals, clinics, and maternity homes. These theological students could make appeals for money for medical purposes. Furthermore, they could pay regular visits to the infirm to comfort and pray for them. [11] They should also convince people, if need be from the pulpit, that Ghanaians should take their children and relatives to the hospital as soon as they fall sick.[12] His reason for wanting the pastors to convince sick people to go to hospital is that in the Ghanaian society "many people, for no reason whatsoever are scared of hospitalization, because they believe that the western type doctor can do nothing about certain types of disease."[13]

It is clear from the above quote that Gastel does not seem to understand or even appreciate the meaning of sickness and health in the mythic worlds of Ghanaians. His other reason for involving theological students in healing further justifies the need for this project. For Gastel, theological students can "help eradicate such thinking."[14] As if is not aware that he is contradicting himself, he goes on to say that there is a need to gain "insight into indigenous medicine and traditional modes of treating patients, [because] many Ghanaians have wonderful knowledge of the use of herbs and plants in general purposes."[15]

The fact that Gastel sees the need to teach the ministry about healing in theological centers is very important. However, it seems Gastel cannot decide what to do with Ghanaian traditional notions of healing which are part of their mythic world. On the one hand he states that theological students can help the healing ministry by teaching Ghanaians to eradicate their traditional beliefs.

On the other hand, he admits that Ghanaians do have good knowledge of dealing with sickness that is of relevance to even Western scientific medicine.

Gastel seems to be interested only in the bio-chemical value of the herbs in indigenous healing which he probably equates to the same functions as drugs in Western medicine with no regard to the holistic nature of Ghanaian traditional healing. Our data in later chapters has shown that the distinction between medicine and religion does not exist in the traditional healing system.

Huppenbauer on his part admits how little the ministry of healing featured in the theological training at his time in Trinity College. He claims that different aspects of 'health', 'disease' and 'healing' were treated in "different theological disciplines". This is done, he believes, in a form suggested by the text book, and is, therefore done often with a typically "Western philosophical approach to the whole problem."[16]

He also claims that the final year students of Trinity College of his time, in their discussions of the theme of the Lordship of Jesus Christ in New Testament studies, gave rise to questions of Lordship with respect to Ghanaians' fear of evil spirits and powers.[17]

He further recalls that the discussions were of interest to the students. We can infer here that matters of healing were of some importance to his theological students. This interest and the fact that they did not apparently address it also suggest a gap between the mythic world of the Ghanaian theological students and that of the missionary imported theological education with respect to healing.

Hupperbauer himself seems to recognize this gap and the need to bridge it when hesitates that the teaching of the healing ministry in theological colleges was not a matter of "additional courses only".[18] Instead, such "courses must be given in the form of a visibly effective co-operation of specialists in different disciplines, such as medicine, sociology, psychiatry and theology."[19] Although we agree with the above suggestion, it will not fully bridge the gap if these disciplines are looked at from Western perspectives without any reference to Ghanaian mythic worlds.

Otoo, then professor at the Ghana Medical School, also added another perspective on the teaching of the ministry of healing in medical sxhool.[20] For

Otoo, the healing ministry "requires certain definite qualities of personality which can only be acquired through Christian discipline."[21] He therefore poses the question: how can a secular government run a medical school and ask students to practice this Christocentric ministry of healing without implying that students should be Christians? He also questions whether there is a "sufficient body of knowledge about the ministry of healing to earn it a respectable place in the curriculum of a medical school". [22] He concludes, therefore, that the teaching the ministry of healing in a medical school is necessary but only possible if the medical school is wholly owned by the Church in which there is a "free hand for Christian influences over and above the academic dictates of the medical curriculum."[23]

Both Huppenbauer and Otoo seem to emphasize a dialogue between Christocentric healing ministry and Western scientific medicine in Ghana to the exclusion of the traditional Ghanaian healing system. What they seem to lose sight of in their approaches is that if this dialogue does not include the traditional mythic worlds' understanding of religion and medicine such a dialogue will be meaningless to Ghanaians who are supposed to benefit from such dialogue. In other words, it is still a Western dialogue conducted on Ghanaian participation.

Otoo on his part seems to imply that it is all right for a Ghanaian Christian to study Western scientific medicine but it is not all right for a Ghanaian Christian to study indigenous healing systems as if both are mutually exclusive.

In our judgment there is an urgent need for Ghanaian pastors and Western scientific medical practitioners to collaborate in their efforts to study seriously indigenous healing systems if they are to offer holistic healing to Ghanaians in general and Ghanaian Christians in particular. But such collaboration has to be based on a sound knowledge of how Ghanaians use their mythic worlds in their experience of sickness, healing and health.

Another landmark consultation on theological education in Africa was held in Legon, Ghana from 21st-27th July, 1986. The programme for theological education (PTE) of the world Council of Churches and the West African Association of Theological Institutions (WAATI) jointly organized this consultation. The papers delivered and the conclusions of the workshops are contained in Ministerial Formation (1986). [24] For items were the focuses of this consultation. These were (1) theology, theological education, and the

Church (2) continuity and change in theological education, (3) ecumenical perspective and dimensions of theological education and (4) the funding of theological education.

In his contribution on theology, theological education and the Church, the then secretary of WAATI made a relevant observation on theological education in Africa as quoted by Pobee, which is worth considering. Pobee reports that the secretary observed that in Africa, ' theological students want degrees to raise their own social status and to improve their financial prospects, while Church leaders are preoccupied above all with consolidating their own institutions and, very often, their own positions within them."[25]

Our interest in this statement is not so much whether it is true or false, but rather how theological education seems to be conducted for these goals with little or no reference to the Africans and their social-cultural, socio-political and economic contexts. Pobee posed the following appropriate questions:

> When and under what circumstances and by what criteria should the structures evolved in the colonial Church be dispensed with and give way to new models? ... what are the true indices of theological excellence? Which textbooks?[26]

We believe that the answers to these questions will come by first investigating the mythic worlds these African Christians bring to the Christian faith. This view seems to be supported by Amirtham. He observed that:

> ... there are certain gifts that God has lavishly showered on African peoples, which clearly only they can bring into the Kingdom. African spirituality, African communitarian life, African experience of the Spirit, to mention only a few. Black is beautiful, is a new discovery and a new identity, a gift of Africa to the dialogue of cultures. God's rainbow of grace includes all colures and shades. The ecumenical spectrum needs Africa to complete its wholeness.[27]

The overwhelming conclusion of the consultation was that African theological education is predominantly modeled after the Northern imported church, ministry and theological education. As these Northern models, received through the missionary era, become so "idolized", it needs courage to change them or even abandon them. Yet this also means the kinds of ecclessiologies inherited need to change in order for the new theological changes to make any serious impact. The conclusions from these consultations provided evidence that the offences were committed, that the "epistemological distances" exist, and that there is an urgent need for a contextualized Christian pastoral hermeneutic with respect to the Churches ministries of healing throughout Africa in general and Ghana in particular.

Since we have established that the offences were committed because of the "epistemological distances" created, our suspicion is that one source of the problem and solutions to the dual systems syndrome may be traced to the kinds of method and nature of the paradoxical role of the indigenous mythic world or what is referred to as culture in theological education which produces the ministers who teach and nurture Ghanaian Christians. We suspect that the degree to which these pastors are able or unable to help their parishioners bridge the gap between indigenous mythic worlds and Western inherited Christianity partially reflects on the method and nature of the paradoxical role of indigenous mythic worlds in the theological education these ministers receive. Therefore, there is some correlation between the method of incorporating culture in theological education and the pastoral attempts to bridge the gap between indigenous mythic worlds and Western Christianity.

There is an urgent need for a critically well thought out process of engaging Ghanaian indigenous mythic worlds with the Christian faith in theological education. This process has to begin with a careful and critical "reflection on both the received model of theological education and the receptor context for which a new model and method are to be evolved."[28] The viability and relevance of such a process is only possible if Africans, in the words of Ukpong, " look inwards into [their] culture for insights as a new sense of direction and a new pattern for a contextualized model of theological education".[29]

This research primarily seeks to explore the viability and relevance of such a model of contextualization by first attempting to gain insights into the interpretative functions of indigenous mythic worlds. For if the mythic world is the source and resource for dealing with life threatening situations such as sickness, then we believe that a Christian ministry of healing "manufactured" elsewhere with some other mythic world cannot be imported wholesale and offered to Frafra Christian converts. Secondly, we will use these insights to propose a hermeneutic of a contextualized Frafra Christian ministry of healing.

Furthermore, the interpretation of symbols in Christian liturgy is inseparably related to the Christian mythic world and the mythic worlds of both Western missionaries and other Ghanaians involved in the Christian ministries of healing. The Frafra Christian converts do not share the same mythic worlds with neither the Western missionaries nor some of the other Ghanaian pastors. How then do we expect the symbols of these liturgies to have the same meaning for the Frafra?

Almost all pastoral theologians will agree with Lartey that the "Church was commissioned by Christ to continue a healing ministry that would point to and embody God's continued care for the people in the world."[30] The questions the Frafra Christian converts like Buo are asking are: firstly, what is the church, and secondly, can the church apply universal criteria in the practice of Christian healing? Whose mythic worlds and whose symbols does the Church use as normative for carrying out such a ministry of healing? Is it ever possible to have a universal normative Christian ministry of healing based on universal symbols from a universal mythic world to carry out the Church's contextualized ministry of healing? Does what the Church defines as Sickness, healing and health necessarily reflect Frafra Christians' views or experiences of sickness, healing and health? Can the Church offer a contextualized Christian ministry of healing that reflects the socio-cultural, psycho-spiritual and socio-Political context of Frafra Christian converts? What type of symbol does the Church use to construct a liturgy which communicates God's love and power to Frafra Christians when they are sick?

These questions have arisen out of a critical reflection upon my own background as a Frafra, and a pastor, as well as my ministry among the frafra Christians like Buo, other Ghanaian Christians, other Christians of different cultures, race, sex, and confessions, and from a critical review of African literature on how to indigenise the Christian ministry especially the ministry of healing in Africa.

The outcome of my reflection in my journey of self-discovery is that the Church can offer a contextualized Frafraf Christian ministry of healing to Frafra Christians who fall sick. Consequently, this research was solely devoted to seeking an understanding of the interpretative function of the Frafra mythic world in kaaba. We then used the insights from such understanding to construct a contextualized Frafra Christian ministry of healing.

There are also compelling reasons from the irreversible changes taking place among the Frafra that necessitate this project. Frafraland and the Frafra are no longer the isolated and insulated villages and people they might have been a hundred years ago. Frafraland, and the Frafra are going through irreversible changes. Indeed, the Frafra are going through what Malinowski calls "tripartite division."

Malinowski observes that throughout Africa there is a tripartite division which is made up of "old Africa" "imported Europe and North American", and the "new composite culture." [31] Consequently, there are three subcultures in this tripartite division. The Frafra, Christians and non-Christians, move in and out of these subcultures. These subcultures are a "compound" or "mixture" or "fusion" of two cultural influences.[32] The "compound" refers to a situation where people hold to the traditional world view, while the "mixture refers to where they mix the "old" and "new". The "fusion" suggests that there is no distinction between the "new" and the "old". Such a tripartite situation poses an even greater problem of a pastoral theological researcher because it is not easy to know where to start.

As already indicated we take the view in this research that we should first try to understand the parent indigenous mythic world which the Frafra use as an interpretative mechanism in their experiences of sickness, ritual and healing and which becomes the primary point of reference when they encounter the new Christian faith.

Fortes investigated the influences of modernity on the Frafra by what he calls contact agents like a dispensary at Zuarungu[33], the then Administrative Capital of the Frafra and found the following. Between 1924 and 1928 the dispensary treated between two hundred and three hundred patients who were mostly civil servants and their families from the south of Ghana. Between 1928 and 1929 "many Frafra people started attending the clinic with complaints of various types of infectious diseases."[34] Fortes attributes this to the "energetic propaganda of the resident medical officer."[35]

According to Fortes [36], while the dispensary has completely displaced the native treatment for yaws, which was lengthy, expensive and unreliable, it has not "influenced the rest of native medicine, which is based on magical principles, either in its technique or in its pharmacopoeia."[37] It can be inferred from the conclusion of this study that the Frafra were selective in what they took from the modern dispensary because some of the Western medical diagnoses were incongruent with those of their mythic world.

The urgent need for the Church to offer a carefully and critically thought-out and relevant Christian ministry of healing to Frafra Christians has also become an imperative due to other recent trends in Frafraland. For example, some Islamic healers known as "mallams" are known to write some verses of the Koran on either paper and/or leather and sell them to those in need. The belief is that these words from the Koran can offer them protection against some spiritual attacks as well help them succeed in their business. These "mallams", who combine Islam and traditional healing, are also readily available for consultation. The concept and function of the healing offered by the "mallam" in Northern Ghana are well articulated by Mbillah.[38]

In the past the traditional healers sat and waited for the sick to come and consult them. At times some of them were even reluctant to go and perform healing rituals. Those who did would not ask for any reward until the sick were completely healed. Nowadays, some traditional healers openly sell their healing powers and herbs in the market and lorry stations. Indeed the increasingly commercialized traditional healing powers and herbs are becoming the fastest growing medico-religious healing businesses in Frafraland today. The influxes of these different, and often conflicting healing systems, are creating a corresponding increase in demands for these services among the Frafra. The Frafra people, both Christians and non-Christians, are constantly shopping for one type of medico-religious healing or another. The deplorable socio-economic conditions and deteriorating modern health services and facilities are also contributing to this spree of shopping for one type of healing or another.

The above situation in Frafraland is compelling the Christian Church as a whole and the missionary-founded Churches in particular to justify their claims about the power of liberation, and wholeness in the Gospel of Jesus Christ. Our contention is that the basis of a uniquely Christian Frafra ministry of healing to the Frafra Christians in times of sickness has to come from insights from a study of the interpretative functions of their mythic world symbolically represented in kaaba.

Frafra Notions of *Kaaba*:

Kaaba is a difficult and complex phenomenon to define and explain in English. In fact, it is even a difficult task for the native Frafra speakers to explain what they mean by it. It seems to pervade all aspects of Frafra life and rituals. Everything in life involves some form of *kaaba*. Before embarking on a journey, hunting or fishing, starting a farm and harvesting *kaaba* is performed.

Life; sickness, healing and health are only defined by forms of *kaaba*. *Kaaba* are the raison d'etre of the Frafra religion, sociology, psychology and ethics. For the Frafra, life is *kaaba* and *kaaba* is life. The meaning and role of Frafra *kaaba* is equivalent to the concept of well being or the Judaeo-Christian notion of *shalom*.

The word *kaaba* is a verb. It is used to describe and interpret different experiences of life. The Frafra perform *kaaba* as both a medical treatment and religious act in the holistic sense. It also has different meanings and purposes. The following are some examples of how *kaaba* pervade all aspects of Frafra life. These examples also show why it is difficult to convey/translate adequately the Frafra notion of kaaba into English.

The Frafra perform *kaaba* for good harvest at the beginning of the farming season, during game expeditions, business undertakings, or any other task. there are also *kaaba* of praises and thanksgiving for successfully accomplishing the various tasks listed above. Furthermore, there are *kaaba* for successful marriages, pregnancies and safe deliveries of new babies. *Kaaba* are what anthropologist might call "rites of passage".

Kaaba, as used in the above situations have similarities with types of prayer in the Christian tradition. *Kaaba* in these situations can imply either prayers of petition, confession or thanksgiving.

There is also a medical usage of this word. When someone is sick and the initial first aid called muuha (plural) (a mixture of dried herbs in the form of balls) does not bring relief, then they ask for *kaaba* from someone in the village who specializes in treating that kind of sickness. The advice most members of the family and the community give is "kika ba kaab" (let them treat it). In these situations kaab may be defined as treat, heal or cure.

There is another word in Frafra that may be a synonym the English words like treat, heal or cure. That word is *teb*. It is used as both a noun and a verb. As a noun it means a male or female healer. *Teb* as a verb connotes the idea of struggling by kicking one's feet. The implication here is that the healer and the sickness are engaged in battle.

A third word, which is used, is *belem*. This is the word Fortes translates as prayer.[39] *Belem* literally means beg, pleas, ask for favours. So *belem* translated as prayer in this case can only refer to prayers of petition. But as we have seen *kaaba* includes other forms of prayer. That is also why one cannot use one Christian meaning of prayer to refer to all types of *kaaba.* The Frafra use *teb* and *kaaba* as verbs interchangeably. So it was difficult to tell whether or not one uses *kaaba* or *teb* as an individual preference, or whether the choice of one or the other reflects on the severity of the sickness.

We also observed that it was very common to have many *kaaba* and *teb* for as long as the sickness exists. It was also a common practice for them to combine a number of treatments at the same time. When asked why they did that, the common response was *"nya pu kat taba"* (roots/herbs do not prevent each other from working.

Field research Methodology on Ritual Studies

Our research begins with a critical investigation of how the Frafra use their mythic world, symbolically represented in *kaaba*, as an interpretative mechanism in their experiences of sickness. But we had to devise an appropriate approach that would enable us to enter the Frafra mythic world and obtain the Frafra self-understanding of their experiences of sickness, kaaba and wholeness. For although my helpers and I are Frafra, by virtue of the influences of Western education, Christianity and secularity, we could not presume to experience sickness, healing and health in the same way as those in the village.

In the light of the hypothesis of the research, the complexity of *kaaba* and their central role in all aspects of Frafra life, the holistic nature of the Frafra mythic world and the stated objectives of the field research, we developed an interdisciplinary qualitative research approach utilizing perspectives from social and human sciences, studies in primary religions, phenomenology of religion, and Christian theology and clinical pastoral education. However, we did not assume that social and human sciences' interests are necessarily the same as those of Christian pastoral theology or a contextual Christian pastoral theologian. We had to pose two questions: (i) what do social and human scientists and theologians have in common? (ii) how do they also differ with regard to the methods they devise to the study of rituals in general and the study of Frafra kaaba in particular?

Bourdillon suggests that social anthropology and theology have a long tradition of studying the ritual of sacrifice. For him sacrifice is at the centre of many cultures of the world and is a main theme in the Christian understanding of humanity's relationship with God through Christ's death.[40]

In the study of the ritual of sacrifice, begin their investigations with animal sacrifices and analyze the meanings of the sacrifices in various cultures.[41] One of the aims of the theologian is to gain anthropological insights and use those insights to construct a theology. A case in point is the theories of substitution and atonement in Christian theology. We believe that the substitution theory of atonement in Christian theology came out of an effort to indigenize Judaism and Christianity in the cultures of the Ancient Neat East, [42] and Judaeo-Hellenistic cultures.

The other thing that theologians and anthropologists have in common is that they both try to analyze their data with the help of other theories or general principles.[43] They can collaborate with each other in some cases to some degree. Yet they also have clear areas of differences. According to Bourdillon, the difference between the anthropologist and theologian does not lie with "theoretical methods of analysis as in the evaluation of communication which analytical interpretation reveals."[44]

The difference is that the task of theologians is to: analyze and adjust the symbolic system of their tradition in order to probe problem areas and to remove inconsistencies, both inconsistencies internal to the system and inconsistencies between the systems as it has been received and contemporary experience.[45]

Social anthropological investigations in non-Western cultures especially in Africa, have always taken seriously the relationship between the mythic world and rituals.[46] So we believe a practical theologian insights from these methods of investigation and analyses from social sciences.

We believe that by its very nature a contextual pastoral theologian's task is to create a dialogue with all disciplines and religions. However, in the dialogue, a contextual Christian pastoral theologian should, in the words of Radcliffe, "attempt to discern the significance and meaning of events."[47] This does not mean that a theologian "will be [so] utterly indifferent to all possible explanations of religious phenomena that are none of his business"[48]

Some sociological explanations can change or even correct some theological explanations. Radcliff offers some examples of areas in which sociological explanations benefit theology:

"Sociology can free theologians from the tyranny of the past ... by showing how the theological statements of his tradition are in fact formulated in languages that reflect the social structures of quite different societies. Then he is liberated from naïve biblical or dogmatic literalism."[49.] The various forms of liberation, black, feminist and indigenous theologies[50] also offer poignant examples of ways in social anthropological explanations can serve theological interests.

We further believe that there is an inseparable unity between the social, the spiritual and the cultural which reflects itself in the unity between symbols, ritual and the mythic world. Such a unity justifies the use of an interdisciplinary method in our investigation and analysis of the data.

Field Research Design

We designed multi-disciplinary qualitative research methods informed by other qualitative research designs[51], and clinical pastoral education methods of data collection such as verbatim.

The Conclusions from our research

The insights of *kaaba* healing as ritual systems through symbolic representation have enormous potentials for constructing a contextualized Frafra Christian ministry of healing. The Frafra oral diagnostic manuals and healing are symbolic construction of Frafra mythic world. The entire ritual system creates a "subjunctive" world in which their mythic world can perform its interpretative functions in times of sickness. A metacommunication between the healer, the sick and the entire community is a necessary condition for the interpretative process between healer, patients and the entire community. The themes of confession as a cathartic exercise, the themes of creation and recreation or renewal, solidarity, of the priest-healer when expressed within the context of yir have much to enrich the Christian ministry of healing to the Frafra Christian converts.

The Frafra believe that sickness is caused by a spiritual contagion in the form of viruses, bacteria and/ physical harm such as a falling branch of a tree hitting somebody. They also believe that humans are agents of spiritual powers who have the ability to mediate and transfer other powers. These beliefs have potential for revitalizing not only the traditional theological concept of God, but also a cross-cultural theology of the Holy Spirit and indeed a cross-cultural Christian ministry of healing within the Church. The holistic approach in diagnosis and treatment of sickness in nya healing can contribute in the debate between medicine and theology, Christian medical ethics and ecological ethics, especially in preventing the importation of environmentally damaging industries and life styles into Frafraland.

In all the yaabnam cases they went to the *boar*. Its influences were both particular and universal, as we shall see later in chapter six. In 96% of the cases, which we studied, the *nya, tiim*, and *baanaam* healers were always called to the patients' house. In only 4% of the cases were the patients sent to the healers' house. These were all children. The reason was that the mothers of these children either had difficulties becoming pregnant and/or in some cases had difficulties giving birth. The women were put in the care of a healer they deemed capable of helping them either to become pregnant or to deliver a healthy baby. The contract between the healer and the parents of these babies was that these babies have become adopted by these spiritual powers.

Therefore any time they were sick it was deemed that they should be sent to these healers first. If he cannot heal then he can call another healer. In some cases the children are known by the name of either one of the ancestors of the healer or the spiritual power responsible for the child's well-being. Frafra names such as Tii(tree),Kugre(stone), and Zure(tail) reflect the circumstances that led to their births. These cases seem to be similar to the circumstances leading to the birth of Samson (Judges 13: 1-25), and Samuel (1 Sam. 1:1-28) in the Hebrew Bible.

In such cases these children became adopted spiritual members of those households. This revelation has implications for the Church's pastoral, evangelical, and mission programmes, which usually presume that these programmes are so beneficial to the Frafra that they should come in their numbers. It also has implications for the primary health care programmes of the government. We can infer from our findings that the Church and primary health care workers should go to the people rather than expect them to come to them.

Although the 4% of the cases are few, they demonstrate the significance of the meaning of names, and the use of rituals in maternity clinics. The findings from our study therefore validate the hypothesis of our thesis that the Frafra healing rituals represented in kaaba offer important insights for contextualized Frafra Christian ministry of holistic healing.

The common method of Christian formation is one in which the Christian Gospel is usually filtered through Western philosophies, psychologies, social anthropologies before it encounters indigenous mythic worlds of followers.

We believe that there is a direct correlation between the paradoxical role of culture in theological christian education and the ability of the ministers to help their parishioners deal with some of the issues of conflict between their mythic worlds and inherited Western Christianity.

We are proposing therefore a working pastoral theological method of contextualization in which there is a direct correlation between contextual theological education and contextualized Christian ministry of healing because we believe the two are inseparable.

Contextualized Critical Pastoral Theological Reflection Method

The challenge for the African Church to find an appropriate African method of doing theology from an African perspective is an area of intense and often conflicting theological debates.[53]

Almost all African theologican agree that African Christian theologies do not need to be dressed in Western concepts. This project is an attempt to add a perspective. For we, like others, believe that it is possible to avoid the approaches by means of which African theologies are dressed up in Western concepts. This is not to suggest that African theologies cannot use insights from World Christianity, Western social/human sciences, the sciences of religion and scientific medical healing systems. Rather, African theologians need to develop a clear process of doing theology in Africa with or without using appropriate insights from other disciplines before we can compare and contrast such African Christian theologies with theologies from other contexts.

We advocate an African theological approach similar to the hermeneutic circle of Segundo, with some variations to suit the African contexts. According to Segundo, a hermeneutic circle is a methodology in which there is a "continuing change in our interpretation of the Bible which is dictated by the continuing changes in our present-day reality, both individual and societal."[54]

The worlds "hermeneutic" and "circle" are crucially important for an African theological methodology. For Segundo "hermeneutic" is about the interpretation while "circle" implies the nature of the interpretation in which there is movement back and forth between a given reality and how that reality compels a new interpretation of the word of God. To Segundo there are two preconditions of the hermeneutic circle. Firstly, there is the compelling question raised by the present reality, which might be strong enough to raise the suspicion of previous ideologically biased interpretation of the Bible. Secondly, the new reality must also be equally compelling to question the old interpretation.[55] Our conclusions from the literature review on the African situation in general and the Ghana context in particular together with results form the field study satisfy these preconditions. However, Segundo's hermeneutic circle needs to be modified in order to make it applicable to the African context.

We are more interested in exploring ways through which Segundo's hermeneutic circle can be adapted and modified in order to be relevant to African reality as well as fulfill the task of a contextual Christian pastoral theologian.

One area of concern in Segundo's hermeneutic circle that needs modification is his notion of changing reality. For African theologians in particular, it is dangerous to concentrate solely on the changing situation. As we have consistently argued most African Christians come to the changing or new situation with their old mythic worlds. Furthermore, the changing or new situation lays a foundation for the future. Therefore to concentrate solely on the changing situation, as important as it is, without any consideration of both the old mythic world and the future represents only a partial approach. We suggest, therefore, a theological reflection method, which is contextualized, critical, and pastoral. Contextual critical theological reflection is an attempt to understand and to critically reflect theologically on the process whereby African Christians use their old mythic world to translate the Gospel in such ways that the Christian Gospel can be a resource to help them in times of sickness. It is simultaneously pastoral because its aim is to seek for ways by means of which the Frafra Christians can experience well being, wholeness, and liberation in the gospel of Jesus Christ.

Its precondition is an honest critical engagement. In other words, it must accept and deal with any possible areas of tension or conflict between Biblical Christianity Western social/human sciences and indigenous mythic worlds. The word "translated" is borrowed from Sanneh.[56] It is adopted here to refer to the kind of complex interpretative mechanism that the Frafra mythic world performs in *kaaba*. It also includes the kind of hermeneutic circle that Segundo advocates,[57] with a modification that we take seriously the past mythic world which they bring with them to the Gospel and the goal or future of this encounter in our critical theological reflection.

The contextualized critical pastoral theological reflection method has four stages in its hermeneutic circle adapted from Segundo.[58] The four stages are the processes of the theological reflection necessary in order to construct a contextual Christian pastoral hermeneutic of healing utilising insights from the indigenous mythic worlds.

The first stage of the hermeneutic circle is to try to understand how a mythic world of a given community is used to interpret or make meaning out of everyday encounters. In our case we begin with how the Frafra use their mythic world in *kaaba* to interpret life-threatening situations such as sickness.

The second stage for a contextual Christian pastoral theologian is to understand critically and reflect theologically on how the old mythic world translates the new situation. In the case of the Frafra we were concerned with how they used the symbols from their mythic world to translate the symbols of their new Christian faith in order to achieve wholeness or well being in times of sickness.

In the third stage, the encounters between the old and new mythic worlds become the data upon which to conduct a Frafra Christian pastoral theological reflection. The process of pastoral theological reflection has to seriously take into consideration the emerging mythic world produced by the encounter between the old and new mythic worlds. The fourth stage is to complete the circle by testing these constructed indigenous Frafra Christian ministry of healing and theological education in the Christian community using a model of faith/praxis reflection in the practice of Christian ministry. It is only then that this constructed and tested indigenous Frafra Christian ministry of healing, and method of theological education, can become the pastoral hermeneutical responses, which can fill Panikkar's "epistemological distance". These responses can then join other models from other Christian sojourners from Asia, Europe, North America in the faith and engage in a North to North, South to South, South to North critical dialectic dialogue in the Church's task to present the liberative power of the gospel of Jesus Christ to all of God's people.

In conclusion, we believe that this contextualized, critical, pastoral theological reflection method is capable of creating and maintaining the unity between contextual theological education and contextual practice of Christian ministry, especially the healing ministry, in Ghana.

Preview of Chapters

This project is located both within African theological discourses on the Christ and culture debate in general and African attempts to indigenize the Christian ministry of healing in particular. Therefore, chapter two offers a literature review of theological, social, anthropological, and literary discourses on the encounter of the interpretative function of indigenous mythic worlds and Western Christianity and modernity.

Chapter Three describes the Frafra: their land, culture, and religion. It also describes the various changes taking place in Frafraland today.

Chapter Four decribes and analyse of the data on Frafra diagnostic and classificatory sayings, or what is referred to as traditional oral diagnostic manual and *nya* healing rituals. The focus in the analysis is to show how the Frafra mythic world functions as an interpretative mechanism, which enables the Frafra to experience holistic well-being.

Chapter Five also is a description and analysis of the Frafra self-understanding of the complex *tiim* and *baanaab* healing rituals.

Chapter Six is a description and analysis of *yaabnam kaaba*. Among the Frafra *nya, tiim* and *baanaab* sickness are caused by external invasions of spiritual powers. So nya, tiim and baanaab healing rituals are used to fight and neutralize invasions at the personal level. Hence they can be referred to as personal healing rituals. But these spiritual invasions are only possible because their ancestors have withdrawn their spiritual protective powers or what is also referred to as spiritual immunity against attacks. Therefore, *yaabnam kaaba* are intended to restore these ancestral spiritual powers or spiritual immunity to the entire community. They can also be referred to as community healing rituals.

References

1. R. Panikkar, Myth, Faith and Hermeneutics: Cross-cultural studies (New York: Paulist Press 1979), p. [8]

2. Ibid.

3. Ibid.

4. K.A. Busia, "Has the Christian Faith Been Adequately Presented?" in International Review of Mission, Vol. 50,(1961), p.[87].

5. Panikkar, Myth, Faith and Hermeneutics (1979), p. [8]

6. Walter J. Hollenweger, "African and Western Medicine in Dialogue" in Abraham A. Berinyuu Pastoral Care the Sick in Africa (Frankfurt: Peter Lang 1987), p,[iii]

7. Ibid.

8. The Ghana Bulletin of Theology (GBT) vol. 3 no.2 (June 1967).

9. W. Huppunbaur, and Frans L. Verstraelen, "The healing ministry of the Church" in The GBT vol.3 no.2, (June 1967), p.[2]

10. Van L. Gastel, "Teaching the healing ministry in the theological center" in Theological center" in The GBT vol. 3 no.[3] (Dec. 1967), p. 20-22

11. ibid. p. 20

12. Ibid.

13. Ibid.

14. Ibid.

15. Ibid.

16. Huppenbaur, "Teaching the healing ministry in theological training" The GBT Vol. 3 no. [3] (Dec. 1967), p.22

17. Ibid.

18. Ibid.

19. Ibid.

20. S. Otoo, "Teaching the healing ministry in medical training programme" The GBT Vol. 3 no. [3] (Dec. 1967), p. 24-25

21. ibid. P.24

22. ibid. P.26

23. Ibid.

24. Ministerial Formation vol. 35 (Sept. 1986)

25. John S. Pobee quoting from Bishop Prince Thompson "why are we here? And Quo vadimus?" in Ministerial Formation vol. 35, (Sept. 1986), p.6,7 2

26. Ibid.

27. Samuel Amirtham, "A vision for theological education in Africa" in Ministerial Formation vol. 35 (Sept. 1986), p. 11-12

28. Justin S. Ukpong, " Contextualizing Theological Education in Western Africa: Focus on Subject" in African Christian Studies vol. 3 no 3 (sept. 1987), p.63

29. Ibid.

30. Emmanuel Y. Lartey, " Healing : Tradition and Pentecostalism in Africa Today", International Review of Mission, vol. LXXV, No. 297, (1986), p.75-81.

31. B. Malinowski, "Introduction Essay : "The Anthropology of Changing African Cultures", in Methods of study of Culture Contact in Africa with introductory essay by B. Malinowski (Oxford : Oxford University Press, 1965), p.viii (published for International African Institute).

32. ibid., P..xviii

33. Meyer Fortes, "Culture contact as a dynamic process" in International African Institute <u>Methods of study of Culture Contact in Africa</u> (1965), p 64ff

34. ibid, p.65.

35. Ibid.

36. Ibid.

37. Ibid.

38. Johnson Apenad Mbillah, Islam and culture with Special reference to the role of the Mallamai of Northern Ghana (M.Phil. Thesis University of Birmingham, Dept. of Theology 1990). See also Jack Goody, "Restricted Literacy in Northern Ghana" in Jack Goody (ed.) <u>Literacy in Traditional Society</u> (Cambridge University press 1969) (119-264), p.20

39. Meyer Fortes, <u>Religion, Morality and the Person</u> (1987), p.23

40. M.F.C. Bourdillon, "Introduction" in M.F.C. Bourdillon and Meyer Fortes, (eds.) <u>Sacrifice</u> (New York : Academic Press 1980), p.1

41. ibid, p.2

42. Robertson-Smith, Semitic Religions (London: Adam and Charles Clark 1984).

43. Bourdillon, and Fortes, eds., Sacrifice (1980), p.2

44. Ibid.

45. ibid, p.4

46. In 1954 an international conference was organized to explore cosmological ideas and social values of Africans. This was a landmark

Conference because it set the agenda for social anthropological studies on African religion and social theories.

The deliberations of this conference were published as a book entitled African Worlds (1954) edited by Fortes and Dierterlin. The participants of this conference explored the importance of the "Cosmological ideas as _expression of moral values in relation to material conditions of life and the total social order" (p.x).

The participants, agreed that traditional beliefs and practices for Africans are issues of over riding value. (p.viii). Therefore, in order to understand African people's cosmological ideas it was necessary to do a comprehensive study of African beliefs and ritual practices. They also realized that since the significance of the cosmological ideas were best observed in their everyday life, ritual practices were the best suited categories to make accessible and investigable African cosmological ideas and social order, as well as such natural phenomena as rain, forest, animals which determine means of production. They suggested that beliefs and use of ritual in these communities partially reflect Africans socio-political system and economic activity. A case in point is the Ashanti of Ghana. According to Busia the Ashanti world is made of two concentric circles. The outer circle is made of the spirits while the inner circle is humans, trees, rivers and hills. At the center is the Great Spirit or the Supreme Being who creates and commands all submission. Priests are chosen by spirit possession usually in the forests. In the political arena the Ashanti Chief is the head and supreme of all local chiefs and commands all allegiance. The Chief is also the embodiment of their spiritual values" (K.A. Busia, "The Ashanti of the Gold Coast" in African Worlds, p. 202). Daryll Forde best summarizes the role of religion in this approach thus: .. ….. religion is studied as a basis for cultural activities and social ties" (Daryll Forde, "Introduction" in African Worlds p.ix).

This conference was more or less an inventory of Western social anthropological scholarship on African culture. They critically examined theories, concepts, methods and definitions from Western perspective used in rendering African religion.

Another landmark work came out of a follow up of the first conference co-edited by Fortes and Dieterlen. In this volume African Systems of Thought (1965), the then leading African social anthropologists focused on religion, beliefs and ritual in both the traditional and modern African Communities.

During this inventory taking it became clear in both conferences that all these methods, theories, categories and analyses broadly reflected the schools the two most colonizing powers in Africa: the French and British schools.

The French School places emphasis on the whole data of knowledge of belief and doctrine, which is subsumed, in African myths and the symbols used in their ritual performances. This school believes that the people embody this knowledge, which is the foundation of their thought and ethics in their social interactions and technology of production.

This interlocking process of belief system and ethics form a coherent and logical system (1965:3). Consequently, for the French, ritual systems are not simple reflections of socio-economic forces and socio-political relations but rather they (rituals) form a coherent and autonomous body of beliefs and concepts.

Therefore, the texts of rituals provided the cosmological ideas, which shape as well as are being shaped by their socio-economic forces and the socio-political relations (1965:11). Ritual texts also provide an important role in which issues of " ... life that are diffused, scattered and fragmented are assembled, interfused and ordered" for the people (1965:11). Hence, the French School sought to relate thought to text and text to context from which it arises.

The British School of social anthropology in contrast emphasized social relations. For this school, the everyday social and political life was inseparable from the beliefs and ritual practices of the people. They start with the everyday social and political context in which ritual and myths are part of the means of social and political communication and organization (1965:4).

47. Consequently, the adherents of the British school tended to concentrate their research on categories such as kinship, economic and political relations (1965:4). In the approach of the British School, the first stage is to pay attention to what they call "the observational data of social positions associated with rituals" (1965:9). The Second stage is to examine the relationship of one particular social structure to the other structured patterns and how rituals fit into the total pattern structure. The overall goal of the British School was to delineate the theory of harmony and conflict in ritual symbolism and belief that reflects the conflicts within the socio-political structure. Therefore African beliefs and ritual

practices such as ancestral veneration/worship, issues of witchcraft, sorcery and possessions were/are mainly "related to such factors as the type of conflict, structural positions of the actors and the shape of development of local groups" (1965:2). See also Ivan Karp, Charles S. Bird, (eds.) Explorations in African systems of Thought (Washington: Smithsonian Institute Press 1980).

47. Timothy Radcliffe, "Relativizing the relativizers: A theological assessment of the role of sociological explanation of religious phenomena and theology today" in David Martin, John B. Mills, and W.S.F. Pickering, (eds.) Sociology and theology : Alliance and conflict (Brighton, Sussex : The Harvester Press, 1980), p. 152.

48. Ibid.

49. ibid, p.161.

50. See Juan Luis Segundo, Our ideas of God (Orbis Books 1973). James H. Cone, A Black Theology of Liberation (Philadelphia : Lippincourt 1970); Sallie McFague, Models of God, Theology for an ecological, nuclear age (Philadelphia Fortress Press, 1989); Aylward Shorter, African Culture and the Christian Church (London : Geoffrey Chapman 1973).

51. Michael Northcott, Research Methods in Practical Theology : The Vocation of Research in Practical Theology. A manual of research guides in Dept. of Practical Theology & Christian Ethics. Judith Bell, Doing your Research (Milton Keynes : Open University Press, 1987); Eileen Kane, Doing your own Research. How to do Basic Descriptive Research in Social Science and Humanities (London : Marian Boyars, 1985).

a. Participant observation

We chose participant observation as the primary method for gathering the empirical data of symbols, key words, phrases, body gestures, physical setting and all types of movements, the different roles of participants in both the healing shrines, homes, sit-in lectures, and shared campus life deemed appropriate. We chose this method because we believed that mere observation would not discover the relationship between sickness and healing in ritual performances as well as class sessions. However, we needed to be extremely conscious of keeping a critical distance between the observer and the observed.

b. Interviews

We conducted two principal types of interviews: the informal and the formal. In most cases we used verbal questions as an introduction to a follow-up interview, or pilot interviews where it was importance to respondents and ourselves.

Knowledge of the language was an asset. However, in order not to lose the critical distance required of scholarship, I used the services of the Wycliff Bible translators in the area to re-translate the information from healer and patient fact sheets, as well as to check for accuracy of the questions, and the responses in the Frafra language of interviews.

Both the formal and the informal interviews were structured. The responses to these questions were to make content analyses easier to demonstrate how they invoked their mythic world and how they used it through the symbolic representation of *kaaba* in their experiences of their sickness. Leading questions, when employed, were used with extra care because the interviewee for ethical and/or social reasons might say A and not B, although s/he might really feel like saying C.

c. Formal interviews.

The formal interviews were more precisely focused on the questions on the fact sheet. We were particularly interested in the relationship between symbolism, rituals, their mythic world, their experiences of sickness as the basis for the efficacy of *kaaba*. Flexibility of this agenda yet consistency on the key issues was fundamental guiding rule.

d. Follow up cases

The cases to follow up for in-depth study were picked from the formal interviews of the healer, the person healed or being healed, and members of their families.

We also attended several market days in Bolgatanga, mainly around the lorry park, the area where animals are sold, and the surrounding traditional drinking bars. The reasons for going to these areas were to meet other Frafra people from different villages and communities that we could not visit, and gather their views of sickness, healing and rituals, the different types of healers, and personal accounts of healing. The aim was to compare and contrast their views with views from other villages and with those we gathered from the designated areas of research in order to obtain a general view of the function of the Frafra mythic world as an interpretative mechanism in their experiences of sickness and healing in *kaaba.*

52. G.K. Nukunya, Kinship and Marriage among the Anlo Ewe (London : University of London, 1969). Also for the difficulties of one not familiar with the context see Geoffrey Tooth, Studies in Mental Illness in the Gold Coast (Ghana) (London : His Majesty's Stationary Office, 1950). See also J.C. Carothers, The African Mind in Health and Disease : A Study in Ethnopsychiatry (New York : Negro University Press 1990).

53. John Parratt, " Theological Methodologies in Africa" in Verbum svd vol. 24 fasc 1 (1983), p.47-62. See also Kwame Bediako, Jesus in African Culture(A Ghanaian Perspective) (Accra: Asempa Publishers 1990)

54. Segundo, The Liberation of Theology (1976), p.8.

55. Ibid

56. Lamin Sanneh, Translating the Message : The Missionary Impact on Culture (Mary Knoll, NY, : Orbis Books 1991). Sanneh has shown in this book how Africans in incredible ways are translating the Christian message into their own cultural idioms, while at the same time the Gospel is transforming African cultures.

    These cultural idioms that they use to translate the message or are being transformed by the message we designate as indigenous mythic worlds.

57. Segundo, The Liberation of Theology (1976), p.7.

58. ibid.

CHAPTER TWO

Literature Review

Introduction

In this chapter we are going to critically review the literature on how far African theologians and others account for how African Christians use their indigenous mythic worlds as the primary means of interpreting and appropriating their newly found Christina faith. We are particularly interested in looking at the models of indigenization they offer and the methods they use to construct these models.

Our contention is that indigenization began from the moment Africans encountered Western Christianity. African Christians began indigenizing Christianity in so far as they had to use their mythic world to interpret and appropriate the gospel preached to them.

The central role of the mythic world in dealing with sickness, the focus of this project, dawned on me in my ministry among Christians of various races, sexes, cultures and confessions. I embarked on an itinerary of a self-critical reflection on how my own spirituality and ministry are shaped by my own mythic world as a Frafra.

So we will begin this chapter with the story of the genesis of this thesis. This story will clearly show the gap between the indigenous mythic world and the newly found Christian faith.

The Story of the Genesis of the Project

The impetus for this project evolved from my own background as a Frafra and my observations of how important the sacrifices offered to ancestors were believed to be as the only means of guaranteeing our well being in Datuku, the village of my upbringing.

Until recently, Datuku was almost completely cut off from modern civilization. Datuku was a seemingly self-contained village made up of people who migrated there to obtain more land for farming. There was the village chief with his council of elders, who settled all social and political disputes. The Tendan (priest of a local shrine) had responsibility for ensuring that there was rain and fertility for good harvest. The Tendan also ensured that the earth was not unduly violated. So he sought the permission of the earth for burials and the appropriate times for funerals, hunting and fishing. The chief and his council of elders, the Tendan, the various cephalic clanships, and family heads were charged with responsibility of the well-being of their members, which they maintained by constant periodic sacrifices (kaaba) to the ancestors.

In Datuku, as in all Frafra villages, everyone knows everybody. Everyone is also related to everybody either through blood ties or by marriage. Every old man and woman is either a “father” or “mother”. In this seemingly self-contained village the inhabitants lived in relative harmony with each other and with nature. The trees, stones and rivers were part of a community of spiritual protectors, guides, and providers of food. The inhabitants produced their own food through communal labour, hunted and fished according to the directions of the village elders.

The most indelible memories of growing up in Datuku were the performance of rituals as part of everyday life. I cannot remember a time when there was not some kind of ritual being performed. The most common ritual was Kaaba.

Kaaba is a key word in Frafra notions of well being. It is a complex word, difficult to define. A brief explanation is already given in Chapter One and more detailed descriptions and analyses will follow in the later chapters.

As children we were always happy to eat the meat from kaaba and more importantly felt a sense of protection they provided. We believed that the more kaaba a home had, the more protected that home was. So it was common knowledge that one did not offend children from homes considered super-fortified through constant kaaba. The people from homes with less kaaba felt less spiritually fortified. They were afraid to go where the super-fortified went. Naturally, children from super-fortified homes became leaders on adventures in the bush. Almost all of us wore a form of talisman on our waists and hands. Wearing these reinforced our confidence of being immuned from spiritual attacks and general physical hazards associated with walking in the bush.

The frequent movement of people with fowls, goats, sheep and cows for use in kaaba was a common sight at houses where someone was sick or recovering from sickness. At sunset we would hear from such houses the sounds of birds and animals being made ready for kaaba. Consequently, our association of kaaba with well being was similar to our association with the breast and mother's warmth, care and protection.

The efficacy of words and actions and symbols used by the healers was a very important aspect of kaaba in our mythic world, from which we derived our sense of identity and meaning in life. A Frafra grows up associating kaaba with fortification against destructive powers and recovery from various forms of harm caused by a destructive power. Therefore, in the Frafra mythic world kaaba and well-being form part of the totality of life.

The Encounter

Datuku was not isolated and insulated as we thought. Colonialism slowly but surely invaded Datuku. A stone building was erected which was called "branchi". On investigation, we discovered "branchi" to be a linguistic corruption of a Hausa _expression "ba mu chi" which means "give us to eat". It was a kind of garrison of the colonial administration in Zuarungu and Nalerigu respectively. This village garrison was responsible for collecting eggs, fowls, and food as taxes for the colonial officers as well as the center of recruitment of men for the First and Second World Wars.

The whole village was filled with awe and fear when some thirty people led by two white men invaded the village and erected their tents in the middle of the village. For tow weeks they would get up in the morning and walk into the jungles and return in the afternoon. Later on, it was learned that they were surveyors who had come to construct roads to connect other parts of Ghana thereby opening up Datuku to modern civilization and later, to Western Christianity.

By 1957 a school was opened in the village and some of us were sent to the school.[2] About two years later a white man appeared. He talked through his interpreter. We wondered whether the white man was a god or human being. His skin and hair looked different from us. Even our food, which we thought every human being should be able to eat, he would not eat. So we asked ourselves if he was a human being like us, and if so, what kind of human being was he?

About six mouths later, another white man came on a motorbike. Both of them kept coming to different parts of the village. The first one we called "pasta" and the second we called "Fada"[3]. The question the Frafra asked was why it was that at times both "Pasta" and "Fada" seemed to be saying the same thing with respect to Jesus yet they behaved towards one another as enemies. Both brought us food and clothing. Later the "Pasta" came with a white woman who we were told would bring medicine to treat babies who fell sick. In the course of time, they erected churches and brought people to teach literacy classes to adults who could not go to school.

The "pasta" and "fada" told us about a garden in which the first human being lived in perfect peace. Then God gave a wife this first human being. Both lived in a perfect condition they called "paradis". Then a devil called "sutani" deceived them and they obeyed him and God drove them out of this "paradis". As a result all human beings inherited their punishment of disobedience until Yesu, God's son, came in order to pay for their punishment. The white men insisted that the disobedience of this couple caused an estrangement between all human and God, and among human beings. They taught us that the sin of this couple has been passed on to us more or less biologically and ontologically. This story is totally different from the one we were told by the elders that explained how our first ancestors sprang from the ground: and that some of the trees stood on their graves; and that we also embodied their spirits because they were reincarnated in our mothers' wombs.

During the month of December they called us to sing and dance after distributing clothing and food. Both "pasta" and "fada" even came to stay in the village for days. They told us that God loved us and gave his son Yesu to die for us. The said Yesu was born of human parents although He was conceived of the Holy Spirit. They further explained that He was born to die for the sins of all human beings including the people of Datuku. And that through his death, God had forgiven us our sins and that if we accepted Jesus, he would save our souls so that when we died our souls would go to heaven. We should repent, therefore, and burn all the protective ancestral symbols, stop believing that animals, rivers, trees, stones were both physical and spiritual, and follow God's son, Yesu Kristo. If we did not believe in Yesu, we would go to hell fire for destruction. In other words, Kaaba to our ancestors did not bring us well-being as we had believed. Indeed, the white men claimed that our ancestors did not exist. After every sermon the "pasta" and "fada" would ask whether we would accept Jesus. The most senior elder in the gathering would respond "Te wom ya" (we have heard).

The problem of who and what Jesus is to the Frafra

The "pasta" and "fada" notion of estrangement between humans and God and among humans was totally different from that of the people of Datuku. More importantly, his notion of God was contrary to the notion of God the people of Datuku had. The people of Datuku, indeed all Frafra, never imagined themselves sinning against God. If anything they sinned against their ancestors, not God. In the first place, they do not deal with God directly. For the people of Datuku and indeed the Frafra as a whole, without kaaba there is no well-being. Well-being means getting a good harvest, more children, having herds of goats, sheep and cows. This means if there is no kaaba, life is not worth living.

After some of his talks the "Pasta" or the "Fada" would ask us whether we believed in God. Everyone would stat nodding. What both "Pasta" and "Fada" did not seem to understand was that belief in God was nothing new. What was new was that their existence to our well-being in Datuku was inseparably related to a wrong act by a couple and the birth of a baby boy elsewhere. This God's son, who the missionaries called Yesu was as new and foreign as they were themselves. The idea that God had a son was also foreign to Frafra belief.

Most of the Bible stories were similar to the stories we used to tell by the fire in the evening. The questions that preoccupied the minds of the elders were how could Yesu a non-Frafra born in a far away country protect their children from the witches, the destructive powers within and without as well as what follow them to the bush while they were looking after our sheep and cows? Who would give us a good yield? The people knew they could always call the name of the Yaab (ancestor) in sudden dangers and he would respond. But as for Yesu, if even he existed, he could only hear the white man's voice. What would Yesu do if in the middle of the night a member of the family were inflicted by some powers within or without?

How could the Frafra bridge the wide gap between their notions of well being and kaaba to ancestors, spirits and cosmos and the "Pasta" and 'Fada's" notion of salvation in Yesu for purposes of preventing our souls from hell fire?

What started as a childhood curiosity, and then a lived experience, hit home in my ministry in hospitals in North America. In these hospitals, I felt the Protestants looking for some signs and symbols beyond prayers and conversation, for a deep and personal communication with their God and interpretation of their sickness. I also saw the eagerness with which patients who were Roman Catholics in similar conditions looked forward to the arrival of the priest or the Eucharistic minister for the Sacrament of the sick.

importantly, his notion of God was contrary to the notion of God the people of Datuku had. The people of Datuku, indeed all Frafra, never imagined themselves sinning against God. If anything they sinned against their ancestors, not God. In the first place, they do not deal with God directly. For the people of Datuku and indeed the Frafra as a whole, without kaaba there is no well-being. Well-being means getting a good harvest, more children, having herds of goats, sheep and cows. This means if there is no kaaba, life is not worth living.

After some of his talks the “Pasta” or the “Fada” would ask us whether we believed in God. Everyone would stat nodding. What both ”Pasta” and “Fada” did not seem to understand was that belief in God was nothing new. What was new was that their existence to our well-being in Datuku was inseparably related to a wrong act by a couple and the birth of a baby boy elsewhere. This God’s son, who the missionaries called Yesu was as new and foreign as they were themselves. The idea that God had a son was also foreign to Frafra belief.

Most of the Bible stories were similar to the stories we used to tell by the fire in the evening. The questions that preoccupied the minds of the elders were how could Yesu a non-Frafra born in a far away country protect their children from the witches, the destructive powers within and without as well as what follow them to the bush while they were looking after our sheep and cows? Who would give us a good yield? The people knew they could always call the name of the Yaab (ancestor) in sudden dangers and he would respond. But as for Yesu, if even he existed, he could only hear the white man’s voice. What would Yesu do if in the middle of the night a member of the family were inflicted by some powers within or without?

How could the Frafra bridge the wide gap between their notions of well being and kaaba to ancestors, spirits and cosmos and the “Pasta” and ‘Fada’s” notion of salvation in Yesu for purposes of preventing our souls from hell fire?

What started as a childhood curiosity, and then a lived experience, hit home in my ministry in hospitals in North America. In these hospitals, I felt the Protestants looking for some signs and symbols beyond prayers and conversation, for a deep and personal communication with their God and interpretation of their sickness. I also saw the eagerness with which patients who were Roman Catholics in similar conditions looked forward to the arrival of the priest or the Eucharistic minister for the Sacrament of the sick.

I further witnessed the remarkable difference brought about by the laying of hands and the speaking of tongues, and the changes, which the charismatic caregivers made in their patients' perception, and responses to sickness. Then slowly, but surely, I started asking myself if these Christians who are born and raised in a Western scientific culture with a scientific world view appeared to find in these rituals helpful ways of dealing with their sickness, how much more the Frafra whose mythic world is structured by those ritualistic approaches they use to deal with sicknesses which they face. It seemed to me that for both Frafra who are sick and patients in Western hospitals, the use of their mythic world as interpretative functions in appreciating rituals made a difference in their understanding of their experience of sickness.

I asked myself continually whether the interpretative functions of mythic world represented in Kaaba can offer some insights to Frafra Christian pastoral care givers? If so, how can a Frafra Christian pastoral caregiver mobilize the Frafra mythic world in a ministry of healing to Frafra Christians in times of sickness. My reflections above are similar to Ela who refers to his reflections as an "itinerary of self-discovery."[4] I was forced by the pastoral needs of the experiences of sickness to embark on this self-discovery. I was forced to ask myself as a Frafra, Western-trained, pastoral theologian how I could translate Western theological, philosophical and psychological concepts into the Frafra notions of kaaba, boar (ancestral earth shrine), yaabnam (ancestors) and yin (personal guardian spirit). So I began pursuing the question of the interpretative function of the indigenous mythic world in healing rituals, and their implication for a Contextualized Christian pastoral care to Frafra Christians when they fall sick.

The Gap Between Mythic Worlds and Western Christianity

We shall present here three pastoral cases of Frafra Christians who are caught up in the "epistemological distance". These cases are also examples of the need to first investigate how the Frafra use their mythic world to deal with sickness before they become Christians. These cases are not isolated ones. They are symptomatic of the general pastoral problems most Frafra Christians face with respect to the Christian ministry of healing.

Case One

Tii was converted at fifty years. Later all members of his immediate family became Christians. Prior to his conversion he was one of the leading diviners in the village. He was known to possess special powers to control all forces with respect to fishing in his village. If for any reason he did not lead any hunting and fishing expeditions, no one would go for fear of being killed by other powers. At his conversion he burnt in front of the church all his paraphernalia of powers for hunting and fishing and also removed all the symbols of his ancestors in front of his house. He cleared his house of anything religious in Talleh belief. He composed songs that are being sung today among Talleh Christians. I visited his family countless times and he and his family gave me friendship and love I will never forget. To our surprise we learnt that anytime he or a member of his family was sick, he would pray fervently first and, secondly, go to consult the bakolog (diviner) and offer kaaba. At his death we discovered that his elder son had made replicas of all that he burnt in front of the church at his conversion.

Case Two

Susan is thirty-five, converted at thirty. She is a mother of three who are all well educated. Since conversion she has become an active member of the congregation. She is president of the women's guild, a local preacher and leads worship regularly. One day she went to the bush to cut firewood. A snake bit her. She cried and screamed until passers-by came to her rescue. They brought her to the village on their shoulders. On arrival she called her catechist for prayers. After that they called the pastor who took hr in his car to hospital. While on her way to the hospital she dispatched her brother to the diviner. A week later she came out. On Sunday she went to church and gave thanks to God and to the members of the congregation for their support. The following day she left for her brother's house. According to eyewitness account her brother kaab an animal and a couple fowls as part of her husband's place and her life in the church and out the church continued as usual.

Case Three

James is the son of a famous church worker. Hr was baptized as a baby. He was raised a Presbyterian. He trained as an Evangelist, and was assigned to a station. Somehow he got an infection on his leg that immobilized him for years. He tried every treatment the doctors prescribed for him. However, the inflection continued. Being on sick leave, he left the parish and went to another village where he pursued traditional treatment, which involved all types of kaaba. Later the sore healed.

Tii, Susan an James are symptomatic of the dilemmas of Frafra Christians whose healing needs have become the quest and questions of this thesis. The quest is to provide a ministry of healing of the whole person with the gospel of Jesus Christ, which can and should mobilize Frafra mythic world, which serves as their interpretative mechanism. This quest for healing of the whole person simultaneously raises questions of how to incorporate the Frafra belief in kaaba and the kind of Christianity, which the missionaries presented to them.

We shall attempt to account for the gap between the Frafra mythic world as exemplified by these Frafra Christians and Western Christianity with Kraft's basic principles of communication theory. In Chapter one we showed that the missionaries committed the three offences stated by Panikkar. We also showed that these offences gave rise to the gap between the Frafar mythic world and Western Christianity and medicine. In this section we shall attempt to account for this gap. For one cannot attempt to bridge the gap until one can account for it.

According to Kraft, effective communication should result in a situation where the receptor understands the communicator as the communicator intends.[5] It is obvious that this was the intention of the missionaries. But the question is, was this possible? The answer to the above question may be found in Kraft's second principle of communication theory. The second principle says that the determinant factor in communication is how the receptor understands.[6] But how the receptor understands depends on whether both receptor and communicator are from the same culture or not. This principle is an important one because it explains the gap between the Frafra receptors in Datuku and the Western missionaries.

The Western missionaries used a language and bodily postures, which were embedded, in their mythic world. Even if their messages were translated in Frafra, their Frafra translators also used Frafra, which is equally embedded, in the Frafra mythic world. Since they did not share a common culture, there is no doubt of the less effectiveness of their communication and its intention based on this principle.

A quote from Samovar and Porter further explains the gap, but more importantly shows the principal role of the Frafra mythic world in appropriating Christianity. They write:

> Meaning ... comes from a reservoir in which all of our prior experiences are Contained. When we encounter a social stimulus, we dip into our reservoir And using our own unique thought process the meaning we deem appropriate and Attach it to the stimulus.[7]

If both the Frafra and the Western missionaries were operating from different mythic worlds, the question still has to be raised: how could the missionaries influence the Frafra since some of them became converted to Christianity?

The other principle of communication is that the most positive communication results from person-to-person interaction.[8] It is true that the missionaries were friendly in the sense that they smiled and played football with Frafra young people. They also gave the Frafra second hand clothes, food and medicine. So all these could impact on the communication. But they lived in bungalows and their private lives in their bungalows remained a mystery to the Frafra. So these influences were too infrequent to create the kind of influence implied by this principle. Therefore, if the messages in communication are made credible or incredible by the quality of relationship between receptor and communicator, then in addition to the gap between mythic worlds, there was a credibility gap, for the Frafra hardly knew the missionaries as they knew the diviners, healers and Tendanam who they lived with in the same communities.

The case for gap between mythic worlds is furthermore supported by Kraft's notion of frame-reference principle.[9] Kraft states: "... if effective communication is to take place, both the communicator and the receptor must be in position to attach similar meanings to the symbols employed."[10]

In order for both to derive similar meanings from the symbols of communication, they have to operate "within a common context or frame of reference,"[11] Since the Frafra and the missionaries did not have a common or similar frame of reference, or what we call interpretative functions of the mythic world, it can safely be inferred that there was little or no effective communication. If there was communication, it was not a dialogue. It was simply instructions for the Frafra to follow. For example, they told the Frafra to stop kaaba. They also asked them to take Biblical and Western names and forget the names of their ancestors, which they were given at birth. The first three converts were renamed Samuel, David, and Joseph. These converts were also strictly warned not to take part in kaaba of any kind. They were not to sing folk songs but only songs with Jesus in them.

We cam also safely infer from the way the missionaries wanted their converts to behave that the missionaries seemed to be interested in culturally extracting the Frafra converts from their mythic worlds. In the light of the evidence, the "fada" and "pasta" could be justifiably called "cultural extractionists". A cultural extractionist is defined by Kraft as a communicator whose: Primary concern ... is to convert receptors to their way of extractionist thinking. Communicators seek to teach receptors to understand and look at reality in Forms of their own models and perspectives.[12]

The fact that the Frafra became and are becoming Christians seems on the superficial level to suggest that the missionaries as extractionists may have succeeded. The fact that the Frafra became Christians cannot be attributed to the extractionists approaches used by the missionaries. The cases we have cited thus far discount such a claim. Furthermore the kind of Christianity imported into Frafraland invalidates such a claim.

The kind of Western Christianity imported Widened the Gap

The kind of Western Christianity exported to the Frafra by itself also contributed to widen the gap. The kind of Western Christianity that came to Frafraland was already in crisis; a crisis created by a new scientific culture. Such Christianity believed that the indigenous healing rituals had nothing to offer Christian theology. In fact, the scientific medical discoveries at least partially coloured how some Western Christians even read and interpreted the healing narratives in the gospels. Some Western theologians including some of the missionaries, who brought their version of Christianity to Frafraland, believe that divine healing had ceased. This apparent denial of the power of the Spirit to heal seemed to find its theological _expression in the doctrine of dispensationalism that rose in Britain in the last century.

The doctrine of dispensationalism, among others, teaches that the gifts of healing and miracles in the Church have ceased, because such gifts are no longer necessary[13]. Although Luther Calvin could not be said to be dispensationalists, some of their writings on the subject of divine healing or miracles echoed the views of the later doctrine of dispensationalism. Luther wrote:

> Now that the apostles have preached the word and have given their writings, and nothing more than what they have written remains to be revealed, no new and special revelation or miracle is necessary.[14]
> Calvin also wrote:
>
> The gift of healing disappeared with the other miraculous powers that the Lord was pleased to give for a time, which might render the new preaching of the gospel fro ever wonderful. Therefore, even were we to grant that anointing was a sacrament of those powers, which were

> then administered by the hands of the apostles, it pertains no to us, to us to whom no such powers have been committed.[15]

In the face of the industrial revolution, advances in social/human sciences, and scientific medical discoveries, Christianity in the West was in a crisis of credibility. Hence, new theological explanations were called for if the Gospel narratives, especially with respect to healing, were to be made intelligible to modern Christians. According to Kelsey, Bultmann also demythologized the Kerygma, to make the message meaningful to modern Christians.[16] Keksey is of the view that for Bultmann:

... all angels and demons, all extrasensory knowledge, the experiences of prophecy and tongues, the value of dreams and visions, as well as every account of healing the demon possessed and the physically ill, must simply be rejected. They did not happen as such. Obviously, since they did not happen then, there is no reason to believe that they will now.[17]

Consequently, western Liberal theology of the nineteenth century that influenced some of the Swiss and German missionaries who came to Frafraland to borrow the words of Kelsey "was bedded down, seemingly complacent, between the idealism of Hegel and the scientific naturalism of Darwin."[18]

Kelsey suggests that the liberal theologians implied that:

> ... any idea of supernatural non-physical reality existing apart from personal psychic material is discarded. The value of history is questioned, and a scientific understanding of the world as a closed system of reality is accepted as axiomatic. The course of nature cannot be broken into or interrupted by any powers beyond 'existence'; instead meaning comes to men as they authentically live in this immediate, conscious situation.[19]

Therefore, such a Christianity in influenced by existential philosophy and scientific discoveries in the words of Kelsey have: ... Swept clean of any idea of Christian healing. On one hand the successes of medicine have made any belief in it unnecessary, and on the other, modern theology has made any belief in it untenable.[20]

It is obvious that this kind of liberal theology which seemed to deny the miracles imported to Frafraland further widened a credibility gap between it and the holistic model in the interpretative functions of the indigenous mythic world of the Frafra. Furthermore, the concept of the Messiah in Judaeo-Christian theology has no equivalent in the Frafra mythic world.

In Frafra mythic world as in most African societies, there is what kirwen calls the "concept of God in the absence of messiah."[21] In other words, the notion of an expected tribal political or religious messiah is absent in Frafra mythic world. Hence, we wonder whether the words used to express western Christian doctrines of God, Jesus as Messiah and the Trinity are relevant to Frafra Christians. In conclusion, the factors in communication and the intrinsic nature of liberal theology of some of the missionaries contributed to the gap between interpretative functions of Frafra mythic worlds and Biblical Christianity. The result is that they produced compartmentalized Christians.

In spite of the almost unbridgeable gap between the frafra mythic world and Western Christianity the Frafra were converted to Christianity. The question is why? Was it because of what Baeta calls "basic human aspirations" [22] associated with "pasta" and "fada" such as providing second hand clothing, food, peri-natal, and neo-natal clinics? What are the saving acts of Jesus Christ that the Frafra have said and are saying "Amen" to? Does what ever constitutes salvation in Jesus for Europeans and North Americans also constitute salvation for the Frafra? We strongly believe that the answers to these questions will come from an understanding of how they use their mythic world in defining and experiencing salvation in kaaba. These questions clearly show that there is a theological conflict between Frafra Christians and Western Christianity that must be addressed.

Wingren points out some hermeneutical and anthropological presuppositions in Christian theologies[23] that partially shed light on the conflict inherent in the encounter of Frafra mythic world and Western Christianity. According to Wingren, there are hermeneutical and anthropological presuppositions in all theologies that produce different types of conflict.

A conflict may arise that is open, deliberate and admitted. In this kind of approach, the theologian makes a deliberate choice of what is peripheral and what is essential.[24] In our view the missionaries were more ignorant than deliberate in their extractionist attitudes towards Frafra notions of sickness, ritual and healing in their mythic world. This is not the only kind of conflict that has arisen between the missionary Christian model of healing based on Western scientific model and the Frafra mythic world interpretation of sickness, healing ritual and health.

There is a second type of conflict that arises due to insufficient historical data. For example, a theologian may sincerely want to present a New Testament fact as it really is. However, due to discrepancies in scripture, theologian lacks sufficient knowledge of the situation to enable him/her to present that fact accurately. This kind of conflict can be corrected by detailed historical investigation. [25] The conflict between the Frafra notion of well being in ritual in their mythic world and Western Christianity is partially implicit but it is not central to this kind of conflict. The conflict is partially implicit in so far as they lacked the knowledge of the central role of the interpretative functions of Frafra mythic world.

A third conflict may arise due to method. In this kind of conflict, a thorough investigation of the Biblical content clearly shows that there is a tension between "the essential parts of the biblical material and the modern theological interpretation." [26] A conflict of this category deserves more critical scrutiny for it is not simply a correction or insertion of the lacking information. Correction strikes at the very conception or grasp of the subject and method of the whole work, the very first presuppositions with which the scholar started the investigation. [27] This conflict demands that all previous methods and interpretation be destroyed or adjusted and a fresh look begins.[28] This third conflict is the one that almost all African Christian theologians have engaged in resolving, and to which this thesis seeks to add a contribution.

Our focus is to understand the interpretative functions of Frafra mythic world in times of sickness through symbolic representation of kaaba in order to determine what insights there are for a constructive Frafra, contextualized, Christian ministry of healing.

The third type of conflict clearly explains why the Frafra Christians in the case we have described turn to the interpretative functions of their traditional mythic world. For them salvation does not seem to be related to going to heaven when they die or avoiding the disobedience of the first couple. Rather, salvation or well being is experienced in terms of good harvests, many children and freedom from evils spirits.

Therefore, for a contextual Frafra, Christian, pastoral theologian, the question is, what hermeneutical approaches and biblical insights, as well as insights from the sciences of religion, human/social sciences, and the interpretative functions of the Frafra mythic world are available to the Frafra Christians for a critical theological reflection on the relevance of the gospel of Jesus Christ in times of this sickness? An appropriate response to the challenge of the interpretative function of the Frafra mythic world to the Church is how to critically construct an indigenous Christian ministry of healing that "can mediate the conflicts with Western Christianity in African symbols, rituals and ideas."[29] But before we do that it is also appropriate here to look at how others have looked at the conversion of Africans to Christianity.

In the next section we shall critically review various accounts of what happens when Africans become converted to Christianity. There are only very few attempts made to offer a theological account of the phenomenon of conversion in Africa from the perspective of practical theology. We are particularly interested with conversion in view of the peculiar responsibilities of a practical theologian as articulated by Forrester. According to him:

> the peculiar responsibilities of Practical Theologyinvolve acting as a bridge between theology and the social Sciences and reflecting critically upon, learning from and endeavouring to renew, reform and strengthen practice and in particular Christian practice.[30]

Such peculiar responsibilities for Practical theologians in general and ours in particular will hopefully provide some clues on how the Frafra use their mythic world as interpretative mechanism in the symbolic representation of Kaaba. Such clues will be the basis for bridging Frafra notions of well being and a Frafra Christian ministry of healing.

Some Western pastoral/practical theologians have used other approaches relevant to their contexts.[31] In these approaches they have used paradigms from social and human sciences as cultural paradigms to dialogue with Western theological debates. In our view these are Western Contextual theological models. Although we can learn from these models of begin with that context.

However, the African Christian theologians are free to use some paradigms from social and human sciences if these will help them in their tasks. But the central role of African mythic worlds in engaging all human and cosmic interactions forces African pastoral/practical theologians to being with the African contexts. One such fundamental theological issue that calls for critical examination from African contexts and yet using concepts from elsewhere is the issue of religious conversion in general and Christian conversion in particular.

Theological Theories of Conversion in Africa

The extensive and intensive debate on indigenization or contextualization in Africa cannot be meaningfully conducted without adequate struggle with the phenomenon of conversion in Africa. We shall briefly explore the discourses on the phenomena of African Christian conversions.

Cronin is one of the few African theologians who has offered some insights on the phenomenon of Christian conversion in Africa. He relies on the work of Lonergan[32] for his theological theory of conversion.[33] According to him Lonergan suggested different types of conversion. These are the intellectual, moral, religious and Christian.[34] He argues that Lonergan's notion of religious experiences is a universal experience in all including traditional African religion.

Religious experience, which Lonergan calls infrastructure, makes possible religious knowledge or suprastructure.[35] Religious experience is universal but it is the suprastructure that is unique to each religion.

Cronin produces seven components of African religious experience to show their universal similarities to all religions or at least to Christianity. These are transcendence, immanence, highest good, ultimate love, sacrifice, ways to God and neighbour, and love supreme.[36] As a result; he claims that these seven universal common religious experiences "are the basis for dialogue and common understanding between the great religious traditions".[37]

The universal common religious experience in all religions according to Cronin is the invisible work of the Holy Spirit.[38] The role of Jesus is to fulfill, make clear or visible the invisible work of the Holy Spirit. Cronin also suggests that according to Lonergan God first sent the Spirit. Later God sent the Son in the context of the Spirit's mission, to bring it to completion.[39] For Cronin, all religions including African religions and Christianity "share something very basic in common, namely, the mission of the Holy Spirit, God's universal, invisible, first communication of himself to mankind".[40] The many varied expressions, symbols, rites; traditions of the different religious traditions are simply different ways of describing the "work of the one Holy Spirit".[41]

Hence, "African traditional religions are just one particular example of the work of the Holy Spirit in the hearts of all men."[42] Cronin therefore concludes that the "Good News does not destroy, disrupt or tear up a local culture at its roots but fulfils transforms and transcends it."[43]

In order to account for the need for the mission of the Church in the light of his thesis, Cronin suggests that the mission of the Church is to present a particular infrastructure to the work of the Holy Spirit. Cronin further suggests that "the aim of the missionary work is to oversee the acceptance and enculturation of that message ..."[44] The missionary brings something, which results in new meanings, values and symbols to the African culture[45] but which is not totally strange or foreign, as the Son and the Spirit are already at work in the religious experience. Hence, he concludes "there is nothing in the authentic religious experience of Africa that has to be abandoned. Baptism is not an uprooting and a rejection of the work of the universal spitit."[46] The suprastructure which the missionaries bring include schools, seminaries, Colleges, preachers, and books, sacraments, hymns and rites.[47]

Cronin's analysis of conversion brings out important insights, which we agree with. These are worth summarizing here. There are aspects of African traditional religious beliefs that may not contradict the Christian gospel. We also agree with his argument that these areas of similarities perhaps make it easier for Africans to accept Christianity. We further agree with him that the spirit of God is at work in Africa and among Africans in ways beyond human understanding.

However, there are some assumptions in his analysis we do not agree with. For example, his generalization that all religious experiences are the same based on his seven principles. Even if that may be the case, it demands more comparative global studies to make such conclusions. Moreover, each religious experience produces its own ethics and terminologies and belief systems. And if we compare the ethics and belief systems of Africans and Christianity we cannot say they are all one and the same. Cronin does not sufficiently justify why African Christians need Mass said in Latin, and later on in English, wine and bread produced elsewhere, and hymns composed elsewhere using other people's mythic world to become the "suprastructure" of African Christian "infrastructure".

As we have seen in Chapter One it is no longer admissible for African Christian theologians to ignore the fact that African notions of salvation, health, healing from African mythic worlds are different from the Western world view from which the missionaries derived their "suprastructure". The experiences of most African Christians in general and the cases we have presented so far are evidences of the fact that in most cases the missionaries may have provided an "anti-suprastructure" rather than "suprastructure" as Cronin suggests.

The review of Cronin's effort has clearly pointed out an important danger associated with applying universal theories. In spite of some of the merits of this approach, the application of universal theories to account for African's conversion to Christianity in most cases ignores the particularities of African mythic worlds, which they use as interpretative mechanisms. When Africans are converted to Christianity, they come with these mythic worlds. Our contention is these mythic worlds determine how they appropriate and interpret their encounters with the Christian faith.

Carmody, a Catholic theologian in Africa offers another theoretical account of conversion in Africa. His theory seems partially capable of shedding light on the phenomenon of conversion. Carmody explores the nature of the pedagogy of conversion in Roman Catholicism in Zambia using Paulo Freire's pedagogical models.[48]

Education is a process of dialogue in which the teacher teaches as well as learns from. Anyone in a leadership position who does not behave dialogically but imposes his/her decisions "manipulates and oppresses". [49] Hence Freire proposes his "problem posing pedagogical method" of education.

Freire, according to Carmody, suggests four levels of human consciousness. In the first level is the intransitive consciousness in which the person directs all energies and gifts to satisfying basic human needs.[50] the second is the level of semi-intransitive, in which persons take facts as given.[51]

The third is naïve consciousness, when the persons may do serious questioning but in a rather "naïve way". The persons at this level are usually attracted to the popular views and hence are susceptible to manipulation and exploitation by the populist.[52] the fourth level is the level of critical consciousness. At this level there is critical analysis and interpretation. Self-confidence and willingness to take responsibility are characteristic signs of those in this stage. The fourth level is usually achieved through "problem posing."[53]

Persons in these various levels of consciousness use two different approaches for learning. The first approach is the "banking" approach. In this approach, learners are depositories in which the teacher deposits knowledge, facts, and information. In the banking approach, students or learners are adaptable and manageable beings. The more students work at storing the deposits entrusted to them, the less they develop the critical consciousness, which results from their intervention in the world as transformers of the world.[54]

The second approach is "problem posing". The learner uses critical reflection on present situations in which problems pose pedagogues through intellect and praxis. This kind of process is "the authentic union of reflection and action. The content of this consciousness is the view that one has of one's existence in the social world and of the power one has determine one's destiny."[55]

According to Carmody, conversion to Catholicism in Africa bears "many of the characteristics of Freire's banking approach in education. The converts were expected to record, memorize and accurately repeat the content".[56] In other words, the converts only received and stored whatever they were taught. In the light of Freire's theory then, Carmody suggests "the converts moved from intransitivity to semi-intransitivity".[57] Like education, conversion for some was of a process of domesticating them in the world of their faith instead of deliberating, questioning and transforming them and their societies.[58] We are of the opinion that Freire's theory and Carmody's application of it shows the difficult processes many African Christian converts go through in order to bridge the gap between their indigenous mythic worlds and their newly found Christian faith.

The missionary-founded Church, almost from the very beginning (and even now), seemed to have left their African Christian converts on their own to devise (however elusive) ways to use their mythic world to make meaning out of their new Christian faith. So indigenization of the Christian faith began with the first encounter of African mythic worlds with Christianity. But what kinds of indigenization are going on and are they all acceptable to these Churches? If any kind of indigenization is not acceptable to the Churches then

They need, for their members models acceptable to the Churches and relevant to their members.

Conversion from perspective of Comparative Study of religions

We shall examine the works of some leading scholarly research on the African Christian conversion phenomena from the perspective of what has been known traditionally as Comparative study of religions. This group consists of missionaries and scholars. So their perspectives offer a combination of the interests of their missionary bodies and academics. These interests are similar to the interests of this project.

The rise of the Independent African Churches[59] and the case of Archbishop Milingo of Zambia[60] seem to be clear evidence that one cannot look at the conversion experiences of African Christians without considering the mythic worlds that they bring to these experiences.

Anderson points out that the fact that Africans accepted Christianity suggests, that "amongst all the new things which repelled, there were also elements which appealed strongly to needs vaguely felt, needs which the traditional civilization and religion had never been able to satisfy."[61] Anderson implies some basic commonalty between African mythic worlds and Western Christianity.

Gray has suggested that African traditional religion played an important role in the way African Christians appropriate Western Christianity. He argues that the African notion of evil and rituals played a dialogical role in Africans accepting as well as rejecting Western missionary interpretation of evil. For Africans "evil was experienced as that which destroyed life, health, strength, fertility and prosperity."[62] Some of the African converts also saw "Christianity" as the latest in a "series of purification or witchcraft-eradication movements, another source of spiritual power, which brought assistance."[63] This understanding of Christianity by African Christian converts was "enormously enhanced as African began to read the biblical healing narratives".[64]
For Gray, the Bible has provided Africans with "protest symbols with an array of different meanings which meet different needs".[65] Some of the African Christians also saw the Christian rituals of baptism, worship and sacraments as sources of power for protection as well as access to the power of Jesus to heal. Other Studies from African independent Churches throughout Africa[66] seem to confirm Gray's views.

It is logical to conclude here that the African Christians use their mythic world to find some similarities with Western Christianity and use these similarities to interpret and appropriate their newly found Christian faith. What happens in the areas in which there are conflicts? These we hope to provide some explanations to in the course of the thesis.

Ethnophilosophical Theories of Conversion

There are other scholars who use ethnophilosophical arguments to account for conversions of Africans to Christianity. A leading pioneer of this school is Horton. He argues that the indigenous mythic worlds in Africa operate on the same assumptions and principles as Western science. For Horton, "traditional religious beliefs are theoretical systems intended for the explanation, prediction and control of space-time events".[67]

He explains that in African cosmology, there are two tiers. The first tier consists of the world of the local community, which is more or less insulated from the larger world. It is in the first tier that social interaction is essential to the total well being of all members and not the larger world. The lesser spirits have direct and more powerful influence on everyday social interaction in the first tier. The Supreme Being on the other hand is responsible for the wider world in the second tier. The lesser spirits are also moral guardians and are constantly called to intervene in any everyday social crises.[68] According to Horton, the social environment, thus providing a clue to how traditional cosmology responds to change, conditions the traditional cosmology. When a new phenomenon breaks through the cosmological first tier and weakens the boundary:

> Its adherents do not just abandon it in despair. Rather, they remold and develop it until it attains, once more, its pristine level of explanatory coverage. The end result, therefore, is a much an instrument of explanation- prediction as was the pre-change cosmology.[69]

The philosophers of the traditional cosmology are those "who see the system as a whole with all of its ramifying implications for the world."[70] These include diviners and priests. They assume a common "interpretative challenge of cosmology and ritual than any one else."[71] There are some diviners and priests who ignore the change. Others try to reverse it. Some will extend and develop the traditional cosmology in such a way as to accommodate the new reality in order to make the new meaningful to the people.[72] Horton emphasizes that African Christian converts accept aspects of Christianity that are congruent to their traditional cosmologie.[73] Where there is no congruence of cosmologies,

Christianity appears "as embarrassing additions to the life of converts."[74] Both Gray and Horton have shown the interpretative functions of the traditional mythic worlds. They have demonstrated the role of the mythic world in interpreting and appropriating the new changes and Christian faith. We believe these insights are helpful for contextualized pastoral purposes.

Current African Theological Models of Indigenization

Nyamiti divides African enculturation approaches into two types. The first group consisted of people who start from the Bible and seek to interpret African reality in terms of Western interpretations of the Bible. So they look for various Western theologies that have some similarities with some aspects of African world view.[75] For example, Mbiti compares the African world view with the New Testament teaching of Christ and concludes that there are some similarities between African mythic worlds and the New Testament writings.[76]

Pobee on his part begins his African theology with the creedal phrase "Christ as true God". He constructs an African theology based on the implication of this creedal phrase in the light of Akan notions of royalty. Pobee develops a cultural exegesis in which he compares the creedal statement and Akan notions of royalty. He concludes from this exercise of comparison that the creedal statement has the same implications as Nana has for Akan. Therefore when Akan Christians call Jesus their Nana, they are calling for standards of royalty in their personal orientation, the structures of societal and economic processes and political forces. The implication of such a Christology is a call for both a personal and societal justice as well as renewal.[77]

There is no doubt that there are similarities between Akan royalty in their mythic world and the biblical images of Christians as a royal priesthood, and holy nation. These similarities have many insights to adapt for Akan models of contextualization. Dickson, another Ghanaian theologian, also uses a similar enculturation approach with the Christian teaching of the cross. He aims to construct a theology of the cross, which is positive and relevant to Akan Christians.

He is of the opinion that Western interpretations of the cross through western thought have rendered the Church's teaching on the cross of less value to Akan Christians. Hence, the Easter massage loses its necessary relevant impact on Akan Christians. He is also of the opinion that some symbols in the Akan mythic world can offer Akan Christians richer and more relevant theology of the cross than is currently offered them. He begins his model of indigenization by comparing Akan notion of death with the New Testament teaching of the cross. He concludes from his comparison that the death of Jesus for Akan Christians is a sign of victory.[78] Here again, we agree that some Akan beliefs concerning deaths have important insights for an Akan Christian theology of death. Both Pobee and Dickson have set agenda for serious efforts for contextual theology in Ghana.

Penoukou has also proposed an African Christological model based on the rituals performed in life and death by the Ewe-Amina in Togo. According to Penoukou life and death is a cyclical process of birth, adulthood, death and rebirth among the Ewe-Amina. He reflects on the life and death of Jesus in the light of his understanding of rituals in the mythic world of the Ewe-Amina. He concludes that Christ can be interpreted as a mediator, liberator and Jete (ancestor): the source of life.[79]

Appiah-Kubi follows the approach as Penoukou and also emphasizes the mediatorial role of Jesus in which Jesus can be experienced as saviour, redeemer, power, liberator and healer.[80]

Sanon, another African theologian, proposes the model of Jesus as head and master of initiation. He bases his analysis of African rites of passage on van Gennep's theory of ritual. He compares the teachings of Christ and African rites of passage in which a person acquires a higher status. He therefore sees the similarities between the African rites of passage through which a person acquires high status and the rites of passage through which Jesus became Messiah. He then suggests that in the rites of passage of Jesus, various symbols and signs are used to incorporate humanity. These symbols and signs include Parables, Solidarity, Cross, Church, Grace and Sacraments. Jesus therefore is now master of initiation as one who has been initiated (Heb. 5:9). In the sacrament of baptism Christians are initiated into Christ's "initiatic community".[81] These three approaches of indigenization are significant noble attempts. However, they seem to be glossing over the traditional theological insistence on the controversial inseparable relationship between the works, and person on the one hand and the divinity of Jesus on the other.

The traditional Christian position is that Jesus was able to atone or mediate between God and humanity because he is believed to be both God and human. But in African rites of passage neither the initiator nor these performing the rituals of passage are said to be both divine and human. The traditional initiates do not change ontologically as with Jesus Christ or in Christian sacraments of baptism. Rather, the traditional initiates change sociologically.

Critical Evaluations

The African theologies that we have reviewed show an awareness of the acute need to write a coherent theology that begins with some aspects of African mythic worlds. The potential for a unique African theological contribution of world Christianity is evident in all these works. They have also shown the potential for a direct encounter between the African indigenous mythic worlds and the biblical images and symbols in the Judaeo-Christian faith.

These theologies usually only emphasize the spiritual and the cultural. They are silent on the physiological, psychological and the socio-political dimensions of African mythic worlds or vice versa. The holistic nature of the interpretative functions of African mythic worlds must be taken seriously by the African pastoral needs of mainline African Christians who suffer at the expense of this filtering method of indigenizing theologies by Western trained African theologians. One reason may be that they seem to have a need to be loyal to Western theological schools where they were trained and the ecclesiological bodies that ordained them. As Nyamiti reminds us "… unless our theology is going to affect positively the life of our church communities, our work in vain, it cannot effect them positively unless it is relevant for their spiritual and bodily needs."[82]

We hold the view that African Christological theological categories such as mediator, intermediary, Nana, Jete (ancestor) victor and conqueror are certainly important categories for the construction of African theologies. However, they can become important categories for the construction of these indigenous theologies if they come out of a critical theological reflection of the direct encounter between African mythic worlds with Judaeo-Christian biblical images and symbols. The method of such a contextualized critical theological reflection is already outlined in chapter One.

Parratt has also made helpful reviews and criticisms of African theologians similar to ours.[83] Shorter has offered a model of contextualized Christian ministry of healing in Africa worth considering here. For him healing is the central theme of both the life and ministry of Jesus and African tradition religions. Therefore, there is an urgent need for an African Christology of healing. He also suggests that there are also similarities between the Galilean healers of the times of Jesus adopted.

Shorter advocates an honesty in the dialogue between African traditional religion and Christianity in which the irreconcilable conflicts must be held up.[88] Yet he seems too quick to gloss over the areas of conflict between Judaeo-Christian faith and African traditional religions. He is also silent on how the relationship between sin and sickness can lead to unnecessary forms of oppression and dehumanization in some healing rites of some African ethnic communities. Furthermore, he concentrates on the spiritual and cultural but ignores the socio-political and socio-economic, as well as the physiological and psychological aspects of healing rituals. In spite of these criticisms, his willingness to engage in a serious honest dialogue between African spirituality with respect to healing and Christianity has inspired this project.

African Independent Churches and the Charismatic Movement

We shall briefly explain here the different meanings and usages of the terms Spiritual Churches, Pentecostal Churches, and African Independent Churches or Independent African Churches in Ghana.

Individuals who were on the whole, not well educated, mostly started the Spiritual Churches. Some of them began as members of a missionary founded Church but eventually came out of them. They claim their power and authority form the Holy Spirit. Hence their name Spiritual Churches. Although they may talk about "holiness" as described by Hollenweger, they tend to use the Bible and the traditional beliefs as complementary or supplementary.

There are mainly three types of Pentecostal Churches. The first type consists of those started by foreign Pentecostal Churches. An example of this group is the Assemblies of God Church. We shall later discuss in detail the Assemblies of God Church when we are discussing the Northern Ghana Bible Institute.

The second type consists of those that were/are started by Ghanaians and later joined by foreign Pentecostal Churches or evangelical individuals/groups. An example of those in this group includes the Church of Pentecost, Ghana, and the many different Apostolic Churches[89]. These types of Pentecostal Churches tend to have well-developed doctrines origins originating or reflecting mostly their influences by their Western partners.

The third type of Pentecostal Church started as ecumenical house churches or what we call in Ghana "Christian fellowship". In the cause of time some of them become Churches. An example of this type is the Ghana Evangelical Society.

The terms African Independent Churches or Independent African Churches are new in Ghana. They are mostly used in Ghanaian academic circles to refer to Spiritual Churches and some of the Pentecostal Churches. It must be mentioned however that the Pentecostal Churches especially those with some form of Western connection or with leaders who are well educated do not like their churches to be referred to as Spiritual Churches.

In this section, and indeed throughout the thesis the terms Spiritual Churches, Pentecostal Churches, Charismatic Churches or movements, and African Independent Churches or Independent African Churches will be used interchangeably for lack of adequate terminology that makes a clear distinction between them.

According to Mullig the spiritual Churches in an urbanizing social structure with new socio-economic structures have become small businesses in which their leaders leaders gain access to economic advantages.[90] Christianity has become a means of advancing to high social status in the new urban social stratification. She emphasizes, "Healing rituals play a key role in transmitting and establishing these new ideological precept".[91]

For example, the role of the leader of the Church of the Messiah, Mulling claims, "is the rationalization and reinforcement of the relationships, characterized by increasing individualization."[92] Therefore the spiritual Churches are more effective vehicles for the transmission of new ideologies for the new social stratification and socio-economic prospects.

Mulling's generalization from a study of one church is too presumptuous of the functions and purposes of spiritual Churches in Ghana in particular and indeed African in general. It is true that some of the leaders come from the lower economic classes, with less education. In some cases the role of founder or pastor offers economic and social advantages. However, there are other leaders and members of such Churches who are part of the middle class. For example the founder of the Christian Action Centre in Accra comes from a wealthy family. Some of his followers are the young Ghanaian professionals whose needs other than economic and social status may not have been met in the missionary-founded churches in which they were baptized and confirmed.

Thus, they left either to either found or join Spiritual/Charismatic churches in order to meet these needs.

Throughout the regional capitals of Ghana there are such churches whose leaders were previously well-paid professionals, and whose members are mostly well paid. Examples include the pastors and most members of the Broken Yoke Foundation in Bolgatanga and the Central Gospel Church in Accra. Therefore, Mulling's theory may be applicable to some leaders but cannot apply to all leaders Spiritual Churches. We will, rather, suggest that other reasons account for the aspects of worship and teachings of these Churches and their ability to invoke the interpretative functions of indigenous mythic worlds through a method of direct encounter between the traditional mythic worlds. In our view one such outcome of this approach occurs when the Judaeo-Christian faith assumes the role of the functions of the interpretative mechanism of the mythic world in response to crisis and change in the daily encounters of their followers.

The leaders of the African Independent Churches and the Charismatic healers offer an alternative to the Western-imported Christianity in the churches founded by Western missionary bodies. Their alternative interpretation is based on taking seriously the traditional mythic worlds in which humans interact with spiritual powers, both for good and evil. The leaders and followers of these Churches seem to use a method of interpretation of symbolic literalism, which partially correspond to the symbols of African mythic worlds. This approach has been hitherto resisted and even condemned by some mainline Churches for some time. In their theological education, they may have deemed this approach as unacademic. However, it seems the trend is changing.

One well-known case is that of Archbishop Milingo of Zambia. At the beginning of Bishop Milingo's healing ministry, the leadership of the Catholic Church in Zambia and the Vatican expressed concern over his healing ministry. In an executive meeting of Zambia Episcopal Conference (ZEC) in November 1977, they advised him to stop his healing ministry, which he did for some time.[93] He was even transferred to Rome which some suspect may been an attempt by the Vatican to remove him from his healing base in which he used traditional mythic worlds to understand Biblical healing narratives. But he continued healing in Rome. This time, his congregation was mostly made up of Europeans. This may suggest that, perhaps, even people in so-

Called developed countries may still operate with mythic world similar to Africans in addition to their secular and scientific worldviews.

In the November 1990 edition of the official newspaper of the Vatican, there was a picture of Archbishop Milingo and Pope John Paul II standing together. [94] What are we to make of this picture of Archbishop Milingo and Pope John Paul II? Was it indication a public recognition of the healing ministry of Milingo? But more importantly, has the healing ministry of Milingo shown the inadequacy of Western Christianity even among Europeans? Has Milingo Archbishop Milingo successfully married the African mythic world and the mythic worlds of Judaeo-Christian faith? Has Milingo at long last demonstrated an approach, which Western missionary-established Churches can adopt to mobilize African mythic worlds if they do not want to continue the impression that Christianity is a foreign religion alien to Africans?

Hollenweger, hleading authority in the Pentecostal movement suggests that people are drawn to Pentecostalism because of the inability of the mainline Churches "to communicate its faith". [95] He further states that:

> whether it [Pentecostalism] exists amongst the agricultural workers of Chile, the Indians of Argentina, the proletariat of North America, the masses of African cities, the Gypsies of France, the members of Swedish trade unions, or the poor of Britain, the function of Pentecostal movement is to restore the power of _expression to people without identity or powers of speech and to heal them from the terror of loss of speech.[96]

Hollenweger reveals an important insight into the functions of the African Independent Churches in that they are forms of protest by the oppressed or marginalized people. Camaroff comes to similar conclusions from her study on the use of ritual by the Tswana church in Southern Africa.[97] However, there are times when Pentecostalism can be used as an opiate or "alibi" encouraging the marginalized to accept their conditions as if it was the will of God for them to be marginalized

This point is supported by Hollenweger himself, when he argues that their ideology of holiness at times tends to reduce socio-political and economic policies and structures to individual sins.[98] Those Pentecostals in the holiness movement do not always see the interconnectedness of the physiological, psychological, spiritual, social and cultural.

In spite of these dangers in their theology and practice, their greatest contribution to the Church in Africa is the extent to which they take seriously the mythic worlds of the Bible and their followers. Most of the founders and leaders in these Churches do not filter the Biblical mythic worlds through Western philosophical, psychological and theological discussions. They use their mythic worlds to interpret the Bible.

In our view these Churches have attempted some models of contextualization in Africa in general. In our observation in Ghana the leaders and members of these Churches are largely unconscious of what they are doing and in some cases some of the leaders of these Churches may deny it when confronted for fear of being inferior to the Western missionary-founded Churches.

We can conclude here that there is no doubt that the Western-trained African theologians and other Africanists that we have reviewed have tried to show through sociological-cum-phenomenlolgical studies that whatever religions the missionaries brought to Africa they were not superior to African religions. They have further demonstrated quite convincingly that African religions are capable of accepting and reshaping Western Christianity through a critical rereading of the Biblical stories. Their efforts must be applauded. However, one cannot help but suggest that Horton's criticisms of some Western missionaries and anthropologists are applicable to some Western African theologians and other African religionists:

The missionaries, modern Western Christian anthropologists are intellectual smugglers. They are busy introducing Greek metaphysical conceptions into African religious thought. The African deities of the books, clothed with the attributes of the Christian God, are, in the main, creations of the students of African religion. They are beyond all recognition to the ordinary African in the countryside.[99]

Some of the Western-trained African theologians developed concepts of God that lie beyond the recognition of ordinary members of missionary-founded churches. Such approaches seem so reductionistic that the traditional mythic worlds are not given their unique roles in their forms of indigenization. So Opoku suggests that although most: if not all, these Churches are in the hands of Africans, there is still the feeling that too much familiarity with African culture would sap the essential Christian flavour from the Church's being and existence.[100]

Furthermore, "such a recognition would compel an attitude of humility in the face of African culture which should contrast sharply with the arrogant and disdainful attitude of yesteryear and from which the church is still trying to free herself."[101]

Consequently, some of these Western-trained African theologians provide models of contextualized which do not begin with the African mythic world in which salvation, health and ritual are inseparably related. They often fail to recognize that the first encounter of African mythic worlds and Christianity started with a form of indigenization. The moment Africans use their mythic worlds to translate Christianity, is a moment of indigenization. Therefore it is incorrect for these theologians to claim thatindigenization of the Christian gospel started with their writings.

There is also a strong attack on the cultural indigenization school mostly from some theologians in South Africa.[102] Their main criticism against the cultural indigenization school is that it often fails to take seriously the issues of socio-political and socio-economic realities of oppression and exploitation in Africa. Hence in 1977 a pan African conference of Third World theologians in Accra declared:

> It is our belief that God's demands of the Churches in Africa is that they not only oppose any form of oppression and suffering but also sever reliance, direct or indirect, with the forces of oppression … Because oppression is found not only in culture but also in political and economic structures and the dominant mass media, African theology must also be liberation theology.[103]

Here again, because the phenomena of indigenization is not looked at from the perspective of the mythic world of African Christians, these criticisms assume that African Christians are not protesting against economic exploitation and political oppression with their mythic worlds.

The studies of Camaroff and Mulling provide clear evidence that Africans use their mythic worlds to indigenize as well as protest against economic exploitation, political and theological imperialism. Therefore a critical investigation of how indigenous mythic worlds function as an interpretative mechanism is vitally necessary to understand how Africans rationalize their encounters with the "new" faith, and modernity.

Traditionalism and Modernity in African Literature

In our judgment a critical discussion of the debate of the interaction of traditional mythic worlds and Western Christianity and modernity in Africa is carried on better in African literature than in theological writings. African literary writers, unlike theologians, provide important literary criticisms of the rapid changes in Africa. These writers draw on their feelings, understandings and experiences to describe and analyze change as well as recreate their respective alternatives for Africa. Their approach is similar to some leaders of the African independent churches.

Some African novelists are asking profound questions about what is happening to traditional mythic worlds in their encounters with Western Christianity and modernity. Ayi Kwei Armah, for example, asks the following fundamental questions: what can one person or even communities do in the midst of such irreversible changes? Can the collective Ghanaian mythic worlds survive? Are Ghanaians justified in embarking on individual or collective goals? What are the contexts in today's Ghana? How does one exercise freedom? What are one's obligations? Is it the family, the clan, the Church, the government, or the employer? Who maintains order: the police, the elders, the ancestors, the military, or the Church?[104]

The contribution of the literary writers in assessing the role of the traditional mythic worlds in their encounter with Christianity and modernity seems to be what Ong calls "the technologizing of the word."[105] The literary writers use the method of technologizing the word to understand and in many cases protest against these changes. It is unfortunate that African theologians appear to be unaware of the fact that African writers are their allies even if they sometimes accuse the Church of being an agent of exploitation, colonialism and imperialism in Africa. We shall provide here a summary of the views of some of the prominent African writers who are allies in our attempts to understand the phenomenon of indigenization even though we are mainly concerned with the theological dimension of indigenization.

Obiechina observes that: through the introduction of literacy, the corpus of Western, indeed world civilization, its institutions and values, arts and sciences, philosophies and theology, its aesthetic values, and the artifacts of its material culture were made available to people of West Africa.'[106]

The main effect of education "was to break the psychic insularity of traditional education and limited physical mobility, and to substitute for it a cosmopolitan and mobile psyche."[107] Riesman similarly points out the effect of literacy on traditional society in which he observes that with literacy, tradition-direction persons shifted to inner-direction.[108]

Chinua Achebe in two of his novels deals with the irreversible influence of Western civilization on traditional mythic worlds through two traditional characters, the character of Okonkwo in Things Fall Apart and the chief priest, Ezeulu in Arrow of God. Both characters fight an almost losing battle with modernity. Through the characters of Okonkwo and Ezeulu, Achebe, in the words of Obiechina:

> ... is able to enter imaginatively into the lives of his traditional characters and to expose the strains to which they are exposed as a result of the descriptive effect of a foreign culture in a relatively stable and self-sufficient culture they grew up in.[109]

Achebe presents a situation in which there are rapidly shifting loyalties and value systems. This shifting occurs between the values of the traditional mythic world and the values of Christianity and modernity.[110]

The power and symbols of the traditional mythic worlds are disintegrating. Even the role of the gods as "ultimate arbiters of human affairs is lost by the people of Okperi disobeying their chief priest."[111] A money economy is introduced; policemen rather than the chief priest, are now responsible for law and order.

In these two novels, Christianity and modernity provide Africans with alternatives to their traditional mythic worlds. The traditional mythic world seems unable:

> ... to regulate the conflicts and stresses which arose from the culture contact. Traditional customary laws became ineffective, not only because their religious basis was undermined by Christianity but because the colonial administration monopolized the use of coercion and so weakened the capacity of traditional societies to exact conformity from their eccentric members or to settle inter-communal strife by the threat of action or by action ifself.[112]

Furthermore, Olney supports the case of the destruction of the traditional mythic world arguing that: the very fact of writing in English or in French already Constitutes a self-determined alienation on the part of the intellectual or evolve since the foreign language and his professional use of it can only remove him from the great majority of non-intellectual Africans.[113]

The role of languages such as English and French in altering the African mythic world is best articulated and protested by Ngugi wa Thiongo.[114] Ngugi wa Thiongo strongly argues that the introduction of foreign languages was an integral part of the colonial agenda similar to the introduction of district commissioners. Foreign languages were "the most important vehicle through which that fascinated and held the soul prisoner. Language was the means of the spiritualsubjugation."[115]

Critical evaluations of African Literature: A Case for traditional mythic worlds

Lerner best offers a summary of the battle between traditionalism, modernity and technological transformation of traditional societies such as the Frafra by some African writers:

> The process of modernization powerfully transforms individual lifeways. The move from the familiar and deeply personal life of a family farm in an isolated village to the strange impersonality of a 'job' in a busy city crowded with unknown persons is one such transformation.[16]
>
> Although Africans have intensely interacted with modernity, we cannot accept the conclusion of some Western-trained theologians and African writers that traditional mythic worlds have lost their potencies to resist change. As already indicated, various researches on the African independent Churches provide a contrary view. Our view is that the use of African traditional mythic worlds as contexts for appropriating meanings in pluralistic African societies is an important key in understanding the Africans' encounters with Christianity and modernity.

A critical analysis of the African novelists rather suggests that the traditional mythic world is transforming Christianity and modernity. Olney seems to support our view when he says "many African writers ... choose to inform the outside world about Africa and the African experience by dramatizing their lives and then taking their own case as representative."[117]

These writers are certainly drawing on old African traditional mythic worlds and some even attempt to use their mythic world to reconstruct an alternative to the changes they experience. Therefore, the writers are indeed unconsciously suggesting that traditional mythic worlds are transforming both modernity and Christianity in ways that are uniquely African. The task of both African practical theologians and writers is to understand how these mythic worlds are translating Christianity and modernity. But our position is that they cannot fulfill such a task unless and until they first try to understand the role of traditional mythic worlds as interpretative mechanisms in their traditional setting.

It is also often argued that people in cities and urban centers are totally disconnected from rural traditional life. So it is concluded that the African mythic worlds have totally disappeared in these people. There is enough evidence to show the contrary. The confessions of Nkrumah regarding his failure to eradicate traditional mythic worlds in Ghana provide us with a clue to the almost impossible task of changing traditional mythic worlds in Ghana. He writes:

> I had to combat not only tribalism but the African tradition that a man's first duty was to his family group and that therefore nepotism was the highest of all virtues. While I believe we had largely eliminated tribalism as an active force, its by-products and those of the family system were still with us.[118]

Nkrumah's admission of failure to make all Ghanaians adopt his nationalism at the expense of traditional mythic worlds, points clearly to the fact that influence of Christianity and modernity are not only limited but also selective on the traditional mythic worlds of Ghanaians.

We suggest that Nkrumah failed, partly because in Ghanaian mythic worlds a person's identity is inseparably related to the family, clan and tribe. The Frafra, the Ewe, the Ga, the Akan to name a few ethnic communities "have not found in the modern state of Ghana the voice of their past, or with the force and living authority of the ancestors."[119] The yaabnam of the Frafra, the Kusah, the Akan and Ga are real to them in a way that the "conglomerate state can never be because the modern state is an abstract entity formed in nearly every case."[120] Nkrumah's modern western approach failed partly because he failed to understand the old traditional mythic worlds as interpretative mechanisms with which Ghanaians operate even in the modern state of Ghana.

In Ghana there is hardly any group of people who have become so rationalized and modernized that they have severed completely their ties with their traditional mythic world. Nabilah in his research on labour migration of the

Frafra from the north to the south has clearly shown that there is a cyclical movement between rural, urban and city dwellers. There is back and forth movement. Those in the village come to their relatives in the cities for money or some kind of help, while the city dwellers go back to the village for funerals and other ritual needs.[121] There is constant reinforcement of traditional mythic worlds even among the young in the urban city dwellers by these cyclical movements. We can therefore infer that there is a constant interaction between the Frafra mythic world with modernity in which their mythic world helps them deal with changes.

Furthermore, in the cities, there are associations of people from similar ethnic groups. For example, the Frafra association in Accra has an inherited Frafra chief's house in Nima. The Frafra in Accra believe that the chief's house performs a symbolic function in terms of their identity in their mythic world and in the isolated and at times hostile Accra urban life. Therefore the interpretative mechanism of the traditional mythic world is enhanced rather than destroyed. The Christians who come to Accra tend to attend congregations in which there is a majority of their ethnic group members.

A number of the Presbyterian congregations in Accra are made of people of the same ethnic group. For example, the Nima Catholic Church is made up of people from the North. The Evangelical Presbyterian congregations are predominantly made of Ewes who worship in the Ewe language. There are also many congregations of other denominations made up of predominantly one ethnic group or another in Accra. There are similar secular and religious ethnic associations of those from Southern Ghana working in the North of Ghana. For example, in Bolgatanga, there is a strong association of Asante. Their chief or Asantehene is the senior presbyter of the local Presbyterian Church in Bolgatanga. The formation of ethnic groups in the cities in Nigeria is also discussed by Lloyd,[122]

The general conclusions we can draw from these cyclical migrations, secular and religious ethnic associations and congregations overwhelmingly support our claim that traditional mythic worlds as interpretative mechanisms continue to play an indispensable role in the people's encounter with Christianity and modernity. Therefore, a critical investigation of the interpretative in any effort to reconstruct a contextualized Christian ministry especially a ministry of healing.

Change and Pastoral Theological Agenda in Ghana

The central role of traditional mythic worlds in the encounter with modernity and Christianity in Ghana cannot be over-emphasized. As already indicated, the unique contribution of Africa to world Christianity lies in a response that starts with the African mythic worlds. Shorter points out the urgent need of such an African response when he writes:

> The Church needs the African theological contribution for her own theological health. This contribution is not going to destroy or alter the universal tradition, but it may operate first of all as a corrective in a number of ways... it may awaken themes in universal Christianity which are dormant or latent ... show that certain elements presented in Africa are essential.[123]

President Banana of Zimbabwe also offered another compelling challenge for the Church in Africa. He challenged third world theologians in general "to seriously consider rewriting the Bible so that God can be liberated from dogmas that make God the property of ethnic syndicates."[124]

The difference between Banaan's view and the intention of this thesis is that we do not think it is possible to make the Bible ethnic free, but it is possible to make the Bible inclusive of all ethnic groups. For the task of African pastoral theology is to provide a holistic ministry that starts with the African mythic world as suggested by both Lartey and Masamba ma Mpolo.

Lartey advocates a model of dialogue between African mythic worlds and theology, the psychotherapeutic psychologies and sociological/cultural anthropology.[125] Masamba ma Mpolo also offers a similar approach:

> The cultural dimension influencing individuals' concept of illness and behaviour responses, should be taken seriously so that sociology and culture which play a significant rolein the development of personality can become part of therapy.[126]

In conclusion, the story of the encounter of the Frafra mythic world and Western Christianity, scientific medicine, and modernity, and the literature review have shown clearly that an "epistemological distance" exists in Frafra Christians in particular and African Christians in general. These evidences have also shown that the "epistemological distance" was caused primarily because the three offences suggested by Panikkar were committed. The literature review from African theological discourses, the sciences of religion, and African literary writers do not only argue that the "epistemological distance" has to be bridged but more importantly that it can be bridged using resources from African indigenous mythic worlds. Indeed, the African theologies that we have examined are important attempts to offer corrective theological responses to make the claims of the Church necessary and relevant to African Christians. This thesis seeks to join in their efforts by attempting a modest contextual Christian pastoral response to the Frafra Christians in the Frafra context.

References

1. This information was obtained from Gabriel Sampana, Senior Presbyter of the local Presbyterian Church. He is a son of Sampana Nabil, the most senior man in Datuku, who had contacts with both the colonial administrators and the early missionaries. Some even said he supervised the building of the branch. Gabriel, his uncle, and his father did supervise the building of the local Presbyterian chapel. He also became the senior prefect of the literary classes held then by the missionaries.

2 From the records of Datoko Primary School and oral history from two village elders.

3. Pasta is the linguistic variation of the word Pastor and Fada for the Roman Catholic priest or father. Later they were used to refer to the Presbyterian denomination and the Roman Catholic Church respectively in Datuku and indeed throughout Frafraland.

4. Jean-Marc Ela, My Faith as an African (Mary Knoll, NY: Orbis Books 1988), p.[3]

5. Charles H. Kraft, Christianity in Culture : A Study of Dynamic Biblical Theologizing in Cross-Cultural Perspective with Forward by Bernard Ramin (Mary Knoll : Orbis Books 1987), p.[147].

6. Ibid.

7. L.A. Samovag, and R.E. Porter, Intercultural Communication: A Reader (California: Wade worth 1972), p.[33].

8. Kraft, Christianity in Culture (1987), p.[149].

9. Ibid

10. Ibid

11. Ibid

12. Ibid

13. Morton T. Kelsey, *Healing and Christianity* (London SCM Press 1971), p.29-30.

14. Martin Luther, "Sermons on the Gospel of St John, Chapters 14-16 *Luther Works*, Vol. 24,p.[367]. However, later in his life he seemed to change his view or added another view. See pages 221 and 233.

15. John Calvin, *Institutes of the Christian Religion*, iv, 18 (1953), p.2:636.

16. Morton T. Kelsey, *Healing and Christianity* (London: SCM Press 1973), p.29, 30

17. Ibid.

18. ibid, p.28.

19. Ibid.

20. ibid, p.30.

21. Michael C. Kirwen, *The Missionary and the Diviner* (Mary Knoll, N.Y.: Orbis Books, 1987), chapter One

22. C.G. Baeta, *Prophetism in Ghana* (London: SCM 1962) ,p.135.

23. Gustaf Wingren, *Theology in Conflict: Nygren, Barth Bultmann*, translated by Eric H. Wahlstrom (Edinburgh: Tweedale Court 1958), p.ix.

24. ibid. Pp.xiii-xiv.

25. Ibid.

26. ibid, p.xv.

27. Ibid.

28. Ibid

29. Kirwen, *The Missionary and the Diviner* (1987), p.25.

30. Duncan Forrester, "Divinity in Use and Practice" in Duncan B. Forrester (ed) Theology and Practice (London: Epworth Press 1990), p.7.

51 David Tracy, in Blessed Rage for Order: The New Pluralism in Theology (New York: The Seabury Press 1978)) has given a broad classification various practical theology models which are partially helpful in determining various practical theological approaches in North America, and Europe. Such models have had direct and indirect influences on pastoral theological models produced from Asia and Africa. Each of these models attempts a Christian attitude to modernity or in the case of Asia and Africa, both modernity and traditional cultural beliefs and socio-political problems. Orthodox Theology. In this approach modernity does not have any relevance to theology. According to Tracy, the aim of such is to "express an adequate understanding of the beliefs of his particular church tradition" (p.24). Such a theology is not interested in any claims of modernity in which scientific, historical and philosophical scholarships and in Asia and Africa traditional cultural and political problems are brought to bear on theology (p.24). Orthodox theology in this sense is a kind of "bulwark against modernity, [traditional belief) and socio-political realities." The task of a practical theologian from this tradition is to develop a reasoned defence of dogmas in the tradition. Liberal Theology: A dialogue between modernity, secularity and Christian beliefs. The task of a practical theologian from this model is a commitment of "basic cognitive claims of Christianity and modernity, secularity". She/he employs critically free and open enquiry on the correlation of scientific, historical, philosophical and religious claims.

Neo-Orthodox Theology. In this approach there is both acceptance and rejection of modernity.p.29ff. For example, they reject liberal interpretations of Christianity.

Radical theology is one characterized by secular affirmations and theistic negations of liberal and neo-orthodox models of theology. God seems alienated from contemporary human situation. The self-referent (believer's perspective) is commitment of the post modern secular and intellectual and moral values. The method of radical theology is one in which the divine or the object-referent (faith in God) in effect offers a reformation of Christianity that denies central belief in God and Jesus as a paradigm of life and the incarnation is seen as a paradigm of another demonstration of freed humanity (p.31).

The Revisionist model is a revised one of the critical correlation method proposed by Paul Tillich Systematic Theology Vol. One (Chicago: The University of Chicago Press 1951), p.56-68. It is re appropriated by Don Browning as a critical revised correlation in Don Browning in Religious Thought and the Modern Psychologies: A critical conversation in the theology of culture Philadelphia : Fortress Press 1987). It is a critical correlation of Christian claims and of the psychotherapeutic psychologies.

Hiltner suggests a perspective approach in which the social and human science, are perspectives in addition to theological perspective and these perspectives must Dialogue. However, for Hiltner, the task of the Practical theologian is to offer a Theological perspective. Seward Hiltner, Preface to Pastoral Theology (Nashville: Abingdon Press 1958).

Campbell points out how Hiltner seems to be unaware of the methodological Difficulties in his argument (Forrester 1990) p.15.

Although Browning, Hiltner, Forrester and Campbell do agree for a correlation Between other disciplines and theology, they differ in approaches with Browning as in hi Religious Thought and Modernism in Psychology ( ). He shows how his method of correlation can be done. His "Revised critical correlation" implies that the claims of other disciplines are as valid as theological claims, especially between the psychotherapeutics and Christian claims of healing. In other words for Browning, both secular psychotherapeutics and the theological resources for healing are equal and hence achieve the same results.

This approach is what Tracy refers to as revisionist model. In this model one has to judge the value of therapy from the subject or what Tracy calls the "self referent" of the revisionist model. Tracy suggests that the revisionist model is a contemporary one in which beliefs, values and faiths of an authentic secularity are similar to the understanding of beliefs, values and faith of authentic Christianity (p.33).

In this model the Divine or what Tracy calls the object-referent undergoes a critical reformulation of both the meanings manifested by our common human experiences and the meaning manifested by an interpretation of the critical motif of the Christian tradition (p.34). Another example of such a revisionist model of Christian experience and definition of God is found in liberation and Feminist theologies.

32. Bernard Lonergan, Method in Theology (London: Darton Longman and Todd 1971) and A Second Collection (London: Darton Longman 1971) and The Third Collection (London: Dalton, Longman, and Todd 1985).

33. Brian Cronin, "Religious and Christian Conversion in an African Context" in African Christian Studies Vol. 3, No. 2 (June 1987), p.19-35.

34. ibid, p.20.

35. ibid, p.22 relying on Bernard Lonergan A Third Collection (1985), p. 57, 71, 116 and 125.

36. ibid, p.27.

37. Ibid.

38. ibid p.29.

39. Ibid, p.30 relying on Frederick Growe, Son of God, Holy Spirit and World Religions. The contribution of Bernard Lonergan to the Wider Ecumenism (Toronto: Regis College Press, 1985), p.8.

40. ibid, p.32.

41. Ibid.

42. Ibid.

43. ibid, p.32-33.

44. ibid, p.33

45. Ibid.

46. Ibid.

47. Ibid.

48. B.P. Carmody, "Conversion to Roman Catholicism in Zambia. Shifting pedagogues" in African Christian Studies Vol. 4, No. 2, (June 1988), p.5-24. Relying on Paulo Freire, Pedagogy of the Oppressed (New York : Continuum 1981) translated by Myra Bergman Rands) and also Education for Critical Consciousness (New York : Continuum 1981).

49. B.P. Carmody, "Conversion to Roman Catholicism in Zambia" in African Christian Studies Vol. 4, No. 2 (June 1988), p.6.

50. ibid.

51. ibid.

52. ibid.

53. ibid. p.7.

54. p.7 quoting from Paulo Freire (New York 1981), p.60.

55. ibid, p.7.

56. ibid, p.11.

57. ibid, p.13.

58. ibid.

59. E. Fasholoe-Luke, Richard Gray, Adrian Hasting, and Godwin Tasie, (eds), Christianity in Independent Africa Bloomington, Indiana State University Press 1978), p.364-369, also see "The African local churches and the world-wide Roman Catholic communion : modification of relationships as exemplified by Llilouguie Diocese" in Fashole-Luke et al (1978), p.76-95, see also Kofi A. Opoku "Changes within Christianity : the case of the Musama Disco Christo Church" in Fashole-Luke et al (eds) (1978), p.111-121.

60. E. Milingo, The World in between : Christian healing and the struggle for spiritual survival (London : Hurst & Co. 1984). Gerrie Ter Haar, Spirit of Africa : the healing ministry of Archbishop Milingo of Zambia (London : Hurst & Co 1982).

48. B.P. Carmody, "Conversion to Roman Catholicism in Zambia. Shifting pedagogues" in African Christian Studies Vol. 4, No. 2, (June 1988), p.5-24. Relying on Paulo Freire, Pedagogy of the Oppressed (New York : Continuum 1981) translated by Myra Bergman Rands) and also Education for Critical Consciousness (New York : Continuum 1981).

49. B.P. Carmody, "Conversion to Roman Catholicism in Zambia" in African Christian Studies Vol. 4, No. 2 (June 1988), p.6.

50. ibid.

51. ibid.

52. ibid.

53. ibid. p.7.

54. p.7 quoting from Paulo Freire (New York 1981), p.60.

55. ibid, p.7.

56. ibid, p.11.

57. ibid, p.13.

58. ibid.

59. E. Fasholoe-Luke, Richard Gray, Adrian Hasting, and Godwin Tasie, (eds), Christianity in Independent Africa Bloomington, Indiana State University Press 1978), p.364-369, also see "The African local churches and the world-wide Roman Catholic communion : modification of relationships as exemplified by Llilouguie Diocese" in Fashole-Luke et al (1978), p.76-95, see also Kofi A. Opoku "Changes within Christianity : the case of the Musama Disco Christo Church" in Fashole-Luke et al (eds) (1978), p.111-121.

60. E. Milingo, The World in between : Christian healing and the struggle for spiritual survival (London : Hurst & Co. 1984). Gerrie Ter Haar, Spirit of Africa : the healing ministry of Archbishop Milingo of Zambia (London : Hurst & Co 1982).

61. Effraim Anderson, Churches at the Grass roots: A study in Congo-Brazzaville. World Studies of Churches in Mission WCC (London: Lutterworth Press 1968), p.44.

62. Richard Gray, Black Christians, White Missionaries (Newhaven: Yale University Press 1990), p.32.

63. ibid, p.22.

64. ibid.

65. ibid, p.38.

66. C.G. Baeta, Prophetism in Ghana, A study of some 'spiritual' churches (London: SCM Press 1962). See also David B. Barret Schism and Renewal in Africa. An analysis of six thousand contemporary religious movements (London: Oxford University Press 1968). S.F. Nadel, "A study of shamanism in Nuba Mountain" in Lessa L. William and Vogt Z. Evon (eds), Reader in Comparative Religion: An Anthropological Approach (New York : Harper & Row1965). M.L. Daneel, Old and New in Southern Shona Independent Churches (The Hague: Mouton & Co 1971). Bennetta Jules-Rosette, African Apostles. Ritual and Conversion in the Church of John Maranke (lthaca : Cornell University Press 1975). Walter J. Hollenweger, The Pentecostals (London: SCM Press Ltd. 1972). Lamin Sanneh, Translating the Massage: The Missionary Impact on Culture (Mary Knoll, : N.Y., : Orbis Books 1991) Robert W. Wyllie, Spiritism in Ghana : A study of new religious movement. Studies in religion 21 (Missoula: Montana Scholar Press 1980). D.Y. Peel, Aladura : A religious movement among Yoruba (Oxford : University of Oxford Press 1968.) and H.W. Turner African Independent Church (Oxford : Oxford University Press, 1967).

67. Robin Horton, "African Conversion" in Africa Vol. 4, No. 2 (April, 1981). See also on "The Rationality of Conversion", in Africa, Vol. 45, No. 3 (1975), p. 219-235).

68. ibid, p.101.

69. ibid, p.102

70. ibid, p.103.

71. ibid.

72. ibid.

73. ibid, p.104.

74. ibid.

75. Charles Nyamiti, "African Christologies Today" in Robert Schreiter (ed) Faces of Jesus in Africa (Mary Knoll, New York : Orbis Books 1992).

76. John Mbiti, Bible and Theology in African Christianity (Nairobi) Oxford University Press 1986. See also New Testament Eschatology in an African Background (London: SPCK 1978)

77. John S. Pobee, Towards an African Theology (Nashville: Abingdon 1979), p.81-98.

78. Kwesi Dickson, Theology in Africa (Maryknoll, New York: Orbis Books 1984), p. 185-199

79. E.J. Penoukou, "Realite africaine et salute en Jesus Christ" in Spiritus Vol. 23, No. 88 (Dec. 1982), p.374ff.

80. Kofi Appiah-Kubi, "Jesus Christ: Some Christological Aspects from African Perspectives" in John S. Mbiti (ed) African and Asia Contributions to Contemporary Theology (Report of a Consultations held at Ecumenical Institute, Bossey 8-14 June, 1976), (Geneva: WCC 1977).

81. T. Anselme Sanon, "Jesus, Master of limitation" in Schreiter (ed.) Faces of Jesus (Marknoll, N.Y.: 1992).

82. Nyamiti in R. Schreiter (ed.) Faces of Jesus in Africa (Mary Knoll, New York: Orbis Books 1992), p.16.

83. John Parratt, A reader in African Theology. (London: SPCK 1985)

84. Aylward Shorter, Jesus and the Witch Doctor : An Approach to Healing and Wholeness (Maryknoll, New York: Orbis Book 1985).
85. A. Shorter, Jesus and the witch Doctor (1985) (London: Geoffrey Chapman 1988) Also Christian Healing and "Traditional Medicine"in Africa Kergyma (1986), Vol. 20 p.51-58. Also see Aylward Shorter African Culture and the Christian Church (MaryKnoll, N.Y.: Orbis Books 1974).
86. Howard Clark Kee, Medicine, Miracle and Magic in the New Testament Times, (Cambridge: Cambridge University Press 1986).
87. ibid, p.2.
88. Aylward Shorter, African Christian Theology (1977), p.157-161.
89. Robert W. Wyllie, "Pentecostalism: Peter Enim and James McKeown" in Journal of Religion in Africa vol. 6 Fasc 2,1974, p.109-122. See also A detail history of the Pentecost Church of Ghana in Christine Leonard A Giant in Ghana (Chichester:Newwine Press 1989) Also see Paul Gifford "Ghana's Charismatic Churches" in Journal of religion in Africa vol.xxiv Fasc 3, August, 1994
90. Leith Mulling, "Religious change and social stratification in Labadi, Ghana: The Church of the Messiah" in George Bond, Walton Johnston and Sheil S. Walker (eds) African Christianity: Patterns of Religious Continuity (NewYork : Academic Press 1979), p.66. Robert W. Wyllie Spiritism in Ghana: A study of new religious movements AAR Studies in religion 21 (Misoula, Montana : Scholar press 1980).
91. ibid, p.85.
92. ibid, p.86
93. Gerrie Ter Haar, Spirit of Africa: The Healing Ministry of Archbishop Milingo of Zambia, (1992), p.24-25.
94. L'Osservatore Romano, November (1990).
95. Walter J. Hollenweger, The Pentecostals, (London : SCM Press, 1972), p.462.
96. ibid, p.459.
97. Jean Camaroff, Power of Power, Spirit of Resistance : The Culture and History of a Southern African People (Chicago University of Chicago Press 1985).
98. W.J. Hollenweger, The Pentecostals (London: SCM 1972), p.549.
99. Horton, "African Conversion" in Africa Vol. 4, (1975), p.224 relying on P'Bitek African Religious in Western scholarship (Nairobi 1970).
100. Kofi A. Opoku in Fasholo-Like et al (1978), p.112.
101. ibid.
102. Kouise Kretschmar provides a good summary of these approaches and

especially the Southern African responses in The voice of black theology in South Africa (Johannesburg: Raven Press 1986). Also Albert Nolan, Jesus before Christianity: The Gospel of liberation (London: Darton, Lonscmar and Todd 1976). Allan Boesak Farewell to innocence : A socio-ethical study of black theology and black power (Maryknoll, New York : Orbis Book 1977)

103. Kofi Appiah-Kubi, and S. Torries, (eds) African Theology Enroute MaryKonll NY : Orbis Books 1979), p.191 and 194.

104. Ayi Kwei Armah, The Beautiful Ones are yet Born (London: Heinemann 1969).

105. Walker J. Ong, Orality and Literacy: The Technologizing of the Word (London: Methuen `982).

106. Emmanuel Obechina, Culture, tradition and society in the West African novel (Cambridge: Cambridge University Press 1975), p.5.

107. Ibid.

108. David Riesman, The Lonely Crowd (London, 1964).

109. Oniechina (1975), p.6.

110. Chinua Achebe, A man of the people (London : Heinemann 1966).

111. Chinua Achebe, Arrow of God (1941), p.157-158.

112. E. Obiechina, (1975), p.229.

113. James Olney, Tell me Africa : An approach to African literature (Princeton : Princeton University 1973), p.289.

114. Ngugi Wa Thiongo, Decolonizing the mind : The politics of language in African literature (Nairobi : Heinemann 1986).

115. ibid, p.9.

116. Daniel Lerner, in The Passing of Transitional Society (Glencoe, lll. 1958), p.52-53.

117. James Olney, Tell me Africa (1973), p.37.

118. Kwame Nkrumah, Dark days in Ghana (New York: International Publishers 1968), p.66.

119. ibid, p.71.

120. ibid, p.37.

121. John S. Nabilah, The Migration of the Frafra of Northern Ghana : A case study of cycling labour migration in West Africa Ph.D. thesis, Michigan State University, 1974.

122. P.C. Lloyd, Africa in Social Change: Changing Traditional Societies into the Modern World (Middlesex: Penguin Books 1967), p.196-202.

123. Alyward Shorter, African Christian Theology (Mary Knoll, N.Y. : Orbis Books 1977), p.31.

124. Canaan S. Banana, "The case for a new Bible" in l. Mukonyora, J.L. Cox, and F.J. Verstraelen (Co-ordinator) Rewriting the Bible: the real issues (Gweru, Zimbabwe: Manbo Press 1993), p.103-123.

125. Emmanuel Y. Lartey, Pastoral Counselling in Intercultural Perspective (Frankfurt Peterlang 1987), p.175.

126. Masamba ma Mpolo, and Wilheimina Kalu, eds., The Risks of Growth, Pastoral Counselling in Context (Geneva : WCC 1985), p.4.

CHAPTER THREE

The Frafra

Introduction

This chapter describes the Frafra context in which the encounter between the Frafra mythic world Christianity and modernity takes place, Western Christianity and modernity were not introduced into Frafraland until the late nineteenth century and early twentieth century. So Frafraland provides a glimpse of the moment of transition from the mono-cultural, rural traditional setting to a multi-cultural, pluralistic urban context. The Frafra are engaged in an intense process in which they are using their traditional mythic world to make meaning out of these irreversible changes impacting on their lives.

There are different accounts of the etymology of the name Frafra. The most popular version is that it was derived from the common informal greeting "frafra". Cardinal, one of the foreigners alleged to have coined the term, writes:

> Grunshi has been further divided by us into Frafra, Grunshi and Kanjaga. The Frafra included all the Nankani, Nabnam and Talansi and is a word derived from a form of greeting spoken by these people who murmur by way of thanks or petition 'fra-fra or fura-ura.'

The Frafra belong to the general linguistic group designated by Rattray as the "Mole Group"[2] which also includes "the Mampelle, Dagbane, Kusal, Nankane or Gotene, Dagare, Nabte, Bulee, Wala and Loberu".

The Frafraland

Until recently, the present Upper East region was part of what was then called Upper region. The Upper region then included the Wala, and the Dagari., these ethnic groups are now in a different region called Upper West region. This explains why in some of the literature on Ghana, the Upper region consists of all these groups of people.

These ethnic groups have philological similarities and common cultural practices and beliefs. It seems we have to talk Cardinal's etymology of Frafra as a supreme example of the colonial significations of the Frafra people that have stayed and may stay with them for some time. Frafra is now the collective name for the three dialects commonly spoken by the groups of this triad with some marked linguistic variations in certain expressions. The three dialects that make up the Frafra are Goreni, Tallen, and Nabet. Throughout this book, Frafra will be used to designate the collective language, geography, religion, and culture of this triad. Where we are referring to one of the three ethnic communities we will say Gorensi for the people, Goreni for the dialect, Talleh for the people, and Tallen for the language, Nabnam for the people and Nabet for the language.

Geography

The Frafra to the south share boundaries with the Mumprusi, those to the north with the Mossi in Burkina Faso. To the North-west the Kasena, to the west the LoDagaba and the east the Kussasi. The Gorensi are at the center, the north, and the north-west. Prior to Bolgatanga becoming the administrative capital, Zuarungu; two miles east of Bolgatanga was the original capital of the Frafra. It must be mentioned that the idea of an admin istrative capital for the triad was invented by colonial administrators for their own convenience. These boundaries were arbitrarily imposed by colonial administrators. This imposition has resulted to fighting, legal suits, and counter suits even up to the time of writing this thesis.

The Talleh are to the south-east of Bolgatanga, sharing borders with the Mumprusi in the Northern region. They are most known in the literature of anthropology because of the extensive writings of Meyer Fortes[4] about them. Their main administrative and commercial capital is Tongo.

The Nabnam[5] are to the east of Bolgatanga, sharing boundaries with both the Kusasi and the Gorensi in Bongo. Their capital is Nangodi. In terms of local councils they used to be grouped with the Goreh in Bongo but in terms of electing a member of parliament to represent them they were grouped with the Telleh. We have not come across any satisfactory reasons for these divisions so far. Now a new administrative district is created for the Talleh and Nadnam. Its administrative capital is in Tongo.

The Frafra live in an areas of about 1,900 sq km. Frafraland is about 500 to 700 feet about sea level. There are a number of rocky hills scattered throughout Frafraland. The highest are about 1,250 feet found in the Tongo and Nangodi areas. There are two main seasons, the dry and rainy seasons respectively. The rainy season starts at about May and ends in October or early November. The peak of the rainy season is in August and September, with varying rates of rainfall.

The rest of the year is the dry season with no rain or else some showers. The temperature ranges between 15 0 and 50 0 degrees Celsius. The humidity also varies from the rainy season to the dry season. The climate is tropical. The vegetation is savannah, the tall and short grasses, shrubs, and scattered short trees all over. Few rivers flow across Frafraland. There are many dams and ponds throughout the area.[6]

Traditional Frafra Spirituality

One of the difficulties of this project is how to translate the Frafra ways of life into western categories without the distortion and reductionism that Western scholars are accused of. It is not only practically difficult to make such separation between religion, culture, and sociology in the frafra mythic world but it is also difficult to find English equivalents to express their categories. One way of getting around this problem is to describe first, without technical jargon from any discipline.

As already noted, the religious, cultural and social form a totality of life. in most cases a religious act is also a cultural and social act. For the purpose of this thesis, we shall designate the religious socio-cultural psycho-social and economical and political as the totality of life. Totality of life suggests that the religious, cultural and social perspectives interact as one in the Frafra experiences of life.

Frafra spirituality is intrinsically related to two main symbols. The first category we designate as geographical symbols. These include trees, rocks, stones, hills, water, rivers, ponds, woods and metal. The second category we designate as biological symbols. These include all types of animals, both domesticated and wild on land and in water and human begins of both sexes, and of all ages and spirits of ancestors.

Frafra spirituality divides the world into two types. These are the physical visible and non-physical visible. The physical visible is both a replica and a continuation of the non-physical invisible. These two worlds communicate and interact constantly with each other. The spatial relationship between the two worlds is opaque from the perspective of those in the physical visible world but transparent from the perspective of those in the non-physical visible world.

The rest of the year is the dry season with no rain or else some showers. The temperature ranges between 15 0 and 50 0 degrees Celsius. The humidity also varies from the rainy season to the dry season. The climate is tropical. The vegetation is savannah, the tall and short grasses, shrubs, and scattered short trees all over. Few rivers flow across Frafraland. There are many dams and ponds throughout the area.[6]

Traditional Frafra Spirituality

One of the difficulties of this project is how to translate the Frafra ways of life into western categories without the distortion and reductionism that Western scholars are accused of. It is not only practically difficult to make such separation between religion, culture, and sociology in the frafra mythic world but it is also difficult to find English equivalents to express their categories. One way of getting around this problem is to describe first, without technical jargon from any discipline.

As already noted, the religious, cultural and social form a totality of life. in most cases a religious act is also a cultural and social act. For the purpose of this thesis, we shall designate the religious socio-cultural psycho-social and economical and political as the totality of life. Totality of life suggests that the religious, cultural and social perspectives interact as one in the Frafra experiences of life.

Frafra spirituality is intrinsically related to two main symbols. The first category we designate as geographical symbols. These include trees, rocks, stones, hills, water, rivers, ponds, woods and metal. The second category we designate as biological symbols. These include all types of animals, both domesticated and wild on land and in water and human begins of both sexes, and of all ages and spirits of ancestors.

Frafra spirituality divides the world into two types. These are the physical visible and non-physical visible. The physical visible is both a replica and a continuation of the non-physical invisible. These two worlds communicate and interact constantly with each other. The spatial relationship between the two worlds is opaque from the perspective of those in the physical visible world but transparent from the perspective of those in the non-physical visible world.

Rituals are the only means of communication between the two worlds. Kaaba is their main ritual for achieving well-being vitality identity and a sense of meaning for those living in the physical world.

Ancestors and boar (shrines) of the earth are also important forms of spirituality in the frafra mythic world. The office of the Tendan (earth priest) is also important.[7] In the Frafra mythic world the power of teng (earth) pervades the religious, social and the psychological dimensions of life.

Teng to the Frafra can mean the physical, geographical environment on which they live: their houses, the tam (soil), tii (trees), zuar (hills)kuga (stones). Teng can also mean an all-seeing omnipotent spirit which gives them food, protects their animals and themselves and interacts with their daily lives. Finally, Teng also refers to the local shrine whose primary task is to ensure the well-being of residents within this locality.

The local sacred spots are the spots on which kaaba are offered. For most Ghanaians in the South these earth shrines popularly called "nana Tongo" are the most protective powers to be consulted in times of difficulties.

These holy or sacred spots are what the Talleh and Nabnam refer to as tengkpan (tangane in Goreni). There can be found in almost any place: a grove of trees, a heap of stones and rivers. These different tengkpana (plural) have direct responsibility for protecting the different clans. Those who offer kaaba at any one shrine are truly kinsfolk.

A senior member of the clan offers *kaaba* to the ancestors on behalf of all the *biih* (descendants) on a particular sacred spot. The *kpeem* (the senior member of the clan) also presides on the sacred spot which represents the supreme *teng* spirit of that geographical location. So *teng* can refer to one particular local shrine belonging to a particular group of clans but it can also consist of a group of clans. In this case *teng* is called boar.

Frafra social and ethical life, and identify are best understood in relation to their *Kaaba* and allegiance to *teng* earth shrine) boar (the local paternal and maternal head shrine).[8]

The Frafra social life seems to be intensely relational or gregarious. Their ethics are also determined by their social relations and the effects of individual actions on the group. This intensively collective social life however adjusts to personal preferences and choices in spiritual and socio-cultural matters but is not necessarily individualistic as in Western societies. The personal choices must always be related to group solidarity and identity. Social ties trace their origin to the concentric circles of relations of founding ancestors of the clan/lineage. The clan/lineage system is closely connected to the earth shrine. Therefore there is a direct relationship between social relations and personality in Frafra mythic world.

Clash of Traditional Mythic world and Modernity in Frafraland

Bolgatanga is generally accepted to be the commercial center for the frafra by virtue of the fact that it is the capital of the Upper East Region (UER) as a whole. Bolgatanga has more of the modern institutions such as, the banks, and government offices are located there. Bolgatanga furthermore has most of the modern social amenities such as transportation, water, communication systems, electricity and a regional hospital. In short, Bolgatanga is more urbanised all the Frafra towns and villages in the UER of Ghana.

Consequently, it is undergoing irreversible changes in almost all spheres of life. The same could be said for Bongo, Nangodi and Tongo, only to a lesser degree. There are people from different parts of Ghana as well as expatriates working as teachers, doctors, nurses, engineers, bankers, Church workers in Frafraland.

The conflict between the old and the new is also clearly visible in Frafra land. Traveling the breadth and width of Frafraland, one observes that the people are in a state of confusion or a feeling of ambivalence towards the conflict between the "old" and "new" in their lives and environments. They wear Western clothing, have transistor radios, televisions, phones, and faxes to mention but a few. Hence they are connected to the larger world cultures. They also use modern cooking tools such as gas/electric stoves and cookers. They use tractors and ploughs for their food production. Some use bicycles to move about at the center of almost every village are both primary and middle schools, a chapel or two chapels representing two versions of the alleged one Christian faith; usually Presbyterian and Roman Catholic chapels respectively, both competing for members not only from the same community but at times from the same households.

On Bolgatanga market days, lorries go to the respective villages to carry people and goods to and fro. In some villages there are government clinics or dispensaries that are often falling apart and without drugs. Those villages without these dispensaries are served by the Presbyterian mobile clinics. They go to these villages at least every fortnight to give pre-natal, natal and post-natal health services. Some villagers have become so used to being picked up by these clinic vans to the extent that they postpone their trips to Bolgatanga to the clinic days in their villages. Those who are Presbyterians feel it is the obligation of the staff to pick them up on their errands.

In Kpalugu in Tongo, there is a huge closed down tomato factory, in Zuarungu near Bolgatanga there is also a closed down meat factory. In Nangodi there is another closed-down gold mine but which at the time of this research was being considered for possible re-opening. In Vea in Bongo, there is a collapsing irrigation project aimed at producing rice and tomatoes for local consumption and export throughout the year.

Since 1970, the U.N., the World Bank and other vehicles of Western capitalism have embarked on giving Frafra people interest-free loans, tractors, chemical fertilizers, ploughs, and building large storage rooms. They have also embarked on massive campaign programmes to persuade Frafra people to cultivate cotton and rice for exports instead of the staple foods such as groundnuts, local sorghum. Naraand and ki (millet). This is made attractive by the provision of local FM radios whose range is confined to the Upper East region on which they listen to news and weather forecasts of good times for them to grow cotton and rice. They can now listen to local, national and international news in their native dialects.

All these drastic irreversible changes give the impression of everything new, the old passing or dying. There is nothing further from the truth than such an impression. As one stands in the heart of Bolgatanga, the "old" imposes itself in ways that are, impossible to deny or ignore. There are the thatched houses standing side by side with modern complex buildings of banks, post offices and air-conditioned multi-national corporation offices.

While one listens to popular American music with a "walkman", one also hears the sweet melodies of humming voices accompanied by maracas and occasionally the drums of diviners in their zona (consulting rooms). One also hears and at times see dee (the funeral procession) accompanied by dance and music and above all the display of spiritual powers by shamans chewing poisonous arrows et not dying. Cutting themselves with knives, yet no wounds piercing spears and knives in eyes, mouths and stomachs, yet no visible sign of cuts or bleeding. These activities defy modern scientific medical explanation.

There are the countless da dut (local beer or pubs) in which people are not just having fun but are also telling oral histories of all the ancestral fame and notable achievements. Among the Frafra, if a musician only sings the praises of an individual present at the drinking bar that musician is not worth rewarding. In the Frafra tradition a musician should be able to recite the achievement of at least the past three generations of that individual. Therefore even in entertainment people being taught or reminded by the traditions they come from reinforce their notion of collectivity.

One also sees even in Bolgatanga traditional judges shuttling back and forth dealing with community conflicts, performing marriage, birth and death rites and legal consultations. One sees candidates for vacant stools, wearing their special protection symbolized in tails, rings, head caps and bangles on their legs wrists and necks. If you dare peek through the heavy smocks, there are symbols of spiritual powers on the chests and waists. One also sees the tendanam (priests of the earth) in shrine attire of skins and head caps of ropes with bundles of tails of animals either offered to shrines or most probably representing shrines they embody and attend to.

There are also signs of occasional sacrifices in the center of Bolgatanga, especially among the rocks at the center, from which it is alleged the name Bolga (sand) and tanga (Rock are derived. At other times, usually in the evenings, one sees people offering their ancestral *kaaba*.

In short, Bolgatanga bears all the signs and symbols of the continuity and discontinuity in the interaction between the "old" and the "new" in Frafraland.

The epitome of this continuity and discontinuity is the Bolgatanga *Nam yir* (the chief's house) the symbol of tradition. It is a large compound of round thatched rooms with a few rectangular buildings roofed with iron sheets. The *zanor* (gate or entrance) is partly a traditional type but unlike the traditional type it has a door attached. At the reception is an air-conditioned room roofed with both grass and iron sheets. The chief sits on a platform raised two to three feet, which traditionally would have represented the founding ancestor or his immediate father or grandfather with signs of sacrifices. Instead, it is decorated with traditional fabric, a western carpet, and traditional leader pillows. The seats for his guests are all (at the last time we saw them) made of modern comfortable leather cushions with all the trappings of a modern board room. We might add that he is a certificated "A" teacher and professes to follow the Roman Catholic faith. He drives a nice Mercedes-Benz car instead of a horse.

Chinua Achebe's novel *Things Fall Apart*[9] seems to depict the clash of modernity and traditionalism in Frafraland as located in Umuofia a traditional village like datuku or any Frafra village. They story begins with the missionaries and British administrators commencing their attack on traditional life in Umofia village. Life in Tongo, Bolgatanga and Bongo at the time of Meyer Fortes[10] and even now can be characterized with the words of Cooley as "a certain fusion of individualities in a common whole, so that one's very self, for many purposes at least, is the common life and purpose of the group".[11] There are also similarities between Okonkwo's community and what Fortes describes about the Talleh[12], one of the Frafra triad. Okonkwo's character depicts aspects of the traditional religious belief system, especially the ancestral powers encountered with the "new" and the conflicts that result from such encounter.

Okonkwo's friend Obierika echoes the feeling of the elderly of the Frafra against modernity thus:

> …our own men and our sons have joined the ranks of the stranger. They have joined his religion and they help to uphold his government… The white man is clever, he came quietly and peacefully with his religion….He has put a knife on the things that held us together and we have fallen apart.[13]

However, we contend that the Frafra mythic world does not only survive but indeed transforms the new into its own frame of reference. Hence it is important for the Church to understand the critical role of the Frafra mythic world as an interpretative mechanism.

Der recounts a story of how the LoDagaba became Christians which indicates how their notion of salvation was different from the "White Father". According to Der, "there were mass conversions among the Dagaba. Christianity emerged as a revolutionary force to ancestral cults and other traditional beliefs".[14] There is a story that seems to explain the mass conversions of the Dagaba:

In 1932 the North_West region was hit by a severe drought that threatened the livelihood of farmers. Sacrifices offered to the local gods produced no rain. This shook the confidence of the people in the power of their gods and their ancestors. In their distress converts and non-converts alike turned to the missionaries for assistance. In July 1932, the Supervisor of the Mission in Jurapa, Remigius McCoy, led a delegation of the chief, his Sub-Chiefs and elders in prayer in the church to ask for rain. Shortly after the service, it rained heavily.[15]

It was recognized by all the missionaries that this incident was the most effective form of evangelism. For it was only after this incident that there was massive conversion to Christianity. This incident clearly shows that salvation for the Dagaba, means more than going to heaven when they die. Therefore, Jesus as saviour for the Dagaba must mean his ability to give them rain in times of drought. Salvation in this understanding is not so much a change in human ontology but provision of daily needs.

Our contention that the indigenous mythic world in Ghana in the encounter with Christianity, and modernity survives is also confirmed by an incident in Tongo. The "White fathers" applied to the Colonial administrator to extend their mission to Tongo. The permission to open stations at Tongo was proceeded by this simple but important incident.[16] Armitage in 1912 led soldier to destroy a shrine at Tongo. His reason was that the shrine was a source of resistance to British rule in the North East of the territory.[17] A historical account of similar incidents which were intended to either scare the Frafra or beat them into submission are recounted in detail by Anafu.[18] These incidents strongly suggest a decisive evidence of the merciful assault of modernity in Frafraland on the one hand and the fierce resistance of the Frafra mythic world on the other hand. Force the *boar* (earth shrine) is comparable to the Christian chapel, Islamic mosque, or Jewish temple. Its destruction by armitage would have had the similar importance to the Frafra as the burning of chapels and mosques is to Christians and Muslims respectively.

The shrine supposedly destroyed by the colonial powers is the same shrine referred to in Southern Ghana as "Nana-Tongo" where people go for all types of spiritual protection even to this day. In the light of the frequent consultations in this shrine even now we can safely infer that the idea of "knocking down" traditional symbols and mythic worlds on the part of modernity and Christianity has at least partially failed.

The introduction of education, Christianity and hospital in Frafraland has meant providing alternative lifestyles to the Frafra. Christianity and modernity have introduced new beliefs, attitudes, technological skills, and ideologies. People are free to move to the urban areas for jobs in which they will be paid money rather than engage in community farms.

Monica Wilson makes an important observation of how modernity alters traditional societies. She observes that modernity changes control of material environment, non-religious and impersonal factor and mobility. The result is less or no traditionalism as traditional societies become connected to global systems. [19]

The change ultimately produces two different modes of apprehending reality. Traditional mythic world apprehends reality through signs symbols and rituals. Western civilization on the contrary "tends to foster a scientific outlook".[20] To some extend these observations are applicable to the Frafra situation. But in other respects they are not.

It is therefore imperative for the Church to devise more effective methods of presenting the Gospel of Jesus Christ especially during times of crises with integrity. This thesis seeks to attempt to offer a direction of how to understand the indigenous mythic world the Frafra Christian converts bring and devise ways to mobilize some of the important symbols of their mythic world in a contextualized Frafra Christian ministry of healing.

References

1. A.W. Cardinal, *The natives of the Northern Territory of the Gold Coast*(London: MacMillan & Co 1921), p.viii.

2. R.S. Rattray, *The Tribes of the Ashanti Hinterland* with a chapter by Professor D. Westermann Vol. 1 and Voll.2.

3. ibid, p.2.

4. Meyer Fortes, *Dynamics of Clanship* (1945) We of Kinship (1949).

5. Detail descriptions of the clanship of the Nabnam, their religion and sociology are given by John M. Hunter "The clans of Nangodi" in *Africa* Vol. 38, number 4, (1968), p.377-411.

6. John sincerely. Nabilah, *The Migration of the Frafra of migration in West Africa* (1974), p.6.

7. Meyer Fortes, *Dynamics of Clanship* (1945)

8. ibid. p.10ff, see also Web of Kinship (1949), p.234ff.

9. Chinua Achebe, *Things fall apart* (London), chapters 14-21.

10. Meyer Fortes, "Culture Contact as Dynamic Process" in *Methods* of Study (1965), p.65-91.

11. C.H. Cooley, *Social Organization* (New York, 1929), p. 23

12. Meyer fortes, *Dynamics of Clanship* (1949).

13. Chinua Achebe, *Things Fall Apart* (1962), p. 124

14. Benedict Der, "Church-State Relations in *Transactions of Historical Society in Ghana,* p.5.

15. Interviews with Fr. McCoy and Bishop Dery, 4, Sept. 1972 conducted by Benedict Der.

16. Der, P.47/48, relying on ADM 56/1/298 Morin to Governor, 2 April 1924, ADM 56/1/298, Ag. Chief Comm. Of N. Province 6 Oct. 1924, ADM 56/1/298, Col. Sec. To CCNTs, 27 October 1924, and ADM 56/1/298, Guggisberg to CCNTs, (9 May, 1925).

17. Der, p56, relying on CO 96/523, Armitage to Ag. Col. Sec 4 (Dec. 1912).

18. Moses Anafu, "The Impact of the British on the Tallensi Political Institutions 1898-1967" in *Transactions of the Historical Society of Ghana* vol. 14, number 1 (June 1973), p. 7-37.

19. Monica Wilson, *Religion and the Transformation of Society* (Cambridge: Cambridge University Press 1971).

20. E. Obiechina, (1975), p. 34.

CHAPTER FOUR

Diagnoses and Nya Kaaba

Introduction

This chapter reports on one of the most common forms of *kaaba*. Firstly, we shall describe the Frafra self-perception of sickness healing, and health in *nya kaaba*. Secondly, we shall use theoretical insights from human and social sciences, studies in primary religions, phenomenology of religion and Christian theology. We will engage the concepts from these disciplines in an analytical, comparative, and dialogical manner to analyze these rituals. The purpose here is to determine whether or not these conceptual frames from other disciplines can provide any insights into Frafra self-perception of how their mythic world functions as an interpretative mechanism in their experiences of sickness, healing and health.

The data was collected from Frafra social interactions between persons of both sexes, all ages, and of different social roles in homes in rural villages and urban areas. Other settings included market places in both rural and urban areas.

Frafra classifications of symptoms and diagnoses of sicknesses

This section begins with how the Frafra classify their symptoms and diagnoses of their experiences of sickness. Among the Frafra there are many types of life-threatening situations. The Frafra use sayings to group these threatening situations. When a woman goes to fetch water, falls down, and the pot either hits her leg and fractures a bone or hurts any part of the body, the Frafra say *boo n bo* (some bad intended action has happen ed). When a man, in the course of farming, cuts his toes, they also refer to this as *boo n bo*. When a child is playing and falls and hurts himself/herself badly, they say *boo n bo*. When someone has a lorry, car or bicycle accident and he or she is hurt, people say *boo n bo*. Almost all *boo n bo* crises involve physical damage, including fractures and cuts. They are characterized by some amount of bleeding.

When one is feeling a rise in body temperature and/or general weakness in the body coupled with loss of appetite, they say *u nengbina n yalek* (his/her body is diluted. When one has a headache with a cold or catarrh, the say *owood nkpe u* (cold has entered him/her). Again, when one has stomach problems of various kinds, they say *puo n doo (puo* pertains to sickness of the stomach). So the translation will be "sickness pertaining to the stomach is troubling him/her). With reference to the elderly, they usually say *pummahuk* refers to sickness pertaining to the stomach of older people. Therefore the translation is "sickness pertaining to the stomach of older people" is bothering him/her.

There are times when somebody will just complain that *u neng n dumit* (his/her body is paining him/her). There are also times a person may experience an acute pain on either the hand or leg which leads to a boil. The Frafra usually say *u nuuk be nuber n mod* (his/her hand or leg is paining). *Mod* refers to the white pus that comes when boils are burst.

The Frafra also use saying when diagnosing sicknesses. The first category of sickness is diagnosed by the saying that *"u tuu yaabnam"* (he/she has gone astray from the ways of the ancestors). This means that one has not behaved according to the ethical codes of the sickness may not have personally committed the offense. He/she could be suffering on behalf of the collective family in which the offense may have been committed either in the past or present. So the offender may be either alive or dead.

This second diagnosis is best summarized by the saying *u galeme kiiha* (he/she has broken the laws of the clans). These are individual punishments for individual acts of disobedience. In both the first and second saying, the causes of sickness are the ancestors. The third diagnosis is also best expressed by the saying that *ba eng me* (they have caused). This diagnosis connotes the idea that someone has deliberately caused this to happen to this individual for malicious reasons. The one who has caused it is usually jealous of some achievement of that individual or his/her family.

At times the one suffering has offended the one causing the suffering. At other times the one causing the suffering simply wants to demonstrate his/her special powers in order to induce fear, and command respect from the larger community.

There is yet a fourth important type of diagnosis of sickness quite different from those already mentioned. The Frafra generally refer to this type of sickness as *tii. Tiih* is the plural of *tii* which means a tree. The Frafra believe that trees and stones can have different forms of life. For example, they believe that stones and trees can transform themselves and become mobile. They roam around in various forms and at various times and can behave like humans. Some of the trees and stones change themselves into human beings and pose as beggars in order to test the generosity or greed of people. So the

Frafra do everything possible to give an unknown beggar something for fear that the beggar could be either an evil tree or stone.

For the Frafra boo n bo. *nengbina n yalek, owoon nkpe u, kiiha* and *ba eng me* refer to the social, physical and spiritual aspects of their social interaction. These classifications seem to be their equivalent of modern scientific concepts of symptoms and diagnoses. These classifications are both similar and different with those of modern scientific medicine. They are similar in the sense that they both operate within a mythic world. But they are also different in the sense that the Frafra symptoms and diagnoses reflect their mythic world in which the medical, religious, social, psychological, political, and cultural and interconnected and interdependent.

When an individual experiences something that disrupts the social, cultural, physiological and spiritual harmony of his or her interactions, then many questions about an individual's body and community ties are raised. These ties are based on ancestral relationships. These sayings such as *boo n bo, ba eng me, nengbina n dumet* diagnose and classify Frafra experience of sickness by invoking the mythic world as the interpretative mechanism.

In the Frafra mythic world, their experience of sickness includes the social, psychological, physical and spiritual. Activities such as fetching water, children playing, falling from a bicycle, and farming clearly suggest that the everyday social activities are both social and spiritual as cited in Chapter Two and earlier in this chapter. Their beliefs in the spiritual powers of wind, stones, plants, and rivers also suggest that the cosmos is both physical and spiritual. Consequently, stones, plants, river have an impact on the social, psychological, physical, cultural, and spiritual in everyday interactions. Thus for the Frafra, there is no such dichotomy of actions as profane or sacred. They are profane and sacred, medical and religious, physical and spiritual at the same time.

The diagnosis of sickness resulting from inappropriate contact with the spirits of stones, trees and wind, and going astray from the laws of the ancestors demonstrate that the Frafra mythic world is one in which the spiritual world is coterminous with their physical worlds. To be healthy means to enjoy the full protection of the spiritual powers including the ancestors because one is in the right relationship with social, psychological, physical and cultural ties.

Therefore when sickness strikes a person, that person is immediately in a transitional state from full participation to little or no participation in community life. that person has also moved from full protection of the ancestral spirits to less protection or none at all. The person and indeed the entire family or community may be described as being spiritually, psychologically, physiologically and culturally in a transitional state. The state is one of less spiritual protection from the ancestors. Sickness, then, is an experience of social psychological, physical and spiritual estrangement.

One can argue that these sayings, which we designate as symptomatic and diagnostic classifications of sickness may in fact be ordinary secular Frafra words with nothing medical and religious intended. But their attitudes and actions towards these sayings suggest that they mean something much deeper and more serious in the Frafra mythic world.

For the Frafra any such serious and deeper meaning must have consequences for their well-being. Well-being must, by definition have religious and medical implications. Therefore we maintain that these sayings are forms of Frafra diagnostic classifications. In our opinion, they are the equivalent of modern diagnostic manuals such as diagnostic system manual I, II, III in modern psychiatry. These sayings suggest what Kirby describes as "Concepts of life."[1]

These sayings are also, in the words of Worsley, "…taken to be epiphenomenona of something deeper."[2] That something deeper may be both universal and particular. In this case that something is health and sickness. According to Parson, health and sickness are universal categories among all human beings in all societies[3]. We will add that it is also particular because the experience of sickness is invariably determined by the particular mythic worlds. The interpretative functions of mythic worlds are particular by definition.

The particularities of the interpretative functions of mythic worlds in sicknesses are supported by Worsley's notion of metamedical context:

> …All medicine has a 'metamedical' context. Medical conceptions of illness and its cure are always embedded within wider frameworks which supply cognitive, normative and cognitive ideals (concepts, values, models, and projects) ultimately within some explicit

metaphysic or implicit 'metaphysical pathos' which may be Hinduism or Western science, astrology or logical positivism.[4]

A "metamedical" system only operates from a particular socio-cultural milieu. Therefore experiences of sickness are culturally bound. The question is: What are the deeper things to be revealed by these particular Frafra diagnostic classifications of sickness? In other words, what do they reveal about the Frafra notion of sickness, health, healing and personality in the Frafra mythic world?

One of the deeper things these oral diagnostic classifications reveal is how Frafra classify sickness according to symptoms or causes of both. These symptomatic and diagnostic classifications show the main difference between traditional Frafra healing systems and Western scientific medical healing systems. Western scientific medical system classifies sickness according to symptoms and causes based on what Worsley refers to as a "biomechanistic framework". He further suggests that "the biomechanistic framework separates nature from supernatural, the social world from the world of nature, and the physical individual from his or her social matrix."[5] The biomechanistic framework of the scientific approach operates with what Worsley describes as "the metamedical isolation and reduction of illness as a purely biological phenomenon with the body conceived as a mechanistic system."[6]

Foster, another research in no-Western healing systems, in his comparison between Western and non-Western aetiologies of sickness, has broadly divided them into two. According to Foster, non-Western cultures such as the Frafra have a personalistic aetiology of disease while Western scientific medicine uses naturalistic etiologies of sickness.[7] Foster defines personalistic and naturalistic thus:

A personalistic medical system is one in which disease is explained as due to the active purposeful intervention of an agent, who may be human (a witch or sorcerer), non-human (a ghost, ancestor, an evil spirit) or supernatural (a deity or other very powerful being). The sick person literally is a victim, the objective of aggression or punishment directed specifically against him.[8]

In a naturalistic system, "disease is thought to stem, not from the machination of an angry being, but rather from such natural forces of conditions as cold, but an upset in the balance of basic body elements".[9]

The Frafra diagnostic classification of etiology, symptoms and treatment implied by *boo n boo, nengbina n yalek, owood nkpe u* and *ba engme* do not make such distinction between personalistic and naturalistic descriptions. The results of Price Williams' study of the notion of sickness among the Tiv of Nigeria are similar to our findings. The Tiv like the Frafra do not regard illness or disease as a category distinct from misfortunes, or from wrong or inappropriate relationships among kinfolk or more complicated matters relating to the misuse of the land.[10]

The pioneering studies of Evans-Pritchard also support our findings that non-Western medicines do not make such clear distinction between personalistic and naturalistic classifications of sickness. Evans-Pritchard concluded from his studies among the Azande that the Azande use both naturalistic and personalistic diagnoses and treatments.[11]

According to Worsley, Janzen in his work in Lower Zaire also concluded from his research that the people of Lower Zaire have a "dialectical, Prometheus models not a mechanistic one, not only of disease but also of therapy".[12]

In our study we did not engage in any kind of universalistic comparisons between Frafra indigenous healing systems and Western scientific medicine. MacLean's results from such comparison between Yoruba indigenous medicine and Western scientific medicine[13] are interesting and in many respects inform our approach. The only difference between both approaches is the intentional pastoral perspective that we bring.

These diagnostic classifications are first and foremost intended to invoke the Frafra mythic world that the sick person, the healer and the community share in common. In that mythic world, symptoms aetiologies, diagnoses and healing are both naturalistic and personalistic, secular and sacred. They are also personal, communal, social, psychological, physiological, cultural and spiritual. One involves all and all involves one.

One cannot deny the important contributions Western scientific medicine has made, is making and will make in both eliminating and treating some life-threatening diseases, and promoting understanding into the nature of some bacteria, viruses, and the human immune system. However, the dichotomy of Western scientific medicine is not found in the interpretative functions of the Frafra mythic system on the basis of their diagnostic classificatory sayings.

The important implication here is that we are critical of Western distinctions between religions and medicine as isolated separate dimensions of human existence. The point that human existence is not compartmentalized into the social, religious, and psychological is echoed by some Ghanaian theologians. For example, Baeta, one of the foremost of Ghanaian theologians writes:

> Traditionally in Ghana, the solution to all problems of ill-health, as of concern or anxiety generally has been sought squarely within the framework of religion. On a world view which assumes the effective presence of numberless spirits and regards all life as one, with no clear distinctions between the material and the non-material, the natural and the supernatural let alone the secular and the religious, or even between man and other created things and beings, this could hardly be otherwise.[14]

Dickson also describes the Akan world view in the following terms:

> ...The chief's role, the relations between members of society, morality, the stages in a person's life (birth, puberty, marriage and death) the practice of medicine, architecture, warfare, traditional education etc. all these are not dissociated from religion in traditional African society.[15]

Lartey, another Ghanaian transcultural pastoral theologian, also holds the view that most if not all Africans have a "relational wholism". The notion of "relational wholism" is one in which "human life is seen in its totality. A human being is a psychospirito-somatic unity. Dichotomic or trichotomic views of life are not adhered to."[16]

Therefore, the distinction between naturalistic and personalistic systems of healing, or between medicine and religion, the sacred and secular, are not useful categories to understand the holistic nature of the mythic world invoked by these diagnostic classifications. *Boo n bo, ba eng me* suggest that something outside one's body even one's community or generation can impact on another person. A mental bad wish by someone somewhere else can affect another person. Like the Anufo, the Frafra notion of "sickness" is not considered simply the loss of health but an entity and a power in itself, caused from within or from outside the individual".[17] Hence, a mental wish by an individual or the community can use a virus, or bacteria as agent of a spiritual contagion to cause sickness in another person.

It also indicates that there is another level of life which actively interacts with the visible, social and physical dimension of life. everything including air, water, lorries, bicycles, can be agents of powers. These sayings, which are also symptomatic medical categories of sickness, suggest that a person can become invaded by spiritual powers because of that person's or a relative's actions. That can disrupt the appropriate social and religious boundaries between persons and between persons and the cosmos. *U tuu yaabnam* (going astray from the ways of the ancestors) also suggests that the social and spiritual equilibrium or boundaries are disturbed. The equilibrium is disturbed because the conditions needed to maintain the unity of the social, spiritual, psychological, and physiological, are not observed. This also applies to the unity with the trees, stones and rivers.

In the Frafra self understanding talk of their social ties implies the spiritual, psychological, physiological and cosmological.

A social conversion implies a spiritual communication with the spiritual invisible powers. Hence, one does not mention some sacred names of places and persons, nor does one curse or swear in social conversation for fear that they spiritual consequences may occur. *Boo n bo, nengina n yalek, kiiha, tuu yaabnam, tiih* are not only ordinary secular medical words, they also invoke a sacred dimension of human existence in the Frafra mythic world.

The Frafra use their mythic world in ordinary everyday words as medical, social and spiritual diagnostic manuals. These findings seemed different from the tendency to render non-Western healing rituals as exotic and hidden on the one hand, and as secular naturalistic medicine on the other. These sayings are in fact the medical, religious, and social symptoms, diagnosis and aetiologies of sickness in the interpretative functions of Frafra mythic world.

Nya Healers

The statistics in Appendix A, clearly suggest that *Nya* healing is by far the most popular form of healing among male and female healers and patients and between adults and minors. *Nya* healing is a combination of acquired knowledge of herbs and the ancestral spiritual powers which one inherits at birth.

Fortes seem to offer a worthwhile explanation on the almost equal number of men and women healers. According to Fortes:

> ...there is a no known society in which the interdependence and complementarity of sexes is not embodied in custom and sanctioned by law and morality. To consider the status of either sex without the other is to distort the reality we are trying to understand.[18]

The point of interdependence and complementarity is also important in *Yaabname* healing rituals of the Frafra. Even though the presider is always a man, the women of the clan or *yir* are always present.

The word *nya* means roots. So *nya daan* means owner of roots. The Frafra use this term to describe a healer who uses roots. *Nya* healers are similar to the *ran (lo) wal* among the dinka as described by Lienhardt.[19] a *nya* healer usually claims his/her healing tradition from the ancestors either from the paternal or maternal side. In this type of healing the spiritual power of healing is passed on to one's *doam* (offspring) accompanied by observation, and instructions for acquiring a knowledge of roots, leaves or bark of trees and the techniques of how to apply them when a particular sickness strikes.

The body of the healer is an extension of both the biological and spiritual powers of his/her paternal and maternal ancestors. Hence, the healer's body is capable of producing healing because the efficacy of the words lies in the powers of the ancestors which he/she embodies. When someone has a sprain from strains due to body postures, the person usually starts with some first aid treatment, usually hot water or oil massage. These days, most people buy mentholatum ointments and/or aspirin or any locally obtainable Western analgesics. Some may wait for a few days to see whether or not they are healed. Others will call for a healer who specializes in treating sprains and fractures. In the following, we shall examine some cases.

Case 1: Bone Setter

A young man twisted his wrist. Within a few hours, his hand began to swell so the immediate local diagnosis was a sprain. They sent for a woman who has known to be the best bone setter in the village. She arrived and after the usual exchange of greetings, she started the healing session. The young man was called to sit in front of the main entrance of the house. She collected fresh droppings of cattle and mixed it with tobacco and ashes. As she mixed them, she was reciting incantations; she called on her ancestors one after the other.

She asked them to come and add their potency of healing which they possessed and had passed on to her. She said, "I am doing the acts on your behalf with the belief that you will come and add the power that will heal so that this young man sleeps like a child."

She lightly smeared the mixture around the wrist and elbow. After that she invoked the blessing of her ancestors. The family head was also responding *Banam ne yaabnam sak* (may our ancestors allow her healing to be effective). Asked what price to pay, she said that she would not charge. Rather, she said that if and when the young man felt healed, he was to do something to show his appreciation. That something could range from buying her cola nuts to weeding herfarm for her.

Case 2 *Zu maahud (*migraine)

A man of about fifty-two years old complained of *owood* (cold) and *zug* (headache). His condition seemed to get worse. It was generally agreed by most members of his family that he had *zug maahud. Zug maahud* seems to be what is diagnosed by western medical experts as migraine headache. He sent one of his children to call the *zub maahud ny daan* (the one who has roots for the cure of migraine headache). The healer sent word that he would come in the evening.

At about sunset, the *nya daan* arrived, bringing some roots and herbs. He sad down, and asked the family to bring a chicken. He tied the herbs in a bundle, then called the man and some members of his family. the *nya daan* held a calabash of water, a chicken and the roots facing the dug *zaron* (the gate of the room) of the man. Firstly, he invited the man who was the head of the family saying *deegen kaab tem* (do the invocation of the healing for me). The man replied aimed at fighting or neutralizing the power of the contagion in its host's body.

The same Frafra belief of sickness as a contagion is made more explicit in the *tiim* aetiology of sickness in the interpretative functions of the Frafra mythic world. Furthermore, *tiim* healing also shows that the Frafra have a holistic experience of daily interactions. The case of *tiim* sickness and healing also implies that in the Frafra mythic world the physical world is coterminous with their spiritual world. These two worlds constantly interact with each other in ways that diminish as well as promote the quality of human life. humans are both objects and subjects of the consequences of the interactions between the physical and spiritual worlds.

The Frafra also share their world with invisible spiritual beings and/or powers. The Frafra seem to have an ambivalent relationship with their world. On the one hand they are partners in healing. On the other hand they can also be used against each other. Hence, sickness is an invasion from without. A power greater than the sick person attacks the sick person and penetrates his/her spiritual defense and assaults its target (the human object) and causes one type of sickness or another.

Tiim healing employs more powerful spirits to fight and weaken the contagion and some cases literally kill it, or rescue the spirit of the victim from its oppressor(s). The *tiim* powers operate through the man who owns them. They are believed to be partially embodied and diffused in their owner's bodily fluids. Hence his saliva, or blood can be contagious. They can also be infused in other media such as herbs roots, water and bones of animals or birds to effect their healing and protective power.

Like *nya* healing, the focus of *tiim* healing is to neutralize the contagion by killing or weakening the invading spiritual power or rescuing the captive spirit from its victim. *Kaaben tete* (do the healing for us). Secondly, he poured water on the ground after whispering to his paternal ancestors to add healing potency. Then he turned to the heap of bundles of the *nya.* he called upon his maternal *yaabnam* to assemble around these *nya* and bring their healing powers. After these incantations, he poured the water on the *nya*. He also cut the last toe of the chicken and allowed a few drops of blood on the *nya.* the man put his nose on the smoke coming out of the *nya.* this act of putting a part of one's body through the smoke, the Talleh refer to as *nyel.* The *nya daan* then picked up a handful of ashes from the burnt *nya* and mixed it with *kpam* (oil, usually shea butter). He rubbed the mixture in the patient's palms and wiped it on the man's face. The Talleh refer to this kind of *kaaba* as *wobeg zug* (message the head with a concoction). The *nya daan* left the chicken in the house until the man was well. Afterwards the man would send the chicken and some gift of gratitude to the healer which they refer to as *lebeh nya* (return the *nya*). it is believed that *ba pu lebeh nya* (if the *nya* is not returned) the sickness can come back and perhaps become chronic.

Analysis

To the Frafra, like the Anufo, in the words of Kirby, "sickness is an entity, a power in itself"[20]. Sickness is a contagion that invades the body. *Nya* healing first and foremost invokes the Frafra mythic world by reconstructing that mythic world with symbols of body, words, plants and herbs, and the spirit of the ancestors. The first question to answer is whether or not *nya* healing is, in the words of Ademuwagun, "strictly disease centred"[21] as in the Western scientific medical system.

In all cases, and in the two cases we have cited in particular, there is certainly a knowledge of herbs and the techniques of using them in various kinds of sicknesses. The technique of mixing cow droppings tobacco, ashes, herbs and oil and rubbing or massaging them into the palms and face, strongly suggest that ny healing is a biochemical or pharmacological type of healing. In other words, it is "naturalistic" rather than "personalistic" healing. The pharmacological component of indigenous healing such as *nya* healing has become an intense area of study by medical doctors and scientists.

Nya healing and Western Scientific medicine

The question which occurs is whether *nya* healing and Western scientific medical healing differ to too great an extent or whether they can co-operate with each other. Western scientific medicine is based on scientific rationality. It also operates by objective physiological and numerical calculations. It defines disease by physico-chemical diagnosis. the treatment is based on mind-body separations. In this concept there is a clear separation of disease from the social, political, spiritual and cultural dimension of life.[22] Helman also correctly points out that:

> ...the 'model' of modern medicine is mainly directed towards the discovering and quantifying of physico-chemical information about the patient, rather than less measurable social and emotional factors.[23]

The Western medical doctor's method of diagnosis is one of relating "...the symptoms to their biological referents in order to diagnose a disease entity."[24] As a result of the development of more sophisticated technology "...the underlying pathological processes are now firmly identified by blood tests, x-rays, scans and other investigations usually carried out in specialized laboratories or clinics."[25] the scientific notions of sickness, healing and health implied in these quotes are different from the Frafra notions of sickness, healing and health implied by *ny* healing. Western scientific medicine diagnoses and heals by solely concentrating on:

... certain physical and biochemical parameters, such as weight, height, circumstance, blood count, hemoglobin level, levels of electrolytes or hormones, blood pressure, heart rate, respiratory rate, heart size or visual acuity.[26]

The Frafra healer diagnoses and heals by emphasizing the unity of the physiological, psychological, and pharmacological, as well as the social, spiritual, and cultural. Therefore, the Western medical models imported into Frafraland urgently need to incorporate insights of indigenous *kaaba* if they are to succeed in presenting themselves as credible models of healing to the Frafra.

International bodies such as WHO, OAU, UNESCO, and WCC have engaged in various collaborative research into indigenous healing systems. According to Bibeau the OAU was among the first Africa inter-regional organizations that showed interest in traditional medicine. The OAU sponsored the first symposium on medical plants and African pharmacopoeia in Dakar in 1968 and a second symposium in 1975 in Cairo.[27] These symposia led to the formation of the inter-African commission on African Medicinal Plants and Traditional Pharmacopoeia as part of the Scientific and Technical Council for Research of the OAU. The main interest of the commission was the botanists, chemists and pharmacists should conduct Western scientific investigations on the plants or herbs used by various traditional healers and assess their chemical compostion.[28]

According to Bibeau these scientists were aware that "...traditional practitioners possess an entirely separate medical system which cannot in any case be reduced only to medicines."[29] Yet they chose to concentrate only on the chemical analyses of the plants and herbs used in indigenous healing systems. These Western-trained scientists used in indigenous healing systems. These Western-trained scientists such as botanists, chemists and pharmacists separated indigenous holistic healing systems into compartments of pharmacopoeia, and the spiritual.

The WHO has not only shown interest in traditional medicine but insisted that its members states from Africa, Asia and the Pacific explore ways to promote integrated health systems. In other words African countries should study their indigenous healing systems and integrate some aspects of these indigenous healing systems with some Western scientific medicine.[30]

The OAU, WHO and WCC came to the realization that it was necessary for their member countries in Africa and Asia to free themselves from dependence on Western imported scientific medicine. They can only achieve some independence by utilizing their local resources.[31]

One can infer here that the cultural medical practices in these countries have something to offer Western scientific medical models. Unfortunately, this research tends to concentrate only on the chemical and biological aspects of indigenous healing systems, rather than the holistic approach that we have seen in the Frafra diagnostic sayings thus far.

There are many criticisms of these attempts by African countries to integrate traditional medicine with Western scientific medical healing systems. The criticisms of Hours of worth considering for our purpose.[32] Hours observes that the brutal attack on and attempts to wipe out traditional African medical practices have failed. Traditional African medicine has not only survive but there are increasing attempts by many African governments to incorporate African traditional medicine into Western medical healing systems. However, Hours is suspicious of the reasons behind the growing interest of African governments in adopting traditional healing systems. He holds the view that Africa governments are not resorting to traditional medicines because they are concerned that the two can work together but because they want to use the African traditional medicine as an 'alibi'.

According to Hours most African governments are too heavily indebted to be able to afford good health services. Even the few health services they have are deteriorating. Furthermore, the population explosion in African countries makes it difficult for African governments to provide good health services for their people. Consequently, African governments, by emphasizing traditional medicine, are embarking on "the apologia for traditional medicine".[33] They use the traditional medicines as:

Institutional alibi, designed to mask the inadequacies of existing policies, in the hope that health problems will be solved by introducing some more or less imaginary dimensions imaginary in that those who call it are, by their own terms of reference, largely ignorant of the real capacities of African medicine.[34]

Therefore, he concludes that they tendency of African governments to do research on traditional medicines or even attempts to incorporate them into modern scientific medicine is no excuse for ignoring "frustrations and anarchy of urban life".[35] It is a substitute for investigating and investing in health services. For him, many African governments use African traditional medicine "as a smoke screen which in any official discussion masks the reality of the true problems".[36]

We are also of the opinion that any attempts to investigate the biochemical nature of traditional medicines or to incorporate them into Western scientific medicine without a serious consideration of the traditional mythic worlds in which they operate are a distortion of these traditional medicines. After these criticisms, Hours goes on to suggest that in African medicine, symptoms are seen as sign of social logic which reflects the prevailing notions of cosmic and of village order".[37]

We partially agreed with Hours' rather cynical reasons as to why some African governments are showing interest in African traditional medicine. However, we disagree with Hours' suggestion that the increased interest in African traditional medicine is due only to the poor economic situation in Africa. Rather, we hold the view that in addition to socio-political and economic factors Western scientific medical systems imported into Africa have failed to take seriously African notions of sickness, healing and health originating in their indigenous mythic words. When some Africans go to Western hospitals, they do so using their mythic worlds to translate Western medicine.

These Africans expect diagnosis and healing that can invoke the interpretative functions of their mythic worlds, and when Western medicine cannot meet African expectations, they lose trust in Western medicine. So they either refuse it or supplement it with traditional medicine. We also disagree with Hour's when he reduces traditional African diagnosis and treatment to social dysfunction. Such an explanation of traditional medicines ignores the holistic functions of the interpretative mechanism of traditional mythic worlds.

Warren set out to determine how the Bono define and classify sickness in order to help the Ministry of Health plan its primary health care programme for them. He used what he call 'ethnoscientific techniques' to determine the cognitive level of defining and classifying sickness as either *mogya mu yadee*

(Naturally caused sickness) or *sunsum mu yadee* (spiritually caused sickness).[38] Warren concludes:

From the classification system here it is evident that the majority of the Bono disease names, as well as the number of cases of ill health, having nothing to do with any spiritual forces.[39]

Warren compiled the bono names of disease and determined the derivation of the words whether the bono implied that the cause of the disease was spiritual or physical. He concludes:

> … the results of this study have given Western medical practitioners operating among the Bono a more comprehensive knowledge of Bono ethnomedical beliefs, one which will provide a more viable basis for the improvement of medical health delivery systems in the area.[40]

His analysis of the notion of sickness among the bono of Ghana shows another example of Western dichotomizing tendencies in some Westerner's study of indigenous healing systems such as *Nya* healing. After a critical reading of Warren's investigation we wonder whether one is reading bono ethnomedical beliefs through the bono mythic world or filtered through Warren's Western concept of disease. Warren seems not to be aware of the complex problems inherent in the inseparable relationship between the name and experience in the aetiologies of disease or sickness in primary cultures.

Our study among the Frafra and other studies in Ghana show that most Ghanaian ethnic communities do not separate the two. We shall cite a few examples to support our objection to Wearren's approach. There is nothing in Frafra diagnostic sayings and *nya* healing thus far described to suggest that the Frafra make any distinction between natural and spiritual causes of disease. the researches of Kirby[41] among the Anufo and Kilson on Ga healers (*tsofatse)* are further evidence that indigenous healing such as *nya* healing does not make a distinction between natural and spiritual causes of sickness.

The Ga healers according to Kilson "utilize both physical and spiritual concepts in diagnosing and treating their patients' complaints".[42] Kilson also suggests "both patients and healers, however, share certain basic assumptions about causative and therapeutic factors."[43] The views of Kilson further support our view indigenous healing rituals invoke their indigenous mythic worlds which serve as interpretative mechanisms to enable these people to achieve wholeness or well-being.

Mensah-Dapaa, a Ghanaian scientific educational attached to the famous Akonnede shrine at Larteh in Ghana, made an important study of the healing methods at this shrine. His findings are worth considering because he reaches different conclusions than Warren's which are a result of hi scientific interest in traditional healing. Mensah Daapa's descriptions of the consultation procedures are similar to those of Yoruba healers as described by Maclean.[44]

Twumasi describes the Asante healing ritual in which the healer uses herbs, roots and barks off trees, and pouring of water on the floor. The healers also recite incantations, cut parts of the body, and rub mixtures of burnt herbs on the body.[45] These actions are also similar to *nya* healing as we have described earlier. The Ashanti, like Frafra, believe that diagnosis and healing are both physical, social and spiritual and other "modus operandi underscores such a belief".[46] However, we disagree with Twumasi's assertion that "germs, viruses and the concepts of protein and vitamin deficiencies (to name only a few of the natural causative agents) do not figure in traditional medical theory."[47] Rather, we agree with Appiah-Kubi that for the akan which includes the Ashtnati:

> …healing must be comprehensive, involving the entirety of the individual, his or her family and the society. Healing rituals include social, psychological, physical religious and herbal remedies all the forces at one's disposal are called upon to combat illness.[48]

For Appiah-Kubi, the herbal aspect of traditional medicine which deals with viruses, germs and vitamins is very important. So he makes a distinction between curing and healing. Curing is the aspect of technical knowledge of the cause and effect of drugs and herbs, acquired by both the Western physician and the traditional healer by training and practice, and the accumulated experience from such. Healing on the other hand:

> …implies the restoring of equilibrium in the otherwise strained relationship between a person, fellow human beings, the environment and god. This process includes the physical, emotional, social land spiritual dimension.[49]

However, we think Appiah-Kubi's distinction between curing and healing is not borne out by our research. The danger implicit in Appiah-Kubi's distinction is the Western dichotomy of the body, the mind or soul, which he himself admits does not exist in Akan cosmology.[50] The two go together, there is cure in healing and healing in cure.

Despite these disagreements, Appiah-Kubi's categories of "wholeness and health", harmony with nature as the source of health" and "interdependence of human beings and their environment" in the akan notions of health and healing are also true of the frafra notions of health and healing. All these studies point to a gap between African traditional medicine and Western scientific medicine imported in Africa. This gap is well articulated by Mensah-Dapaa. After a critical observation of the methods of treatment, analysis of cases treated, and biochemical analysis of the herbs used in treatment, Mensah-Dapaa concluded:

> ...There are gaps in medical science as practiced in Africa which could be filled by traditional healing methods. There are numerous gaps in African traditional healing methods which should be filled by medical science.[51]

Mensah-Dapaa goes on to assert that "...a medical school for Ghana without a Department of Traditional Healing would be most unrealistic and un Ghanaian."[52] His reasoning is based on the argument that:

> "...not all diseases in Ghana are due to bacteria, viruses, spirochetes, parasites, malignant tumours or nutritional deficiency. There are ailments in Ghana whose root cause can be found in witchcraft and juju."[53]

This gap is similar to the gap created between the interpretative functions of the Frafra mythic world and imported western Christianity. Consequently, the Church cannot offer any relevant indigenised ministry of healing to Frafra Christians, unless and until the Church takes seriously the interpretative functions of their indigenous mythic world in indigenous healing rituals.

Nya healing as a religious phenomenon

The studies from Ghana, and other research into African healing systems support out opinion that *nya* healing is neither strictly "disease-centred" nor is it only naturalistic as in the case of Western scientific medicine. *Nya* healing is also religious. Yet we cannot call *nya* healing sacrifice as in Semitic religions because the fowl in the second case is not killed. In other *nya* healing in which we observed and participated there was no killing of animals. Most traditional theories of sacrifices are often associated with notions of substituting the animal killed for a human life, and the propitiation and expiation of sin.[54]

In our view the *nya* healing ritual in which a bird or an animal is killed suggests what Ruel calls "non-sacrificial ritual killing". We agree with Ruel that the sacrifice in the case of *nya* healing is one in which the fowl "acts as a vehicle rather than a surrogate and the ritual itself is concerned with broader impersonal qualities of life and well-being rather than the personalized deities or spirits that are commonly addressed in sacrifice.[55] In Case Two, only the toe of the fowl is cut. It is an offering in which the life of the bird is not important. Although the ancestral spirits are invoked to effect healing, they are not addressed as the cause of the sickness.

In *nya kaaba*, the ancestors of the healer and the patient are invoked. However, they are invoked not because they caused the sickness but rather, the Frafra believe that the efficacy of the healing rests in their powers. The sickness is caused by a spiritual contagion, therefore *nya* healing fights this contagion through herbs, words, water and bodily fluids. *Nya* healing may be rendered in the words of Fernandez as follows:

...In essence, a system enacted correspondences. A metaphor (and related topics) is the statement, explicit or implied, or a correspondence between some subject of thought in need of clarification and an object that brings some clarity to it.[56]

In ny healing the Frafra deal with the correspondences between their experiences of sickness and the interpretative functions of their mythic world. In the Frafra mythic world they believe that human beings can become agents of spiritual powers. They can also use these powers for good or evil. Therefore sickness can be caused by another human being or a spiritual power other than ancestral spirits. This can take the form of a virus, or bacteria, physical harm such as being wounded in an accident, or cut by a cutlass on the farm, to name but a few examples. This purpose of ny healing is to counteract or fight this spiritual contagion in its host's body.

The ancestors are said to reincarnate themselves. So the *nya* healers derive their healing powers from them. In some cases the ancestor is said to reincarnate herself/himself in that person. From the day of conception, the biological embryo also has spiritual, social, psychological and cultural ties based on this belief. The ties are reinforced in the culture by the fact that people call this child by names that express their relationship with this ancestor. For some the child may be called father or mother, while for others he/she is called grandmother or grandfather. Hence the ancestral connection is spiritual, social physiological, psychological and cultural. One involves all and all is in one.

This belief is responsible for two inseparable types of causes of sickness and healing. Unfortunately, Westerners like Fortes have treated them separately: the healing to neutralize the contagion and the healing which addresses the reason why it is possible for the contagion to invade its host body.

Nya healing is only concerned with the first. The second inseparable component of this belief will be described and analysed in a later chapter on *yaabnam* healing. The Frafra have a saying which summarises the efficacy of *nya* healing. They say, *Lan ka y nyaab nya u ku tuon kaabe* (if it is not the roots of his/her ancestor, he/she cannot heal).

The belief in the origin of the herbs also adds weight to the efficacy of *nya* healing. In most cases, the roots and herbs are collected from trees or plants that are believed to have grown out of the graves of the founding ancestors of the healers. So the spiritual and physical relationship between the ancestors of the healer and the roots and herbs is literal.

This is why the strictly biopharmacological investigations into the herbs used in indigenous healing cannot diminish or negate the spiritual healing potency of the herbs. It also explains why even if these herbs are used for their biochemical properties, the Frafra will still approach *nya* healing from both biochemical and spiritual perspectives according to the interpretative function of their mythic world.

Nya healing works by invoking the holistic functions of the interpretative function of the Frafra mythic world; the basis of a belief in the human agency of spiritual powers as well as the ability to mediate and transfer these powers for good or evil. No single theory from any one discipline can offer the holistic understanding we are looking for in these rituals. We shall therefore attempt a holistic approach by designing *nya* healing as a phenomenon of symbolic representation.

reincarnate herself/himself in that person. From the day of conception, the biological embryo also has spiritual, social, psychological and cultural ties based on this belief. The ties are reinforced in the culture by the fact that people call this child by names that express their relationship with this ancestor. For some the child may be called father or mother, while for others he/she is called grandmother or grandfather. Hence the ancestral connection is spiritual, social physiological, psychological and cultural. One involves all and all is in one.

This belief is responsible for two inseparable types of causes of sickness and healing. Unfortunately, Westerners like Fortes have treated them separately: the healing to neutralize the contagion and the healing which addresses the reason why it is possible for the contagion to invade its host body.

Nya healing is only concerned with the first. The second inseparable component of this belief will be described and analysed in a later chapter on *yaabnam* healing. The Frafra have a saying which summarises the efficacy of *nya* healing. They say, *Lan ka y nyaab nya u ku tuon kaabe* (if it is not the roots of his/her ancestor, he/she cannot heal).

The belief in the origin of the herbs also adds weight to the efficacy of *nya* healing. In most cases, the roots and herbs are collected from trees or plants that are believed to have grown out of the graves of the founding ancestors of the healers. So the spiritual and physical relationship between the ancestors of the healer and the roots and herbs is literal.

This is why the strictly biopharmacological investigations into the herbs used in indigenous healing cannot diminish or negate the spiritual healing potency of the herbs. It also explains why even if these herbs are used for their biochemical properties, the Frafra will still approach *nya* healing from both biochemical and spiritual perspectives according to the interpretative function of their mythic world.

Nya healing works by invoking the holistic functions of the interpretative function of the Frafra mythic world; the basis of a belief in the human agency of spiritual powers as well as the ability to mediate and transfer these powers for good or evil. No single theory from any one discipline can offer the holistic understanding we are looking for in these rituals. We shall therefore attempt a holistic approach by designing *nya* healing as a phenomenon of symbolic representation.

Nya healing as a symbolic representation

In our attempt to analyse *Nya* healing as symbolic representation, we believe some insights from psychoanalysis will be helpful as we have already indicated. However, it is not every psychoanalytical theory that is appropriate in helping to analyse all Frafra types of healing. Psychoanalysis and psychotherapy mostly deals exclusively with the psychical world of a person with no reference to that person's socio-cultural and political context. There are some merits with such approaches.

In this approach we are primarily concerned with the pre-Oedipus stage if development where symbol formation is critical for the child's sense of identify. We are relying on the similarity between symbol formation and use in play therapy and symbol formation and use in ritual. We also want to avoid the tendency to elevate psychoanalysis and psychotherapy to the status of a secular religion. As Kegan aptly points out, such an approach leaves the impression that "the solution of life's ills could be found in universal psychotherapy."[57]

The Frafra do not separate the religious from the social and that psychological. They experience life as a totality or what we have been describing as an interconnectedness of the social psychological, spiritual, and religious and the cultural. We are interested here in looking at symbolic formation and its role in play therapy in the object Relation schools pioneered by Winnicott. We believe that there are compelling similarities between *nya kaaba* as symbolic representation and symbolic play in play therapy that allows the latter to offer helpful insights into the former.

The similarities between symbol formation and symbolic play as part of bringing up a Frafra child, and symbolic formation and play therapy, also convinces us that the latter can help us gain insights into the interpretative function of the Frafra mythic world in the symbolic representation of *nya* healing.

In our opinion the process of mythic world formation and its use as interpretative mechanism among the Frafra is similar to Christian mythic world information and its use as an interpretative mechanism as part of Christian nurture among new converts to Christianity. We strongly believe therefore that symbolic representation in play therapy has potential as a conceptual tool for giving us insights into how the Frafra use their mythic world as an interpretative mechanism to achieve well-being, as well as for the construction of contextualized Frafra Christian ministry of healing. Freud conceptualizes play as an autotherapeutic process. He writes:

It is clear that in their play children repeat everything that has made a great impression on them in real life, and that in doing so they address the strength of the impression and, as one might put it, make themselves master of the situation. It can also be observed that the unpleasurable nature of an experience does not always suit it for play. If the doctor looks down on a child's throat or carries out some small operation on him, we may be quite sure that these frightening experiences will be the subject of the next game; ...As the child passes over from the passivity of the experience to the activity of the game, he hands on the disagreeable experience to one of his play mates and in this way revenges himself on a substitute.[58]

The healer re-enacts a social context in which the sick person and his/her community experience life anew. By re-enacting their common mythic world they manipulate the symbols to get rid of this unpleasant experience.

Nya healing then constructs a social reality in which the passive attitudes of the sick person and his/her community become active. Their repressed feelings become expressive, and the blurred meanings they attach to their experiences become clearly focused.

Nya healing of the old world of pain or hurt is brought into focus with the potential world of healing or comfort. The symbols constructed in play provide the child with opportunities to play our his/her feelings of tension, frustration, insecurity, aggression, fear, bewilderment, confusion. In similar ways in *Nya* healing the Frafra reconstruct their mythic world which they use to express and maintain their interconnectedness and all aspects of their well-being.

Nya healing as in play therapy, is a phenomenon of representation of symbols in which the symbols are not "organized in terms of taxonomic structures or classification hierarchies but in terms of event schemata or scripts that are skeletal frameworks of everyday events".[59] *Nya* healing as symbolic representation is also an event representation phenomenon. The processes by means of which the symbols are constructed, reveal multiple levels of meanings for the participant. It must be emphasized that for the Frafra, there is a direct correlation between the symbols in *nya* healing and their mythic world.

The interpretative function of their mythic world is best understood by Bretherton's comparison between the healer and a mature artist:

Mature artists in their fictive event represent play much more consciously with the potential map-territory confusions and destructions and with the paradoxes of metacommunication than do young children. Some try to pack as many layers of meaning into a literary work or painting as possible. Others try to eliminate meaning altogether and play only with texture of paint and language. Some try to imagine alternative worlds or utopias, others tease an audience with inappropriate or omitted metacommunication, and yet others explore the paradox of levels of creating plays with plays and pictures with pictures.[60]

There are two words that make clear the significance of using symbolic play as concept for understanding how the Frafra mythic world functions as an interpretative mechanism in *nya* healing. The world "map-territory" is one of them. A map of a place such as London is London represented on a paper that one can put in one's pocket. With the map and the skill of reading maps one can go to London and visit any places of interest. Yet there is a difference between the London on paper and the physical territory of London. One cannot read through the map of London and claim to have been to London. The map serves as a representation of the territory of London and yet it is not London. Similarly, ny healing as a ritual system is a "map-territory" of the Frafra mythic world.

The other word is "metacommunication". "Metacommunication" connotes the idea that there is a common basic understanding presumed by child, therapist and parents, or the artists and audience that is necessary for them to know when an action is literal or non-literal. For example, metacommunication is a prerequisite for the mother to know when the child is actually crying, or play crying.

Metacommunication is also necessary to distinguish reality from "make-believe". However, one cannot define "make-believe" as simply deceptive or false representation. One should rather compare "make-believe" reality in representation with actual life reality as the map of London is to the territory of London.

In *nya* healing the healer uses different metacommunication options to project a shared mythic world and shared realities in the mythic world represented by shared symbols. The "make believe" in *nya* healing enables the sick person to create subjunctive variants on situations they face. Hofstadter offers an important explanation of the term "subjunctive world":

> The manufacture of subjective worlds happens so casually, so naturally, that we hardly notice what we are doing. We select from our fantasy a world, which is close, in some internal mental sense, to the real world. We compare what is real with what we perceive as almost real. In so doing we gain some intangible kind of perspective on reality. Think how immeasurably poorer our lives would be if we did not have this capacity for slipping out of the midst of reality into soft 'what ifs!'[61]

Such unity between the shared mythic world and the creation of subjective variant situations in *nya* healing makes it possible for the Frafra mythic world to engage in its holistic interpretative functions.

The construction of all mythic worlds in general and the Frafra mythic world in particular is best understood by Winnicott's ideas on the formation of transitional objects and transitional phenomena in children. When a baby is born, the baby has no sense of independent existence from the mother. Both the baby and the mother are one as far as the baby is concerned.

In the course of time, the baby kicks, clenches her fist, and slowly replaces the breast with her thumb. From the thumb, the child begins to favour an object that is not the mother. In most cases parents allow the child to become emotionally attached to this object. This object varies from child to child as well as culture to culture. In one culture, it is a teddy bear; in another it is a hand band.[62] Winicott calls this total experience of child and transitional object as "transitional phenomena." The transitional phenomenon is the cultural symbol formation process.

Anna Freud refers to such objects as the thumb, the teddy bear, the talisman and hand band as "transitional objects".[63] According to Winnicott transitional objects and transitional phenomena are the:

Designation of the intermediate area of experience between the thumb and the teddy bear, between the oral eroticism and true object relationship, between primary creative activity and projection of what has already been projected between primary acknowledgement of indebtedness.[64]

shared symbols. The "make believe" in *nya* healing enables the sick person to create subjunctive variants on situations they face. Hofstadter offers an important explanation of the term "subjunctive world":

> The manufacture of subjective worlds happens so casually, so naturally, that we hardly notice what we are doing. We select from our fantasy a world, which is close, in some internal mental sense, to the real world. We compare what is real with what we perceive as almost real. In so doing we gain some intangible kind of perspective on reality. Think how immeasurably poorer our lives would be if we did not have this capacity for slipping out of the midst of reality into soft 'what ifs!'[61]

Such unity between the shared mythic world and the creation of subjective variant situations in *nya* healing makes it possible for the Frafra mythic world to engage in its holistic interpretative functions.

The construction of all mythic worlds in general and the Frafra mythic world in particular is best understood by Winnicott's ideas on the formation of transitional objects and transitional phenomena in children. When a baby is born, the baby has no sense of independent existence from the mother. Both the baby and the mother are one as far as the baby is concerned.

In the course of time, the baby kicks, clenches her fist, and slowly replaces the breast with her thumb. From the thumb, the child begins to favour an object that is not the mother. In most cases parents allow the child to become emotionally attached to this object. This object varies from child to child as well as culture to culture. In one culture, it is a teddy bear; in another it is a hand band.[62] Winicott calls this total experience of child and transitional object as "transitional phenomena." The transitional phenomenon is the cultural symbol formation process.

Anna Freud refers to such objects as the thumb, the teddy bear, the talisman and hand band as "transitional objects".[63] According to Winnicott transitional objects and transitional phenomena are the:

Designation of the intermediate area of experience between the thumb and the teddy bear, between the oral eroticism and true object relationship, between primary creative activity and projection of what has already been projected between primary acknowledgement of indebtedness.[64]

The above explanations offer insights into why the symbols of *nya* healing are inseparably related to the Frafra mythic world. These explanations also shows why these symbols are cultural transitional objects of the Frafra mythic world as well as reasons as to why *nya* healing provides holistic healing.

Conclusions

It is obvious from our investigation that a contextualized Frafra Christian Ministry of healing must begin with understanding the role of the Frafra mythic world as an interpretative mechanism in indigenous notions of sickness. This includes causes, diagnosis classifications and healing rituals. The insights of *nya* healing as ritual systems through symbolic representation have enormous potential for constructing a contextualized Frafra Christian ministry of healing.

One of the most important insights for such a ministry is the need for Frafra Christian theologians to construct a Frafra Christian Ministry of Healing that can utilize the Frafra mythic world.

The Frafra oral diagnostic manuals and *nya* healing are symbolic constructions of their mythic world. The Entire ritual system creates a subjunctive world for their mythic world to perform its interpretative functions in times of sickness.

There are important insights, which can be used to construct a contextualized Frafra Christian ministry of healing to Frafra Christians who fall sick. The need for a metacommunication between the healer, the sick and the entire community makes it further imperative that a contextualized Frafra Christian ministry of healing begins with the Frafra mythic world. For without a metacommunication between the Christian pastoral care giver and the Frafra Christian who fall sick, the care giver cannot create a subjunctive world nor will the symbols used in the liturgy of healing have anything in common with the indigenous mythic world.

Consequently the mythic world cannot function as an interpretative mechanism since the meanings attached to the symbols are incomprehensible. This is because both pastoral care givers and Frafra Christians are operating from two different mythic worlds.

The notion of sickness as a contagion and the Frafra belief that humans are agents of spiritual powers have important implications for Frafra Christian pastoral care. They also have potential for revitalizing the traditional theological concept of the image of God a cross-cultural theology of the Holy Spirit and indeed a cross-cultural Christian ministry of healing of the Church. The holistic approach in diagnosis and treatment of sickness in *nya* healing can also contribute to the debate between medicine and theology. Christian medical ethics and ecological ethics.

Reference

1. P. Kirby, *God, Shrines and Problem-solving among the Anufo of Northern Ghana* (Berlin: Dietrich Reimer Verlag 1986).

2. Peter worsley, "Non-Western medical Systems" in *Annual Review of Anthropology* Vol. 78 (1982), p.329

3. T. Parson, *Social Structure and Personality* (New York, Free Press/Collier-MacMillan Ltd., 197).

4. Worsley, (19820, P.327.

5. ibid. p. 317

6. ibid, p. 321

7. G.M. Foster, "Diseases Etiologies in Non-Western Medical System" in *American Anthropologist* Vol. 78 (1976) p. 75

8. Ibid

9. Ibid

10. D.R. Prince-Williams, "A case study of ideas concerning disease among he Tiv" in Z.A. Ademuwegum et al *African Therapeutic Systems* (London: Crossroads Press for Africa Studies Association (1979), p.27

11. E.E. Evans-Pritchard, *Witchcraft, Oracle and Magic Among the Azande* (Oxford, Osford University Press (1937), p. 448

12. Worsley, (1982), p. 325

13. Una Catherine Maclean, *Magical Medicine: A Nigeria Case Study* (London: Penguin Books 1971).

14. C.G. Baeta, "Christianity and Healing" in Orita Vol. 1 (1965), p. 51.

15. K.A. Dickson, *Theology in Afra* (London: Dalton, Longman and Todd 1984), p.47.

16 E.Y. Lartey, "African Perspective on Pastoral Theology: a contribution to the quest for more encompassing models of pastoral care" *Contact* Vol. 112 (1980), p.7

17. Kirby, (1986) p. 88

18. Meyer Fortes, "informants" in *L'Uomo* vol. Iv, no.2, (1980), p. 363.

19. G. Liehardit, *Divinity and Experience: the Religion of the Dinka,* (Oxford: Clarendon Press 1987)

20. Kirby, (1986), p. 88

21 Z.A. Ademuwagun, "Problem and Prospect of Legimitizing and Integrating: Aspects of Traditional Health Care Systems and Methods with Modern Medical Therapy: The Igo-Ora Experience" in Ademuwagun et al *African Therapeutic Systems* (1979), p. 161.

22. Cecil Helman, *Culture, Health and Illness* (19840, P. 65 also see a history of development of Descartes influence on Western world with respect to healing discussed in A. Erwin H. Ackernecht, *A Short History of Medicine*(New York: The Roland Press 1955), p. 110f and F. Capra, *The Turning Point: Science, Society and the Rising Culture* (London: Fontant 1983), p. 122ff.

23. ibid p. 66.

24. ibid p. 66-67.

25. ibid p. 67

14. C.G. Baeta, "Christianity and Healing" in Orita Vol. 1 (1965), p. 51.

15. K.A. Dickson, *Theology in Afra* (London: Dalton, Longman and Todd 1984), p.47.

16 E.Y. Lartey, "African Perspective on Pastoral Theology: a contribution to the quest for more encompassing models of pastoral care" *Contact* Vol. 112 (1980), p.7

17. Kirby, (1986) p. 88

18. Meyer Fortes, "informants" in *L'Uomo* vol. Iv, no.2, (1980), p. 363.

19. G. Liehardit, *Divinity and Experience: the Religion of the Dinka,* (Oxford: Clarendon Press 1987)

20. Kirby, (1986), p. 88

21 Z.A. Ademuwagun, "Problem and Prospect of Legimitizing and Integrating: Aspects of Traditional Health Care Systems and Methods with Modern Medical Therapy: The Igo-Ora Experience" in Ademuwagun et al *African Therapeutic Systems* (1979), p. 161.

22. Cecil Helman, *Culture, Health and Illness* (19840, P. 65 also see a history of development of Descartes influence on Western world with respect to healing discussed in A. Erwin H. Ackernecht, *A Short History of Medicine*(New York: The Roland Press 1955), p. 110f and F. Capra, *The Turning Point: Science, Society and the Rising Culture* (London: Fontant 1983), p. 122ff.

23. ibid p. 66.

24. ibid p. 66-67.

25. ibid p. 67

26. Ibid.

27. G. Bibeau, "The World Health Organization in encounter with African Traditional Medicine: Theoretical conceptions and practical strategies" translated from French by Sandra Mahaniah in Ademuwagun et al *Africa Therapeutic Systems* (1979), p. 187.

28. Ibid.

29. ibid, p. 182

30 *Official Records of the WHO* No. 229 Geneva 1976. Also see Annual report of Director General to World Council of Health and United Nations in *Office Records of WHO* No.22, Geneva 1976, also see McGilvary, J.C., *The Quest for Health and Wholeness,* (Tubingen: German Institute for Medical Mission (1981), Chapters 4, 5 and 7.

31. *G.* Bibeau, (1979), P. 184.

32. B. Hours, "African medicine as 'Alibi' and as a reality" in *African medicine in the modern world* (seminar held in the center of African studies, University of Edinburgh, 10, 11 Dec. 1986), p.40.

33. ibid, p.45

34. ibid, p. 46

35. Ibid.

36. Ibid.

37. ibid, p.48
38. Dennis M. Warren, "The role of epic analysis in medical anthropology: The case of the Bono of Ghana in Ademuwagun et al *African Therapeutic Systems* (1979), p.36.

39. ibid, p. 42

40. ibid.

41. Kirby (1986).

42. M. Kilson, *African urban kinsmen: The Ga of Central Accra* (London: G. Hurst & Co. 1974) p. 89-95.

43. ibid, p. 91

44. Una C. Maclean, Magical medicine: A Nigerian Case Study (1971).

45. Patrick Twumasi, "Ashanti traditional medicine and its relation to present day psychiatry" in Ademuwagun et al *African Therapeutic Systems* (1979), p. 111, 237.

46. ibid, p. 237

47. ibid, p. 238

48. Kofi Appiah_Kubi "Religion and healing in an African community: The Akan of Ghana" in Lawrence E. Sullivan (ed) *Healing and Restoring* (New York, Macmillan Publishing Co. 1989), p.215-216.

49. ibid, p.216

50. ibid.

51. W.S. Mensah-Dapaa, "Observations in traditional healing methods in Ghana" in Ademuwagen et al *African Therapeutic Systems* (1979), p. 113.

52. ibid.

53 ibid.

54. E.E. Evans-Pritchard, "The meaning of Sacrifice among the Nuer" in *Journal of Royal Anthropological Society* Vol. 84 (11954), p.21.

55. M. Ruel, "Non-sacrificial ritual killing" in *Man* Vol. 25 (1990), p.323.

56. James W. Fernandez, "Analysis of Ritual: Metaphor correspondences as the elementary forms" in *Science* Vol. 182, (1973, p. 1366.

57. Robert Kegan, *The evolving self: Problems and process in human development (*Cambridge, Massachusetts: Harvard University Press 1982), p. 254.

58. Sigmund Freud, *Collected psychological works* (1955), p. 16.

59 Inge Bretherton, "Representing the social world in Symbolic Play: reality and fantasy" in Inge Bretherton (ed) *Symbolic Play*(1984), p.5.

60. ibid, p. 37.

61 D. R. Hofstadter, *Godel Escher, Bach: An eternal golden brain* (New York, Basic Books 1979), p. 443.

62 D.M. Winnicott, *Collected papers* (London: Tavistock Publishing 1958), p.229.

36 Ana Freud, *Normality and pathology in childhood* (London: Hogarth Press and the Institute of Psychoanalysis 1965).

64. Winnicott, *Collected works* (1958), p.230.

CHAPTER FIVE

Tiim and *Baanaab* Sickness and Healing

Introduction

Tiim and Baanaab sickness and healing systems are also important among the Frafra. However, they are some of the most difficult types of healing systems to investigate because most of the healing sessions and objects are not visible to the naked eye. Some aspects of these healing rituals area also done in different locations yet they are supposed to have effects on the sick person in other locations. As we can see from the statistics there are fewer people involved in them as compared to other healing rituals. That makes it so difficult to become part of the inner circle of participants of the healing ritual.

Perhaps the problems stated above may have accounted for why Fortes in all his extensive writing on the Talleh, never deals with or even mentions in passing *tiim* and *baanaab* healing. In spite of these difficulties we had the privilege of being part of some *tiim* and *baanaab* healing.

We shall briefly describe some cases of *tiim* and *baanaab* healing. We observed that most cases of *tiim* sickness were very sudden and more acute. They did not involve blood letting. Some cases of *tiim* and *baanaab* also involved mental confusions.

Types of *Tiim* and *Baanaab* sickness

there are different types of *tiim* and *baanaab* sickness. The most common type is caused by witches. The Frafra believe that the *soi* (witch) has the ability to leave his/her body to engage in spiritual ritual hunting, eating or damaging his/her victims. Once they take possession of a person's spirit, then that person becomes physically sick and may eventually die. Researchers whose works are specifically concerned with the phenomena of witches include Evans-Pritchard[1] and Grottanelli[2] to mention a few. About fifty years ago, Fortes reported that the phenomenon of witches was not of too much concern to the Frafra in their daily interactions.[3] In our research the findings of Fortes half a century ago were confirmed.

There is another type of *tiim* and *baanaab* sickness. This type of sickness is caused by a spiritual power by person(s) a spiritual power to cause physical harm or sickness on other persons. In addition to causing physical sickness, these spiritual powers can also cause infertility, unsuccessful business adventures, destroy marriages, and family relationships.

Earlier on we indicated that in Frafra mythic world they believe that plants, trees, rivers, and stones also have spirits. These are the spirits that are used to cause sickness as well as healing . these types of spiritual powers are similar to what Kirby describes as "territorial spirits".[4] Kirby says territorial spirits live in a particular locality in a particular human community or in the wild.[5]

Kirby seems to imply that "territorial spirits" are geographically fixed spirits. On the contrary, the Frafra notions of territorial spirits are both culturally located in their mythic world as well as geographical. Even though they perform their ritual on some sacred spots, they also believe that wherever they are, the "territorial spirits" are with them. They further believe that these spirits can move across rivers and mountains. Therefore they can be sent to Accra about four hundred miles from Bolgatanga or across the Atlantic Ocean.

This point is supported by a story of a young Frafra woman in London. Beatrice is a well educated woman. She is married to a British man. They have lived in London for five years. Life has been difficult for them. She has been in and out of hospital. Her husband was laid off. She told us that two years ago she received a letter from home saying that a neighbour was jealous of her prosperity and was contacting territorial spiritual powers to go and destroy her prosperity. She said she ignored it at first. But as a result of what has happened to her family she believed that it was directly the result of the "territorial spirits" sent to her in London.

Another important example is the frequent consultation at a shrine in Tongo by many different people from Southern Ghana. In southern Ghana the name "*Nana Tongo"* is associated with the most powerful territorial localized earth spirit in Tongo. It is believed that *Nana Tongo* can give its consultant's money, children, protection against business failures as well as rescue them from very threatening situations. *Nana Tongo* is a cave in the rocks of a village called Tenzug about six miles from the Catholic Church in Tongo. People come from Accra, Kumas, Takoradi, and Tamale to consult *Nana Tongo* with the belief that the spiritual powers of *Nana Tongo* will always be with them. So territorial spirits are not solely localized as Kirby suggests. They are both particular and yet universal.

We have personally been involved with three graduate students from different parts of Africa in the U.K., whose cases are similar to that of Beatrice. Therefore the definition of territorial is not solely a geographical location, but more importantly, cultural in various mythic worlds.

There is also another type of spiritual being of the wild different from those described above. These are commonly referred to by the Arabic term *jinn.* Kirby defines *jinn* as:

...non-localized and associated with the wilds the uninhabited, undomesticated areas beyond the village space and farmlands, in particular places overgrown with thick underbrush or large trees such as are found along streams. They are thought to roam about and behave much as men do in society. they are thus often conceived of as having the corporeal substance of diminutive men having families with wives and children.[6]

Similar description of *jinns* or wild spirits is offered by Trimingham,[7] Lewis,[8] MacDonald and Masse.[9] In Frafra *jinn* are called *baabibih.* The *jinns* can both inflict as well as heal sickness. All these types of sicknesses involve on form of *tiim* or another.

Tiim healings rituals

Tiim healing is mainly concerned with sicknesses caused by spiritual powers. The types of healing they offer are similar to the *mathian gok*among the Dinka as described by Lienhardt.[10] They are also similar to Kirby's third type of healers among the Anufo.[11] This type of healer uses spiritual powers whose main goal is to look for the spiritual contagion in its host's body and destroy it or undo what another power has done. The Frafra believe that spiritual powers can be controlled by humans for evil in terms of causing sickness and for good in terms of preventing spiritual powers from carrying out their intentions.

These spiritual powers have names known to their owners, or controllers. In some cases these spiritual power work through materials objects such as roots, herbs, tails of animals, cloths, amulets, and pots, which Kirby calls "shrine objects".[12] Similar observations were made about these types of healing phenomenon among the Ashanti b Rattray.[13] According to Kirby the Anufo like the Ffrafra believe that:

> ...the inert power contained within earthly substance can be unleashed through correctly combining them, at which point it becomes a distinct

spiritual entity with a name, and is capable of being applied to treat sickness or counteract offensive magic.[14]

in some cases the *tiim* owner would come and give to the sick person some herbs to drink, and a message. At other times he would also come and give the sick person an amulet made of cowries, heads of animals and dried tails of animals.

The *tiim* owners or agents usually do the consultations in their homes. Below are two out of many accounts of *tiim* consultation we were privileged to be part of. These two cases are typical of all those we observed.

Case one of *tiim* sickness and healing

A man took us to his *tiim*. A small clay pot was placed on a three fork branch of a tree. Inside the pot were some barks of a tree, the top of the cover of the pot was covered with blood and feathers of different birds. He explained that he healed by looking inside the pot to determine the cause of the sickness. In other words the pot serves as a kind of spiritual x-ray, or laboratory instrument that identifies the spiritual virus. He also said he could talk with the spiritual powers in the pot. The spirit roams about independent of their owner or agent. However, he always calls the spirit home for consultation in the night.

Any time he was offering a chicken to the spirit, he did not cut the throat. He instructed the spirit power to kill it. we shall present here two eye-witnessed consultation. He placed the chicken on top of the cover of the pot. He told the spirit power to kill the chicken. As far as we could see he did not apply any pressure nor did he hit it. however in about ten minutes the chicken was dead.

At another time it was a dog he killed. He tied the dog to the stick supporting the pot. He kept instructing the *tiim* to kill the dog. In about twenty minutes the dog was dead. As much as we could observe it was not sick before and he did not hit, suffocate, or in any way physically harm it.

Case two of *tiim* sickness and healing

My brother married a woman about six miles away from our village. According to tradition, the girl spent the first night with the most elderly woman in the house. The second day she spent the night with her husband. This was during March when the weather was very hot in the evening. On the third night my brother, his newly wed, my wife and I decided to lie in the open yard as the weather was extremely hot.

At about 4:30 a.m. my wife and I decided to go to our room. Shortly after we went in, my brother and his wife also went into the room. An hour later my brother came to ask me whether his wife was with us as she was not in their room. We woke up and asked the others in their rooms but she was nowhere to be found. We decided to wait at least a day and see what would happened. To our surprise she was in her sister's house, six miles away, at about six o' clock that morning.

She said that a few minutes after she and her husband went into their room she heard a voice of someone calling her to come out so that they could go and cut firewood in the bush. She came out and followed this person who she said she could not identify, until the person disappeared just about a hundred yards in front of her sister's house. So naturally she went into her sister's house early in the morning.

According to her sister and her band, when she arrived, she was cold and confused. Her brother-in-law is adept in *tiim* symptoms, so he had no problem in diagnosing a *tiim* sickness. He went into his room, opened his *baar dok* (pot of water and roots imbued with special powers) and took some water from the *tiim* pot for her to drink. He rubbed his hands with some concoction and massaged her head, face and entire body. She felt well after resting for a few hours.

They sent for her father who came and asked why she was there. She told her story to her father. she was apologetic to her father and pleaded with him to let her come back to our house for she loved her husband. She also added that she could not understand why she came all the way to her sister's house.

Since she said she wanted to come back to my brother, her fathers decided to send someone to inform our family what had happened as well as ask them to come for the girl. After the messenger told the story, my brother consulted with the most senior members of the family and they told the messenger that they wanted her to stay wither parents for a few days while the had further consultations among themselves and their *yaabnam* (ancestors). As soon as the messenger left almost everyone gave a sigh of life. the elder of the family said, "*Te banaab n ta na kad poua kan nya la bah*" (our ancestors have come and drive this woman away). So the marriage was annulled.

As a Christian and a researcher, this case raised very difficult questions. For example, was it a case of the demonic possessions as in the biblical stories.

Was it that my brother slept so soundly that he did not hear the voice, or was she suffering from hallucinations that no one else could hear? The distance between our village and the other village was such that one could not travel it in two hours. Certainly, no Frafra woman would travel through those bushes unaccompanied at that time of the morning. So why was she not afraid? As a pastor, this case raised questions of how much understanding of Frafra mythic world is urgently needed in my ministry and the ministry of the local Presbyterian Church, if we are to address the pastoral issues of Frafra spiritual powers with the gospel of Jesus Christ.

In our descriptions and analyses of Frafra diagnostic sayings , and *nya* healing, we concluded that nya healing is based on the belief that the sickness was caused by a spiritual contagion. Hence *nya* healing was

The call to be a *Baabaab*

The signs of anyone who is to become a *Baanaab* vary from individual to individual. the signs range from mild forms of ill health to very sever psychotic episodes. There are other signs that can be economic factors.

As stated already, the Frafra believe that there are wild spirits in their world. These wild spirits are different from the spirits of the ancestors, the *boar* or *tenkpan* (earth shines) or the spirit of trees stones and water. The *kodgboreh* or *kikito* (spirits or genes) are wild spirits that can be semi-domesticated. By semi-domesticated, we mean that these spirits have independent existence but put their power under the goal of human control. They live both at home; in human social settings such as attending markets. They also invisibly move about with their owner who is their medium. They eat human foods prepared and kept in rooms. They exchange conversation with family members, friends and neighbours. They travel long distances within a short span of time.

Rituals of initiating a *Baanaab*

When shall describe a case of how one became a *baanaab*. Tom is forty two years old. He has a secondary education. Now he works as a librarian in Ghana. He recalls that after school he became employed. Later on he married. He and his wife had two children. He said, he started experiencing unusual "things". He recalled that some items were disappearing from their house. He wondered whether someone was stealing his money as he was often short of money. His wife and family were frequently sick. Suddenly he realized that he had become impotent.

He said that as a well educated person, he went to hospital immediately. The doctors ordered all types of laboratory tests. All the test for suspected diagnoses were negative.

All his x-rays of lungs, brain and other parts of the body were negative. He went to the western trained doctors for about a year and was beginning to feel very worried because the prospect for correct diagnosis and treatment was becoming bleaker and bleaker. Someone came to him and in the course of his desperation and suggested to him to *Baanaab n dolu* (*Baabibih* are following are following him to let them into his life).

According to him, he immediately dismissed this but the thought lingered in his mind. He exhausted Western medical advice and treatment available to him, yet he was not cured. He then decided to try the suggestions from his friends and family. he went back to the village. They told him that there are two rites to perform in order to become a *baanaab.*

The Telleh and the Nabnam called the first rite *ve. Ve* connotes the idea of fermentation. It can also mean failing to show up or the penultimate in ritual performance or achieving a goal.

It is difficult to describe the *ve* process because it is not open to the public. We shall briefly consider what we gathered from some well informed persons and one that we were fortunate to observe.

***Ve* rite**

Before and during the initiating a baanaab one's *yaabnam*(ancestors) are consulted. The family in the extended sense assembles; go to the bakologo to ask for permission of their *yaabnam.* They offer *kaaba* to all the *yaanaam* of both the paternal and maternal ancestors of the candidate. After they have *kaab* the *yaabnam*, they call a most respectable experienced practicing baanaab *to* initiate the new one. This is where it was difficult to either see personally or obtain any consistent account of the process. Indeed, most people were afraid to disclose what they claimed to know for fear that the *kodkpareh* or *kikito (jinns)* would attack or inflict a severe punishment on them and/or their families.

All the informants who indicate that they experienced *baanaab* will go and speak to *Kodkpareh* to tell them that the candidates had accepted to have them in their house.

What most accounts agreed upon was that, the experienced *baanaab* will perform some secret rites to express the willingness of the candidate to be used as the agents or medium of the *kodkpareh*. So the word *ve* expresses the idea of the rite of the penultimate before being fully initiated into the society or cult of *baanaab*. It is a limininal state in which the candidate is not like an ordinary man anymore and yet not a full *baanaab*. The period between ve and *Gbaa*, the second and last rite varies from candidate to candidate.

Baa rite

The world *gbaa* means to catch. It connotes the idea of chasing or seeking after that which one seizes with or without that thing or person's consent. It can also mean to elope with a woman as happens in some types of marriages.

The *gbaa* rite is a process in which the *Baabilih* or *kikito* are forcefully taken from the wild and become semi-domesticated under the control of the candidate. He consults them at will and wherever the control of the candidate. Consults them at will and wherever he goes or sends them they go. But they are invisible to ordinary eyes. When one is ready to *gbaa baabibih* (trap *Baabibih*) they consult an experienced *baanaab*. They brew *daam*(local beer), offer *kaaba* as well as prepare assorted delicious foods. The *baanaab* is supposed to use his *baabibih* to entice the others to come and eat the food. The Frafra believe that the *baabibih* have a craving appetite for the Frafra delicacies.

At about midnight, the *baabaah* assemble. They go with a *koleg* (a bag made of animal skin). They will disguise themselves and display the delicacies. The domesticated *baabibih* will deceive the others to come and eat and drink. As they engage in the food, he will quietly pick them up forcefully into the bag. At times he catches two or more depending upon their reaction time.

When the others take notice, they shout, and fight back by throwing stones and other objects. Those caught in the bags also scream or cry. Most people who claimed to have witnessed such said they did hear their words and protest. Others also said they saw the stones they drew. The *baanaab* will run away quickly to the home of those fighting for their release. They will then perform various rites for those caught to forget their places of abode in the wild as well as put them under the full control of the *baanaab* it is only after this second rite that the *baanaab*. It is only after this second rite that the *baanaab* becomes recognized as a healer in Frafraland.

The major differences between the *jinns* and humans are that they are invisible to humans. They also move about in different ways; they walk, fly, come into a room through small holes and windows. They can also go wherever the *baanaab* goes. They move in numbers of twos or threes. They can also contact others of their kind in the wild. In other words, some *baabibih* are domesticated while others are wild. The *baabibiih* are the same as *jinns* and refer to the same spiritual beings. So we shall use the two names interchangeably.

In both *tiim* and *baanaab* healing the owner or agent contracts with the powers under his control to perform spiritual tasks on behalf of their clients. Later on, they offer rewards to the spiritual powers. He can throw them away or acquire other powers to supplement them.

The *baanaab* in some cases is a diviner. In fact, the word *baanaab* is the title for a diviner, even though they are two separate functions and one can be one without the other. The *baanibih* are not diffused in the bodily fluids of the *baanaab.* They are believed to have independence. They can decide to help or not. This is the main difference between *baabihiih* and *tiim*.

Case of *Baanaab* healing

One day Basima came back from the market in the evening and fell very sick. One of my informants rushed to tell me the story. When we went to visit him it was obvious that he was in pain. He sent for Nagben, a prominent *baanaab* in the village. The *baanaab* arrived, looked at him and told him that he would come back in the night after he consulted his *baabibiih.*

We went to the *baanaab*'s house at about eight o'clock in the evening. He covered himself with a long straw mat at a corner between a wall and his room. He started first by humming. Later, he sang the praises of the *baabibiih* and called the name of the *baabibiih.* After about fifteen minutes, there were knocks on the wall and a discussion between the man and what sounded like two different voices of two people.

One of the voices asked who was calling. The man answered that he was. Another asked why. The man asked them to come in. Both voices seemed to express reluctance. The man persuaded them by promising them a precious gift. We certainly heard what seemed like people climbing the wall to come in. we also heard what sounded like foot steps landing from a height. After the settled, the man told them that his friend was about to die and he wanted them to help.

One of the voices said that was no problem. the other said they knew it before coming. Indeed, he said he saw what happened. He told us that one of the man's neighbours hated him, so he went and gave him (his spirit) to a tree to kill him. So they would both go and ask the tree to release the spirit of the man. The man and those around thanked them. Again we heard what sounded like steps climbing the wall. The voices were also becoming faint as if they were moving further away from the house. The séance came to an end and we left. The sick man was well in about three days.

We shall describe another incident that occurred in a village. This incident is not a healing case as such but it helps us to understand the operation of these *baabibiih.* A man had a big goat that used to give birth to twins. Indeed, this goat was a financial investment for this man. In the early evening he saw the oat in his house, however the goat suddenly disappeared from the house. He looked in all his neighbours' stables but could not find the goat.

He was so worried he decided to consult a *baanaab* at about nine o'clock in the night. We went to the *baanaab*'s house. The process of calling the *baabibiih* was as already described. When the *Baabibiih* came they said one of his neighbours had stolen it to go and sell. However, they promised to go and release it. at dawn, when the man woke up, he saw his goat standing in front of his gate.

Analysis

We have already stated that it is difficult to investigate these types of healing. These cases are the difficulties. We had no way of verifying how the *jinns* released the spirit of *Basima*. We also had no way of observing the *jinns* going to release the goat. All we saw was the consultation and the result of the requests at the consultation. We could not tell whether the *baanaabnam* (plural) were simply skillful ventriloquists or that they actually spoke to spiritual powers. We could not also tell whether the goat coming back was a coincidence or not. The ethical question for a research is whether he/she is involved in deception or genuine phenomenon? We assumed the latter.

Throughout our field research we found that these types of sickness and healing could occur at any lime of the day, week and month. Form the data in the appendix A, we can infer that they also affect men, women and children.

The healers or agents were all men. From the findings in the appendices, it is also clear that they are not as popular as *nya* and *nyaabnam* healing. We may infer here that they may be considered by the Frafra as specialized types of healing.

Tiim and *baanaab* healing seemed t be types of healing that also exist in India.[15] They are also similar to Geertz's description of ilmu among the Javanese[16] in Indonesia.

Both *tiim* and *baanaab* healing rituals in the light of play therapy are symbolic representations of the Frafra mythic world. The questions to answer are what *tiim* and *baanaab* healing in these symbolic presentations reveal about the Frafra mythic world and how the Frafra mythic world functions as an interpretative mechanism to offer healing?

Traditional theories of religion and the phenomena of *tiim* and *baanaab* healing

Tiim and baanaab healing rituals reveal a concept of interdependency between humans and spiritual powers for good or evil. So they offer an important religious perspective in healing rituals. But scholars in the discipline of what is traditionally called Comparative study of religion do not agree on the perspective that it offers. Some may call this kind of healing religious, while others consider it as magical.

Tylor offered some distinctions between the two and are worth mentioning. For Tylor, religion is concern with personal being while magic is concern with impersonal beings.[17] Religious acts serve public interest while magical acts serve private interest.

Beattie defines magic as"...the acting out of a situation, the expression of a desire in symbolic terms; it is not the application of empirically acquired knowledge about the properties of the natural substances".[18]

Although these are two simple distinctions they are by no means simplistic. In one sense we can say that *tiim* and *baanaab* healing are magical rather than religious. The reason is that they use powers that are supposed to function like humans but who were not visible to us. Indeed, some of the actions of these healers may even seem as if they are playing tricks on their patients. However, a careful critical evaluation of these phenomena in other religions including

Christianity strongly suggests that we cannot be sure that they are not based on "empirically acquired knowledge".

We shall give some reasons why it is difficult to call them magical acts without being guilty of one religious bias or another. Firstly, we cannot help but to ask who determines whether they are empirically acquired or not and what are impersonal about them to designate them as magic.

Secondly, we do not also see what is impersonal about these healings in order to categories them as magical and those of the healings of Jesus, or millingo to call those religious.

Thirdly, the similarities between the Christian beliefs in the person and works of the Holy Spirit and the Frafra beliefs in the persons and works of the spiritual beings do not justify calling one religion and the other magic.

The evidences for the personal attributes of Frafra spiritual beings in *tiim* and *baanaab* healing cannot be ignored from the cases that we have cited. Furthermore, for the Frafra, the *jinns* are like human beings who talk and are seemingly intelligent, yet they are invisible and can enter rooms through small holes as we have described.

Fourthly, these healings also had both private and public dimensions. For example, in the case of Basima his healing is both personal and public. For although his healing by the *Baanaab* was privately directed to him, the entire family also benefited from his healing.
In our opinion there may be elements of both in most religions. The problem is that it is difficult to draw the line. Because what is to the believer religion may appear to the observer as magic and vice versa. And even for a believer at one time an act may be considered as religious but at another time the same act may be considered by the same believer as magical for one reason or the other.

One the basis of the above reasons we cannot call *tiim* and *baanaab* healing as either religion or magic. Even if we designate them as religious, there is still the question of how we define religion.

Evans-Pritchard disagreed with the use of psychological and sociological theories to account for the origin of religion.[19] The benefit of his criticisms for our project is the need to explore a holistic approach.

We shall now cite a case to demonstrate how impractical, indeed it is impossible to make a distinction between magic and religion in human behaviour towards the sacred. We cannot even assume that if one is well educated in either Ghana or in the West one does not believe or practice magic and religion in one's behaviour towards the sacred.

A well educate couple had been married for five years. They lived in Accra. They were Christians. For four years they had tried all forms of Western medicine to have a baby including a trip in London, but all failed. Attempts by their relatives for them to see a *tiim* healer failed. Out of desperation, they went to consult *tiim* in tongo, four hundred miles from Accra. The *tiim* healer told them that another spirit has hidden her womb. So they should go back to Accra for he would let his *tiim* go and release the womb.

Six months later the woman was pregnant and I saw the child on my visit to their house for this interview. Although we cannot be certain that it was the *tiik* that was solely responsible for the pregnancy, we cannot also rule its role out completely. However, the point here is that this couple was sophisticated people who went to consult *tiim*.

Mensah-Dapaa a scientist has also reported similar cases in his observations in the Akonnede shrine at Larteh.[20] It seems *tiim* and *baanaab* healing can be wholly analyzed as either magical or religious act. They can only be understood by taking serious the Frafra mythic as the basis for their efficacy to heal. However, by taking seriously the Frafra mythic world does not imply that those engaged into them do not have a knowledge of modern scientific medicine.

The woman who became pregnant, the goat released, the chicken and dog that died in our presence in the cases that we cited may be indications that these types of healing are based on a kind of "empirically acquired knowledge" from the perspective of the believer's mythic world.

The case of the couple at least suggest that one could be sophisticated and yet hold on to such a mythic world in which the belief in *jinns* is a reality. Perhaps, the healing ministry of Milingo in Italy may be one more evidence of the fact that belief in spiritual powers to heal and modern scientific medicine are not mutually exclusive as some writers like Field, Mulling and other social theorists on contact-culture referred to earlier seem to suggest.

The phenomena of *tiim* and *baanaab* healing cannot be fully accounted for, but reducing them to only the social, the moral, the psychological, or the cultural explanations. Rather, *tiim* and *baanaab kaaba* demonstrate the interconnectedness of the social, moral and spiritual, psychological and the cultural in the Frafra mythic world. It is holistic healing.

These cases have shown that *tiim* and *baanaab* healing, as rituals systems are symbolic representation of the Frafra mythic world. They invoke the interpretative functions of their mythic world to address the issues that they perceive as are real that threaten the balance of the interconnectedness of life and thus ensures their well being. In *tiim* and *baanaab* healing rituals the interconnectedness is expressed and an interpretation made possible by a relationship between symbols and belief system of humans as agents of spiritual powers who mediate or transfer these spiritual powers. But the question not answered is: how does the belief in the human agency of spiritual powers in which humans mediate or transfer such powers offer healing?

In our opinion, the phenomenon of *tiim* and *baanaab* healing may be one that the study of religious phenomena from the Bible may offer some insights into. Our attempt is not to determine the falsehood or truthfulness of *tiim* and *baanaab* healing. Throughout this thesis our attempt is to try to gain insights into the Frafra self understanding and use of their mythic world to achieve wholeness through heir various types of healing rituals.

The phenomenon of human agency of divine spiritual powers

We shall turn to studies of the belief system of the mythic world of the people of the Bible. These studies may not only provide us with insights into the belief in humans as agents of spiritual powers and their ability to mediate or transfer such powers, but indeed show comparable models of contextualized Christian ministry of healing.

We shall begin with Mills' treatment of the belief in human agency of spiritual powers in Hellenistic Judaism and early Christianity. Mills relies on the "Sword of Moses" text, which is the basis for her view that in Hellenistic Judaism Moses is perceived as an agent of divine power.[21] the belief in Moses as an agent of divine power is the basis for Moses' ability to perform "miraculous signs and wonders the Lord sent him to do".[22] According to Mills "Moses did wonderful things by virtue of having a direct line to God; hat line was the possession of God's name".[23] The significance of the possession of God and the name, Mills suggests, is he belief that "to know someone's personal name was to have access to their very life-energy and to be able to effect that energy, for good or ill."[24]

In the Moses tradition, we do not only have an example of a human being becoming an agent of divine power, but also an inseparable relationship between the physical and the spiritual worlds.

Solomon is another biblical figure whose life shows that humans can be agents of spiritual powers as well as use those powers for good or ill. Solomon is anointed King (1K1:34). Solomon by this anointing becomes not only a political leader but also a divine agent. In Solomon, Mills suggest:

We have a picture of the king as the focal point of all that is happening in the interchange between God and his people. He is the main channel of divine blessing for the people of cursing for their enemies, and of success and prosperity in the land.[25]

Even his weaknesses do not nullify his role as divine agent for his people. Accounting to Josephus:

God granted him knowledge of the arts used against demons for the benefit and healing of men. He also composed incantations by which illnesses are relieved, and left behind forms of exorcisms with which demons are driven out.[26]

According to Mills, Josephus gives two different traditions of Solomon. The first tradition was that Solomon is a philosopher-sage. The second tradition is that Solomon "was a demon-controller and an exorcist".[27] the sources of the power to both traditions are the "active power of the Deity working in and through him".[28] The symbol of the divine power was in his ring. Mills relies on some writings of Josephus who also claims to have witnessed a demon casting event. Mills suggests that the seal of Solomon's ring:

features in most of the magical material concerning him. It forms the focal point of Solomon's power. It is by virtue of the power invested in the ring that Solomon can control demons. This means that the ring is seen as containing divine energy and presence. What makes for that presence seems to vary. The Aramaic bowls Solomon's ring is likened to that of the great seal of the universe, ring engraved with the ineffable name. In Josephus, Solomon's ring has power because it has a special root under the seal, which root can exorcise demons. In the Testament of Solomon the ring is described as engraved. Later Solomon's seal is shown to be pentangle: a magical sign, which symbolizes healthy influences and so guards against evil forces. Whatever form the ring is thought to have taken it always remains the channel of Solomon's power and the tool, which he therefore passed on to his descendants as a means of aiding them also against demonic influences.[29]

The belief in human beings as agents of spiritual powers that can mediate and transfer power is also operative in the synoptic traditions and early Christian tradition of healing.

Although the New Testament writers differ in their theological emphases which mainly reflects the pastoral needs of their audiences, they all agree that Jesus is both a historical person, born in a particular place and time, yet he has not only an inseparable relationship with God; the divine power declared at his baptism. And because he is or possesses this divine power, he can employ that power to heal a leper (Mk1: 41), cast out the demon (Mk 1:21f), speak words that effect the wishes intended (Mk 7:31f), control natural forces such as wind (Mk 4:7f), and raise the dead (Mk 5:22f).

Mills further suggests that the New Testament writers present Jesus as "an itinerant exorcist healer and teacher"[30], who initially finds acceptance from the crowds insofar as he provides liberation from the practical evils in their lives. According to Mills, in Mark's gospel, "…the human agent and cosmic setting mutually reinforce one another"[31].

Jesus as Initiator of faith

Nolan, a South African New Testament scholar offers contrary views to those of Mill's and Shorter's views stated earlier. According to Nolan Jesus was different from the exorcists, holy men, physicians, which doctors and sin diviners of his time.[32]

For Nolan, although Jesus used saliva (Mk7:33, 8:23) and made physical contacts with sick people (Mk 1:31, 41; 6:56; 8:22), Jesus "…never made use of any kind of ritual formulae, incantations or invocations of names."[33] He furthermore argues that when Jesus used "spontaneous prayer (Mk9:29), … his understanding of what was happening such cases differs widely from that of the holy men who prayed for rain of cures."[34] Unlike the holy men who depended on "… their own holiness their own esteem in the eyes of God; Jesus relied upon the power of faith. It is not prayer as such that effected the cure, it was faith."[35]

Nolan frequently uses the phrase 'your faith has healed you' (Mk 5:34, Mt. 9:28-29; Lk 17:19) as the main evidence for his argument. For Nolan the frequent use of this phrase by Jesus "...immediately lifts Jesus out of any of the contemporary categories of physician, exorcist, wonder-worker or holy man."[36] When Jesus said "Your faith has healed you" Nolan suggests Jesus

> ... is saying in effect that it is not he who has healed the sick man, it is not by means of some psychic power that he has or by some special relationship with God. Nor is it to be attributed to the effectiveness of some magical formula, nor even to he simple medical properties of saliva. He is not even saying, at least not explicitly, that the man was healed by God. 'Your faith has healed you'.[37]

the difference between Jesus and his contemporary healers was that for him "everything is possible for anyone who has faith." The man who has faith becomes like God-all-poweful".[38] Faith is what made possible the healings of Jesus. However, Holan cautions that this kind of faith:

> ... is not the same as psychosomatic influence of powerful suggestion which affects a cure by means of what is called 'overpowering therapy'. It is a conviction that something can and will happen because it is good and because it is true that goodness can and will triumph over evil.[39]

So this faith is based on the power of goodness. However, this conviction on the power of goodness does not work alone. It works on the belief that God is good to humans therefore God's goodness can and does "triumph over evil. The power of faith is the power of goodness and truth, which is the power of God. The success of his healing activity must be seen as the triumph of faith and hope over fatalism."[40]

Therefore "Jesus was the initiator of faith".[41] The faith Jesus initiates is also contagious. It sets forth the liberation process. In a sense it is that kind of faith that makes miracles happen. However, miracle in this context is not defined in terms of what humans call ordinary and extraordinary. It is based on God who has no such limits. This kind of faith operates in a mythic world in which "...the world is God's creation and whatever happens in the world, ordinary and extraordinary, is part of God's providence."[42]

Conclusion

Our view with respect to these two seemingly contrasting positions is not so much of whether or not Jesus was an exorcist healer like his contemporaries. Rather, our view is that at the symbolical level, the hearers and followers of Jesus could only understand and appropriate the faith he initiated from the perspectives of their mythic world.

Also at the functional level, they had to use their faith in symbols and belief systems based on their mythic world in order to apply the same to experience the power of God as goodness over all in the healing of Jesus. Even Nolan himself seems to be aware of this when he said "we must have some kind of ;position, some kind of vantage point or perspective, if we are to see and understand anything".[43]

These two seemingly contrary positions are reconcilable. The mythic world of the exorcist healer of Mills and Shorter, and Nolan's idea of "Jesus as initiator of faith" are very helpful insights in our project.

It is this kind of mythic world in which these two views operate that we see in the Bible and which we believe has been passed on to all Christians in all cultures. However, it seems some forms of Western Christianity have since moved away from or repressed this mythic world. Hence, to some Western Christians, such a mythic world is a stumbling block to healing, but to the Frafra Christians, it is a natural gate to faith in Christ.

It is this mythic world of the Frafra Christians that makes a major constructive contribution to the varied debate between theology and medicine in Frafraland and perhaps even in the West where the debates are complex and controversial. It must also be stated that *tiim* and *baanaab* healing does not render Western scientific medicine redundant. Rather, they add another perspective to holistic definitions of sickness, healing and health.

Scientific medicine does not need to fail before *tiim* and *baanaab* healing can be consulted. The *tiim* and *baanaab* healer and Western medical practitioners can collaborate to provide holistic healing based on their holistic understanding of healing as we have seen. *Tiim* and *baanaab* healing demonstrate other explanation of events in life beyond what humans see and know.

It is therefore the task of the church in Frafraland to devise a contextualized Frafra Christian ministry of healing that can mobilize the Frafra mythic world of *tiim* and *baanaab* healing. The African Independent Churches are partly pulling crowds in Africa because they are appealing to *tiim* and *baanaab* types of healing in the mythic worlds of most of these African Christians.

In conclusion we can say that although *tiim* and *baanaab* healing is difficult to investigate and analyze, they can offer insights which can revitalize the Churches' teaching on the power of the Holy Spirit in the lives of Frafra Christians.

Moses, Solomon, Jesus, *tiim* and *baanaab* powers heal by calling upon the name of the spirit whose power is the source of healing as well as invoking the faith of good that triumphs over evil. Jesus heals in the name of the God who was revealed to Him at His baptism by invoking a triumphant faith.

Therefore *tiim* and *baanaab* healing in Frafra mythic world provides them with a deeper understanding and appropriation of the Biblical healing stories as well as mobilizing the faith in the power of the spiritual powers to neutralize evil spiritual contagions.

It is not only through the name of Jesus that Christians are incorporated into the body of Christ. But the faith that accompanies knowing the name of Jesus strikes at the core of Christian identify and the source of power for Christian witness and mission. Therefore there are enough similarities in both Biblical Christianity on the theme of "knowing the Name of the spiritual power, indeed embodying that power" and *tiim* and *baanaab* healing ritual that can enrich a contextualized Frafra Christian ministry of healing for Frafra Christians when they fall sick.

References

1. E. E. Evans-Pritchard, *witchcraft Oracles and Magic Among the Azande* (Oxford: Claredon Press 1937)

2. V.L. Grottanelli, "Witchcraft: an allegory?" in Fracis X Grollig and Harold B. Haley (eds.) *Medical Anthropology (*The Hague: Mouton Publisher 1976, 321-329)

3. M. Fortes, *Religion, morality and the person* (Cambridge. 1987) p. 329

4. Jon Kirby, God *Shrines and Problem solving among the Anufo of Northern Ghana. (1986). P. 57*

5. ibid

6. ibid. p.61

7. J.S. Trimingham, *Islam in West Africa* (London, 1959), p. 235

8. I.M. Lewis (ed) *Islam in Tropical Africa* (London: Hutchinson University Press 1980), p.60

9. D. B. MacDonald and H. Masse, *Jinn Encyclopedia of Islam* (New ed. Vol.2), (Leiden 1965), p. 547 548.

10. Godfred Lienhardt, Divinity and Experience (Oxford: Clarendon Press, 1987).

11. Jon Kirby, (1986). P.64.

12. ibid, p.65.

13. R.S. Rattrary, *Religion and Art in Ashanti* (London, 1927), p.24.

14. Jon Kirby (1986), p.65

15. Stephen Funchs, "Magic Healing Techniques among the Balahis in Central India" in Ari Kiev (ed) *Magic, Faith and Healing* (The Free Press, 1964), p.121 138

16. Clifford Geertz, *The Interpretation of Culture* (New York, Basic Books Inc., 1975).

17. E. B. Tylor, *Primitive Cultures* (London: Murray)

18. J. Beattie, *Other cultures: aims methods and achievements in social anthropology* (New York: The Free Press, 1964). P. 206-239

19. Evans-Pritchard, *Theories of Primitive Religion* (London: Clarendon Press 1965).

He made important criticisms on the wrong use of psychological and sociological theories to analyze the so called Primitive religions with the intention to trace the origin of religion. (chapter 2 & 3 p. 20 99). His conclusion after a critical review of these theories is that "…for the most part the theories we have been discussing are, for the anthropologists at least as dead as mutton, and today are chiefly of interest as specimens of the thought of their time." (p.100). His reason which we agree with is that these theories assumed that the Westerners "…were at the other end, and that because primitive men were on a rather low technological level their thought and custom must in all respect be the antithesis of ours. We are rational primitive people pre-logical, living in a world of dreams and make-believe of mystery and awe; we are capitalists, the are communists; we are monogamous, they are promiscuous; we are monotheists, they are animists, pre-animists or what have you, and so on" (p.105). In spite of his positive arguments against the wrong labelling of the so called the primitive, he still makes a distinction between magic and religion. Indeed he uses such a distinction of an example in which these theories are wrongly applied. He says "…To try to understand magic as an idea in itself, what is the experience of it as it were, is a hopeless task". (p.111). For him hostile environmental factors must be taken into consideration in any attempt to understand both. He wrote "…from it are derived magic and religion, at first and undifferentiated, though later each goes its own way." (p.116). We can see clearly his distinction between magic and religion. He makes similar distinctions in *Witchcraft, Oracles and Magic among the Azande* (London 1937)), Beattie also offers important criticisms of the distinction between magic and religion in his book *Other Cultures* (London: 1966). Chapter 12 13 p. 202 240.

Another example is what he called "ancestor cult". Later we shall discuss in detail the notion of ancestor cult and raise our objections to it.

20. W.S. Mensah-Dapaa. "Observations in traditional Healing Methods" in Z. A. Ademuwageun et. al (eds) *African Therapeutic Systems* (Massachusetts 1979) 110- 113

21. Mary E. Mills, *Human Agents of Cosmic Power in Hellenistic Judaism to the Synoptic Tradition* (Sheffield: JSOT Press 1990), P. 37.

22. ibid.

23. ibid, p. 38

24. ibid, p.40

25. ibid, p.50

26. Josephus, *Jewish Antiquities* Books V-VIII, Leom, London 1934.

27. M. E. Mills (1990), p. 52.

28. ibid.

29. ibid, p. 144.

30. ibid, p. 99

31. ibid, p. 108

32. Albert Nolan, *Jesus before Christianity: The Gospel of Liberation* (London: Dalton, Longman & Todd Ltd. 1977), p. 30.

33. ibid.

34. ibid.

35. Ibid.

36. ibid, p. 31

37. ibid.

38. ibid.

39. ibid, p.32.

40. ibid.

41. ibid.

42. ibid.

43. ibid, p.4.

CHAPTER SIX

Yaabnam Kaaba

Introduction

In our previous summary conclusions, we said sickness is caused in two ways and affects the Frafra on two levels. The first cause is external which involves an invasion from without that affects a person. *Nya, tiim,* and *baanaab* healers are solely concerned with using spiritual powers, medical techniques and herbs to neutralize the internal invading spiritual powers and/or the contagion in the form of viruses, physical activity such as falling and being hit by pieces of wood. Therefore, for the lack of an appropriate term, we shall designate *nya, tiim* and *baanaab* healing ritual as personal healing.

This chapter is a report of how the Frafra account for why they are attacked by the spiritual powers in the first place and how they use their mythic world to interpret and prevent such attacks. In our research, we asked the Frafra to explain why they are attacked by spiritual powers, or invading spiritual contagions in the first place. The Frafra answer was that someone must have done something that made the ancestors to partially withdraw their protective powers from the community. As a result, evil spiritual powers invade them. In some cases, it is not that the person suffering did something wrong that caused the ancestors to partially withdraw their protective powers. Rather, the one suffering may be suffering on behalf of the entire (y*ir)* family. The actual offender is different from the one suffering and may be either dead or alive. This etiology of sickness is similar to the Hebraic notion of the sin of the fathers being visited upon the sons to the third and fourth generations. (Exodus 20:5). They have to address the particular offense; offender and the offended ancestor(s) in order to fully restore the protective powers of the ancestors to the entire community. *Yaabnam kaaba* is the healing ritual for restoring the spiritual protective powers to the community. Hence, we designate them as community healing rituals.

However, it must be stressed that in the Frafra mythic world *yaabnam kaaba* are inseparably related to any particular personal *nya, tiim* and *baanaab* healing ritual for particular afflictions at particular times on particular person(s). This inseparability of personal and community rituals will become obvious in the cases we shall cite later. In all types of community healing rituals, the members of the clan and their ancestors are involved. It is therefore helpful to describe and illustrate here the Frafra clan system.

The Frafra Clan System

The Frafra social, psychological, physiological, spiritual and cultural relationships are best described by Fortes as a web. An illustration is given below to explain the intertwined complex web of eccentric circles of the Frafra spiritual and social relationship. A marries B, AB give birth to C, C marries D, CD give birth to E, E marries EF also give birth to G, G marries H, and GH have a child I ad *infinitum.* AB are the *yaabnam* (plural) of C,E, G, and I. AB are also the ancestors addressed *yaabnam kaaba.* Portions of the sand from the graves of AB are put in a container. This container represents the founding ancestors of all descendants of AB and is called the *Dugun boar* (shrine within the room). All descendants also refer to themselves as members of a *yir*. The *yir* connotes the idea of household. In other words, the clan in a ritual context is referred to as yir.

In the case of *nya* healing, all descendants inherit whatever healing powers one or both founding ancestors had. In contrast to *nya* healing, the healers in *yaabnam kaaba* are not the most senior members of the clan who preside over the shrine of founding ancestors. It is the ancestors.

The term *dug* and its symbolic meaning during the *kaaba* has very important implications for our purposes. It refers to the children out of copulation in one room seems to provide the basis of the Frafra identity, unity and source of protection and healing.

The founding ancestors AB regulate the social, economic, political and religious lives of all members of the clan. A clanship or *yir* may be likened to an amoeba. It functions as a whole. One segment of the clan in any social interaction involves the whole clan. Consequently, the behaviour of the part has consequences for the whole and vice versa.[1] Therefore, *kaaba* to the founding *yaab* requires the presence of the preventatives of every unit such as descendants of CD, EF, GH. The same applies to issues of jurisprudence and all matters that relate to members of the clan. Fortes describe the Frafra clan system as "an embryo of future organization".[2] All the children of AB are always referred to as *biih* (children) and the clan as a whole is referred to as *yir* (house). Members of the a clan are children of the clan. In the Frafra understanding they embody each other as well as the *yir* and not individuals in the Western sense. The sense of corporate or collective personality in *yir* is an important concept to understanding *yaabnam kaaba* as community healing rituals.

The graveyard of AB in cases where they are buried together or the graveyards of A and B respectively becomes the sacred ground(s) of that clan. All objects in these spots are sacred and are designated as the symbolic presence of their ancestors. The phenomenon of trees as symbolic presence or "hierophant" of the sacred, is well articulated by Eliade[3] Fortes on his part refers to this spot as the "shrine, which symbolizes the identity and common ancestry of the entire maximal lineage".[4] The Frafra call this spot *diaboog* (one can literally translate it as headquarters). A word of explanation of what Fortes calls "maximal" and "minimal" lineages is in order. AB is the maximal lineage of all descendants. But CB is the minimal lineage of only their children and their descendants. In *yaabnam* healing a number of these ancestors are always involved in causing sickness and healing.

Cases of *yaabnam kaaba*

When sickness strikes, two things happen. The head of the household usually sends someone to call the appropriate healer. Sometimes the head of the house waits till the healer arrives. At other times he leaves immediately to the diviner. In all cases that we studies, after the Teb has finished treating the patient, the head of the household went to find out from the diviner which ancestor was offended and what ritual must be performed to remove the wrath of the ancestor(s).

Case A

A woman went to the bush to pick up sheanuts. She climbed a sheanut tree to shake off the sheanuts. Unfortunately, a branch broke under her weight. As she landed the branch hit her leg and fractured it. Her friends brought her home on their shoulders. They sent her to hospital. She was discharged and after three months she was up and about. During her stay in hospital, her husband consulted the diviner. The diviner told him that *yaabnam* who were responsible and why they allowed the incident to occur.

The diviner explained that when her husband was about to marry "*Lada to me, ba da kum te u*" (things were difficult and his father wept on his ancestors). The ancestors then made it possible for him to marry his wife opened her womb and she gave birth to children. They also protected the children until they were now grown up and employed. The ancestors felt their son had not been grateful for the responsibility they had taken to make him "somebody".

They withdrew their protection. He should offer the ancestors a sheep with dam (local beer) in order for them to restore their protection. The man and all the senior members of his clan set a day to offer the *kaaba.*

Another explanation will clarify the use of ancestors in the singular and plural. They believe that although one ancestor may be the cause of the sickness, all the ancestors are called upon as a group in the healing. The principle of corporate or collective identity in which one involves all and all involve one underlies *yaabnan kaaba.* In the evening of that day all the elders, the young people and the most senor women of the clan who are married elsewhere assembled. The *kpeem* (the most senior member of the clan) squatted on top of the *boar*, a symbol of the ancestors. It is a mud-raised platform of about two feet high and three feet in circumference in a circular form, shaped like a head and shoulders as if someone was sitting with arms folded.

They assembled in a small semicircle around the symbol of their founding ancestors. He knocked the top or the head with his right hand, picked up the mixture of water and sorghum and said:

Mba a (my father) all your children have assembled before you, calling you this evening. Call your fathers and mothers to come and assemble with you here this evening. Also call you children. For without you, we will not be here. It is because of you that there is good sleep in this house. We have assembled here with our grandchildren to give you water to drink and to offer you your sheep. For we admit that you are right to ask for water and a sheep. We *belem* (plead) with you to take these offerings and protect us from bad trees, stones, witches and wizards and any evil eye. Ensure that there is good health in this house. Let your children prosper in whatever they do. Let your *duam myerek* (your offspring) increase. Let food come. For we entrust ourselves into your *baanam, ne e biih* (your mothers and fathers and your children.

The text of this incantation is similar to other texts translated by Fortes.[5] After these incantations, he poured the mixture of water and flour on top of the head of the *Boar,* cut the throat of the sheep and allowed a few drops of blood on the head. Then all clapped and said *tari, tari*, (Amen, Amen).

The sheep was skinned and the meat shared. The liver was roasted and pasted on the head of the *Boar.* The meat was ritually shared. The most senior male of the clan got the head and one of the (*gber*) hind legs and the sheep. The next senior male member got hind legs of the sheep. Another senior male took the (*bok)*front leg, and the next took the last front let. The women of the clan collectively got the portion between the chests and legs which the Frafra call *sai*. The same work is used for waist and womb of the woman. It is important to note that when a woman is menstruating, the Frafra say *u luu sai* (her waist has fallen). The *aheh* (the children of all the women who have married elsewhere) took the neck.

Case B

B is a young man of twenty one. One day he went to the market with his friends. He came home after about two hours in the market. He complained of a headache. According to him, the headache became intense, coupled with vomiting. He was sweating profusely. Within a short time all members of the house were called home. His father got up and removes the heads of the *Boar* (mud constructed symbols of the ancestors). He told them that unless his son was healed, they would not receive *kaaba*from him. He quickly sent for a *tiim* healer.

The *tiim* healer arrived with a gourd of water from the *tiim dok (tiim* pot). He also had a tail and some pieces of charcoal. He immediately gave the tail to B to hold in his hands. He asked him to drink the water from the *tiim dok.* He ground the charcoal into power, mixed it with oil and smeared his forehead, arms and legs and also the walls of the room in which he slept. He sat for about thirty minutes and left to consult his *tiim*. He came back and reported that the spirit of the young man had been bewitched and hidden by a powerful spirit. So he asked for pieces of kola, a black cat and a chicken. He left, and returned the following morning at dawn with the news that the spirit of the young man had been released.

As far as we could see, the young man started feeling better slowly, and in about a week he was eating well, walking around though quite tired. The healer had told the young man's father that if his son recovered fully, he should offer his *tiim*, a dog, five chickens and some money. This was the beginning and end of that part of the healing. While the young man was sick, his father, in addition to calling the *tiim* healer, consulted a *bakalog*. The *bakalog* told him that many years ago, there was an epidemic in the village. The ancestors were called upon and they protected their *yir* and no one died from the epidemic. The ancestors were promised a cow then. But they have failed to fulfill their promise. So the ancestors withdrew their protection and that is why a spiritual power attacked a young man in order to remind them of his debt.

After B was well enough, the head of the clan announced a day on which the cow would be offered to the yaab. On the evening of that day all the heads of the clans and the seniors sisters and some of their children assembled at the (*daboog*) ancestral headquarters. There was a big tree in front of the house.

The belief among the family was that the tree grew out of the grave of the founding ancestor. So the tree was the symbolic presence of the "hierophany" of the spirit of their founding ancestors. They assembled in a semicircle. The head of the family rose up with the mixture of the sorghum flour, water and a fowl, He said:

My father, call your father, his father, assemble our *yaabnam*. All of the assemble on your tree. Have you heard? We, you r children, have assembled this evening. We had sleepless nights, we had no one to go to. So we called upon you and you told us that you would rescue your children, and that if there was health, we should give you a cow. It is true, you deserve a cow. Your children have built a house[i.e. married and have had children and they also have their own children]. Your *doam nyerek ya* [your offspring] have spread. Today your name is mentioned everywhere. You have truly overcome the evil powers. You have protected us from *Tiim* and *Kuga* [stones]. You have diffused any bad utterances or wishes against us. Your house is full of farmers. So we have called you to give you water, fowl and your cow. So receive your water.

He poured the mixture on a stone leaning against the tree and some parts of the tree. A text of another prayer collected by Fortes is similar to this text.[6]

Then he cut the throat of the fowl, allowed a few drops of blood on the stone and some parts of the tree, and let the fowl on the ground. It struggled and turned back down, legs up. While he was reciting the above prayer, all those assembled clapped their hands and said *tari, tari.* After that the young men put the cow down ad cut its throat. A few drops of blood were sprinkle on the same spots on the tee and stone. They retired till the livers of the fowl and cow were roasted and brought to the one who presided. Then they all assembled again. He again said:

You collect your liver. Let there be good yield on our farms. Let our young ones marry, let there be multiple births. Hide all evil targeted at any of us. Protect us during farming expeditions.

All those assembled kept clapping and saying *tari, tari.* The meat was shared accordingly as already described in the other text. Everybody left in high spirits to their various homes. Throughout our research all cases of *yaabnam kaaba* were almost in the same form and working as the two samples. The position of the fowl has an important significance in *kaaba.* After a few drops of blood on the symbols of the ancestors, the fowl left on the ground to struggle. If it lies upside down then it is a sign that the *kaaba* is accepted.

In all cases that we saw the fowl always turned upside down. We have not been able to find any other explanation. When we asked a veterinary technical officer he was not able to offer any explanation based on his knowledge of veterinary science.

Analysis

The findings from Appendix A suggest that in almost all sickness the Frafra use *yaaba kaaba* in addition to other types of healing. It is a healing in which the presider is not the healer. Apart from the fact that he is the oldest male of the *yir*, he also has no other special powers or relationship to the ancestors than any other member of the *yir.*

The role of women in *yaabnam kaaba* is not clear. They are involved but they cannot preside if even the oldest member of the clan is a woman. We shall later attempt to account for the role using insights from symbolic representation later.

Fortes' psychoanalytical theories and *yaabnam kaaba*

We will begin our critical analysis of the Frafra communal healing rituals worth Fortes social and psychoanalytical analyses of the Frafra religion, sociology and *kaaba.* Fortes have become a world renowned social anthropologist for his work among the Talleh, one of the three ethnic communities collectively called the Frafra. As already mentioned the three ethnic communities share much in common. So what he says about the Talleh is also applicable to the Nabnam and the Gorreh. We shall briefly review here Fortes' attempts to use psychoanalytical theories in gain insights into ancestors, *boar,* and *kaaba.*

The type of *yaabnam kaaba* described thus far is usually designated as ancestor worship. According to Fortes:

...There is general agreement that, whenever, it occurs ancestor worship is rooted in domestic, kinship and descent relations, and institutions. It is described by some as an extension of these relations to the supernatural sphere, by others as a reflection of these relations, yet again as their ritual and symbolic expression.[7]

In ancestor worship:
the congregation of worshippers invariably comprises either an exclusive common descent group, or such a group augmented by collateral cognates, who may be of restricted range, or else the worshippers in a give situation may comprise only a domestic group, be it an elementary family or family of an extended type.[8]

For Fortes, a strict definition of ancestor worship:
...presupposes geneonymy, that is the commemoration of ancestor by name. In the paradigmatic case...ancestors are worshipped by name and the names are perpetuated in lineage genealogies and personal pedigrees in an accepted generation sequence. Moreover, these genealogies are equally essential for the correct constitution of congregations of worshippers, for exact focusing of their ritual service, and for the organization of social relations in all domains of social structures.[9]

There are many features of *yaabnam kaaba* that are similar to some features of ancestor worship as stated above. Therefore, it can be inferred that *yaabnam kaaba* in all intent and purposes are forms of ancestor worship. But, like Fortes we have some difficulties calling *yaabnam kaaba* ancestor worship. Fortes impression is that the "...Ga give ritual reverence to their dead forbears but do not have ancestor cult in the precise sense in which..."[10] the term ancestor worship implies.

He goes on to make an important comparison. Fortes write:
...Catholics have a cult of saints...and says masses for named dead; Jews commemorate them by name in the course of the celebration of the New Year and their Day of Atonement, as well as on the anniversaries of particular deaths, yet we do not consider Catholics or Jews to ancestor worshippers.[11]

In many respects the saying of masses for named dead and commemoration of the dead by name may be similar to some forms of *yaabnam kaaba.* Yet, if Catholics and Jews are not to be ancestor worshippers, e cannot also equate *yaabnam kaaba* to acts of ancestor worship. We can further infer from the above comparisons that some of these Western categories such as ancestor worship or cults may be either ethnocentric or religiocentric. Therefore if we accept that *yaabnam kaaba* is an ancestor cult, we may be accepting the implied ethnocentrism and /or religio-centrism clearly pointed out by Fortes. For him, in any given culture there is what Field called "dogma personality".[12] Fortes defines "dogma personality" as,

> an accepted formulation, be it pragmatical, mystical, or naturalistic of physical and psychological constitution of man. It establishes the conceptual premises and the symbolic images of nature, causes, and consequences of death and of relations between the living and the dead. It serves as the warrant for the core and observances by means of which the experience of the individual's death is irrevocable is reconciled with acquiescence in the continuity of the living community.[13]

In the light of the concept of "dogma personality" we can infer that *yaabnam kaaba* "is a representation of the social capacities and potentialities with which a person is endowed in virtue of his social roles and relationshis."[14]

The concept of "dogma personality" has offered important insights into the social function of *yaabnam kaaba*. We shall continue to review the value of the ritual of *kaaba* to *boar* in the Frafra mythic world using Fortes' psychoanalytical concepts. according to him, *boar* "is a reflection of the premise that a person is a person primarily by virtue of his or her lineage membership."[15] This notion of collective identity or the notion of " I am because I belong" is an important belief worth exploring in order to understand healing rituals among the Frafra, the Akan, the Ga, and the Ewe of Ghana.[16] It also shows the interplay of ritual personality, and community in the Frafra mythic world in particular.

Fortes translate *belem orka* as prayer. The distinction between *kaaba*, and *belem* was already explained in Chapter One and we suggested *kaaba* is indeed the Frafra prayer with multiple levels of meaning. For Fortes, prayer to the Frafra serves as a "cathartic exercise".[17] Prayer is the process through which the Frafra take control of a situation by representing "themselves in the idioms of their customary beliefs and ideas."[18] Prayer as a public ritual act serves as a means by which the underlying cause of the crisis is exposed. By revealing the hidden cause, prayer for the Frafra becomes a kind of public confession in which the individual and the society make known the hidden causes.

Prayer as a public confession is a cathartic exercise in which the words have the desired effect of "enabling the crisis to be grasped and interpreted and finally mastered…" in two ways.[19] Firstly, the public confession makes it possible for public acknowledgment of fears and feelings of vulnerability and guilt for the offences caused to the ancestors. Secondly, the people praise their ancestors for the benefits they have received from them, as well as reclaiming their rights of protection in the future.[20] *Kaaba* as a public confession "is the primary medium for the catharsis because it puts into words what the act of sacrifice can but symbolize."[21] The symbolic communication in prayer enables the Frafra to express their feelings of dependency on their ancestors and the other mystical powers which are of central importance[22] in the Frafra mythic world.

There is no doubt that in Fortes' psychoanalytical conceptual categories, *kaaba* as cathartic exercise have important therapeutic values for the Frafra and also important implications for a contextual Frafra Christian ministry of healing. However, the psychoanalytical perspective of *yaabnam kaaba* offers only one perspective. We need a holistic approach so there is the need to go further and ask: What roles do the symbols of water, blood and *boar* play in the confession? We believe the rites of passage school represented by Gennep, and Turner may also offer us some insights from the perspective of symbolic interactionism and representation as we have already demonstrated in *nya, tiim* and *baanaab kaaba.*

The rites of passage school and *yaabnam kaaba*

We shall concentrate on the works of Gennep and Turner to determine the insights they may or may not offer on how the Frafra mythic world functions as an interpretative mechanism to achieve wholeness or well being in *yaabnam kaaba.*

In our attempt to use various theoretical concepts to determine if they can offer us any insights into the interpretative functions of the Frafra mythic world in *yaabnam kaaba* we cannot help but heed the warning of Dickson that theories

"...often contribute to sterility of thought when indiscriminately applied."[23] Therefore, all theories we shall use to provide us insights will be critically appropriated with care.

Van Gennep categorized most rituals as "rites of passage" which he "subdivided into rites of separation, transition rites and rites of incorporation."[24] Van Gennep further suggests that "the typical series of rites of passage (separation, transition and incorporation) furnished the pattern for ceremonies of sacrifice...".[25]

The question raised here is whether *yaabnam kaaba* can be categorized as rites of passage in the light of Van Gennep's theory of rites of passage. *Yaabnam kaaba* are forms of sacrifices. But it is not clear whether to treat them as rites of separation, transition or incorporation. If we apply Van Gennep's theory to *yaabnam kaaba* we have to determine which rites of passage they are? Furthermore, his theory seems to imply a linear notion of sickness and health. We believe that the Frafra do not perceive life to be on linear progressive stages. Instead, when they are sick, they believe they are in a state or condition of vulnerability to attacks.

Furthermore, even if there are stages of purification, estrangement or what he calls liminality in sickness, it is still not clear from an Gennep's theory what the Frafra are separated from and to what they are incorporated? Therefore it is difficult to classify *yaabnam kaaba* as either rituals of separation, transition or incorporation on the basis of linear concepts of human evolution as these terms may imply.

We shall consider next Turner's modification of Van Gennep's theory with respect to the Ndembu. Like the Ndembu, the Frafra during *yaabnam kaaba* use religious modes and frames of references through sets of symbols to define their estranged community of biih from the yaabnam. The symbols of both the Ndembu and Frafra have complex referential meanings[26] although the meanings to the Frafra and Ndembu may differ. In times of sickness, it can be said that they community of *biih* are in a liminal state. The texts of prayers suggest that they are very much aware of their status of *biih* of the clan. The sitting arrangements, and the way they share the meat also suggest their awareness of structure.

There is, however, one important difference and similarity between the liminality of *yaabnam kaaba* and the Ndembu ritual that Turner describes.

According to Turner, the liminal period in Ndembu ritual is not only one of the "acquisition of "gnosis" of theogony, cosmogony and mythical history of the initiates of the society but also a change that affects the initiates" ontological transformation."[27] On the contrary in the Frafra *kaaba* there are no initiates *yaabnam kaaba.* An important similarity between the two rituals is their therapeutic effects on the Ndembu and the Frafra.

The therapeutic effect of the healing rituals of the Ndembu and the Frafra is achieved through the ability of rituals to symbolize the feelings, mime the social drama that produced the conflict as well as resolve the conflicts. The symbolism and mimesis achieve health through what Turner calls a "three 'teli structure' process."[28] These are manifest sense, latent sense and hidden sense. The manifest sense refers to explicit aims of the ritual while the talent sense refers to the common sense awareness of what the people understand about what they are doing. The hidden sense meaning of the ritual is largely unconscious. It relates to perennial experiences shared by all members of the community.[29] All the above will seem to be applicable in *yaabnam kaaba.* The social, psychoanalytical, and symbolical concepts of Fortes and Turner have offered important insights which we believe will enrich a contextual Frafra Christian ministry of healing. So it is imperative that we explore a religious dimension in our analyses in our attempt to provide a holistic approach.

6.5 Traditional theories of sacrifice and *yaabnam kaaba*

we shall briefly review the traditional theories of sacrifice and determine whether or not they can provide us with any insights into *yaabnam kaaba* and vice versa. Evans-Pritchard divided scarifies into two different types. He called the first type confirmatory sacrifice. This type of sacrifice is "...concerned with the social relations...changes of social status and the interactions of social groups".[30] Confirmatory sacrifice in our view is similar to what is referred to as "life crisis rituals" by Turner.[31] These rituals deal with helping individuals and communities to make a smooth transition from one social status to another. These include puberty, and marriage rites to mention only two.

The second type is peculiar sacrifice. This type of sacrifice is, concerned rather with the moral and physical welfare of the individual and is performed in situations of danger from the intervention of spirits in human affairs often thought of as being brought about by some faults. In such sacrifices ideas of propitiation and expiation are prominent and their purpose is described by words which have the sense of bargain, exchange and purpose.[32]

Evans-Pritchard's peculiar sacrifices are also similar to Turner's rituals of affliction.[33] Based on Evans-Pritchard's distinction we can say that *yaabnam kaaba* are peculiar sacrifices and not confirmatory. But a critical examination of the cases we have cited show that one type of sacrifice runs into the other. In the cases we cited the reason for sickness was that the ancestors withdrew their protection because their sons did not offer sacrifices of gratitude to the ancestors for making it possible for them to marry. Marriage is no doubt one of the rites of passage. So it can be argued that *yaabnam kaaba* can be described as confirmatory. But the sacrifices cannot be confirmatory because their aim is not for the men to marry but to pay debts of gratitude.

The words of the ritual presider clearly show that the *kaaba* are more of a peculiar type. Moreover, the Frafra have different rituals for marriages quite different from *yaabnam kaaba.* So it is difficult to generalize that *yaabnam kaaba* are either confirmatory or peculiar. For the purpose and meanings to the participants are not always clear. If even they are to the participants, they are not always obvious to an observer. In some cases the profession and the motive of the observer even complicates the problem of determining the purposes and meanings of these community healings rituals. A case in point is the interpretations of sacrifices by social/human scientists, scientists of religion and Christian theologians.

Social/human scientists and theologians disagree on the intention of peculiar sacrifices. For example, Bourdillon suggests that the tension between social anthropologists and theologians is that social anthropologists are mainly concerned with relating what people say and believe to the patterns and social relationships in which they live.[34] Theologians on the other hand are interested in the "systematic search for meaning to symbols and their use."[35] Subsequently, we agree with Bourdillon when he says that although the:

> ...social dimension is usually significant in the explanations of why people use particular symbols and perform particular rites but it does not always help in the interpretation of what they understand and what they intend to achieve.[36]

These argument above also explain why our analysis of *yaabnam kaaba* is neither solely based on the social nor religious terms. For it seems in the interpretative functions of the Frafra mythic world, there is a dialectical relationship between the social and religious. So we need insights from social/human sciences as well as religious ones. The question to address is how do the Frafra achieve spiritual protective powers of their ancestors necessary for personal, family and the community's well being? In the cases we have cited, what is important is that the lives of the animals are symbols of life, therefore it can be inferred that the killing of the animals means the transferring of life to the clan members.

Yaabnam kaaba like other similar rituals may be described as "...a basic human language rooted in man's social nature and pervading his social environment."[37] According to Hubert and Mauss sacrifices such as *yaabnam kaaba* are both for the purpose of exiation and consecration. They are expiational because they re-establish "...the broken convenan".[38] They are also forms of consecration because consecration either acquires a character the victim did not have or "...ride himself of an unfavourable character with which he has been affected; he has raised himself to a state of grace or has emerged from a state of sin."[39] Since Christians can read their perspective on their word sin, its usage here needs careful analysis. On the surface the notion of consecration seems to suggest that the wholesale application of traditional Christian categories or meanings of these words can offer a helpful explanation of *yaabnam kaaba.* It is worth restating the difference between the Frafra notion of sin and the Western Christian interpretation already indicated earlier. From what we have seen so far, the failure to show gratitude invokes anger of the ancestors and the anger leads to withdrawal of protection. So we can use a Christian notion of grace here and simply that the descendants are restored to a state of grace.

However, the offense and the *kaaba* to address the offense do not change the ontology of the offender or community. It is not the removal of the fallen Adamic nature as in some traditional Christian teaching. An illustration will make this point clear. For example, if a pet or a child misbehaves, and the owner or parents refuse to play with the pet or called or accompany it/her/him for a walk, it does not change the ontology of the pet or child. It is the quality of the relationship strained by a particular act that must be addressed.

The notion of sin here means that an offense has caused a temporal poor quality relationship between the protector and the "protected". So even if grace is used here, it must mean improving the quality of the relationship and not the removal of the inherited Adamic sinful nature. The Frafra believe that an offense caused by a member of the family dead or alive can affect another living member. This belief is similar to the Biblical notion of the sins of the fathers being visited on the sons onto the fourth and fifth generations (Exo.20:5). The idea that sin is the cause of sickness can also create an impression that one can apply wholesale all Christian notions of sin to that of the Frafra *kaaba.* The point to note carefully here is that for the Frafra the descendant is not born with sin. Rather, she is born into a situation in which the relationship with the ancestors is affected. Hence she/he may not enjoy their full protection. Hence, in *kaaba* particular acts are addressed not universal human ontology as implied by some Western Christian notions of sin and the atonement of Christ. This is marked difference between Frafra religious anthropology and Western Christian anthropology. That is why it is dangerous to use wholesale a concept from one tradition to understand the other. Furthermore, the notion of destroying one life in order to restore or improve the quality of another life raises other unresolved controversies in religious notions of sacrifice, which must be addressed in both tradition.[40]

Traditional Judeo-Christian theories of sacrifice

The above warning does not in any way mean that insights from Judeo-Christian tradition may not offer helpful insights into other religions and vice versa. Rather, it suggests a critical appropriation of insights from one generation by another. This is the task in this section of the analysis of *yaabnam kaaba.*

Jewish sacrifices have become the bases of many Western Christian rituals today. Theories of atonement in Christianity, came out of Jewish sacrifices. A classical example is the works of Gustaf aulen.[41] Therefore, the use of Judeo-Christian theories of sacrifice in analyzing *yaabnam kaaba* may provide us with paradigms of Christian indigenization for the Frafra context.

Gift Offering

Gift offering is one of the theories in Jewish sacrifice. According to this theory, sacrifice is a means by which humans offer gifts to a god or God. The reasons for this gift include rewards or gratitude for favours.[42] In *yaabnam kaaba* we observed that those assembled are sober and remorseful in their mood. The texts clearly express their failure to express their gratitude for favour. Their mood and words are more confessional for failure than a sense of gratitude. In the texts that are cited, the presider at the healing ritual is primarily concerned with their vulnerability or the way they are exposed to dangers because they failed to offer the due reward. They seem to be primarily apologizing for failure to offer a reward to one kind or another.

Therefore we cannot designate *yaabnam kaaba* as a gift. Although there are some forms of *kaaba* for which the gift theory offers adequate explanation. For example, gift rituals in Frafra occur mostly after good harvests, successful business endeavours, safe deliveries of women, hunting and fishing expeditions.

Meal Theory

The second most common explanation of sacrifice is the meal theory.[43] the meal ritual was performed during what the Israelites referred to as a peace offering. It expressed the idea of having a communal meal or fellowship with the gods. The ritual was based on the covenant between the gods and the offerer. In the case of Israel sharing the same food with God was an act of making themselves holy by renewing the covenant (Ex. 24:11). The reasons for meal ritual are similar to those of *yaabnam kaaba.* The composition of those assembled, the portions of the meat of the shared, the pasting of the liver on the sacred sports, and the responses of *tari, tari* may suggest that *yaabnam kaaba* are rituals of renewing of ancestral ties by sharing a common meal.

This type of sacrifice was a kind of sacrifice originally meant to express the cordial relationship between God and those who worshipped that God. It was a happy occasion and excluded those who in one way or another were deemed unclean (Lev. & :11ff). the ritual also raised expectations of divine favours, kindness or blessings.[44]

The main feature of the peace offering was a communal meal. This communal meal signified a good relationship with God. It is both a religious and social feast (1 Sam. 9:13, 2 Sam. 6:19, 15:1-11, Neh. 8:10, Psalm 22166). The sharing of a meal was symbolically sharing life, and well being between God and believers. Furthermore, the sharing of life also established a covenant between God and the believers.[45] The eating as part of *yaabnam kaaba* is based on an already existing relationship.

However, *yaabnam kaaba* are intended to repair, restore a broken or weakened relationship between children and their ancestors. *Yaabnam kaaba* cannot be described as celebratory rituals.

Furthermore, in *yaabnam kaaba* the emphasis is more on how the meat is shared rather than the eating of the meat. It is only the liver that is put on the alter and eaten by some of the participants. But from what we could observe, it was not compulsory for all present to eat the liver, not even the presider. The

Frafra do not seem to have an explanation of why they put the liver on the altar. We suggest that the liver is a symbol of blood which may also be intended to express the blood ties that bind all of them together. In this case the sharing of a meal with the gods may be an important theme in *yaabnam kaaba*, but it is not the focus. Rather, the theological theme of renewal, of covenant blood ties through common ancestral ties offer theological insights into the explanation of *yaabnam kaaba* and offer important theological themes for a contextual Frafra Christian ministry of healing for Frafra Christians.

Burnt Offering

In burnt offering, the animal is burnt for the god(s) to whom it is offered. The ritual is performed in order to appease the ego. The animal is supposed to represent the life of the one offering the animal it emphases the theme of "...self-surrender...".[46] It could be offered by anyone and at any time. It was based on the covenant between God and Israel in which the people of Israel were expected to keep themselves holy before God (Deut. 6:5; Lev. 22-26; Exo. 29:37). Although the theme of dedication in burnt offering is also present in *yaabnam kaaba,* it is not the main emphasis. The animals in the cases cited are not burnt. The meat is shared among members of the clan and eaten. So burnt offering does not offer a comprehensive understanding of *yaabnam kaaba.*

Guilt and Sin Offerings

According to Gayford, the meaning and purpose of guilt offering are given in Lev. 5:14, 16:6, Num. 6:6-10. it was performed as a kind of compensation for sins or wrongs committed against God. It atone for the sin in its moral aspect.[47]

Sin offering is similar to guilt offering and in some cases the same as guilt offering. In sin offering the blood is poured inside the horn of the altar.[48] Sin in the eyes of the Semites was not only individualistic. All these offerings were required if one failed to give a worthy community witness. Any inappropriate behaviour rendered that person unclean. That person was considered as if he/she were sick. In order to mace the person healthy, clean, or holy, sin offering is performed. According to Robertson Smith, the sin offering consists of two phases.[49] In the first phase, the one contaminated was separated form the contaminating context. Sin offering was an act of cleansing or making holy. The idea implicit here was that the blood of the animal in sin offering was holy or clean. Hence anything it touched or represented became holy or clean. Hence the altars of the tabernacle were male holy or pure by the sin offering (Exo.29:35-37; Lev. 15:15-19).

The second phase was dedication. Once cleansed or purified by the sin offering, the person was considered dedicated or made holy for the gods or God. So cleansing and dedication are the reasons behind blood sacrifices (Ezek. 42:20; 22;26;Lev. 26:19; Exo. 29:36).[50]

In conclusion, the themes of cleansing, dedication, and confession from Semitic religion are important insights in *yaabnam kaaba*. We can also conclude that *yaabnam kaaba* serve the similar theological purposes that sin offering rituals serve. However, one cannot understand or even assume the theological reality being communicated in oral forms of communication, unless one looks at the entire performance. Therefore, we want to avoid an approach through which *yaabnam kaaba* are analyzed in terms of only one theological theme or social theory at the expense of other themes and theories. We have to avoid such an approach in order not to lose the holistic nature of healing invoked in *kaaba*.

Symbolic Representation in *yaabnam kaaba*

We shall turn to the symbolic representation in play therapy which, we believe, offers a holistic approach as is evident in previous analyses. The symbolic representation evokes all the symbols and the entire mythic world that interprets them in such ways that the various themes or motifs thus far evidenced by the theoretical concepts from sociology, culture, psychoanalyses, and religion. Like *nya, tiim* and *baanaab* healing, *yaabnam* healing is effective because it is a symbolic representation. *Yaabnam* healing rituals is symbolic representation are similar to forms of transitional phenomena in play therapy.

In both *yaabnam* healing and play therapy the faith of the child and the ritual participants provide another realm of reality in which the subjective and objective, the social and religious, the secular and the sacred worlds meet. The content of the faith of participants consists of symbols and meanings are in their mythic worlds. In the case of the Frafra mythic world, their faith in *yaabnam kaaba* is one in which the physical and spiritual worlds are co-terminous and dynamically influence each other. The content of the mythic world consists of belief in a constant dialectic interaction between humans and their ancestors, humans and spiritual powers for good and/or evil by knowing their name. The actors and actions in *yaabnam* healing are associated with events that are invested with meanings. As already indicated, the bodies of those gathered around the boar are symbolic and represent the intertwined complex eccentric circles of social and spiritual "web" of the Frafra mythic world.

Yaabnam kaaba as a ritual system creates a subjunctive world. The notion of subjunctive world here is similar to the idea of altered states of consciousness. The kind of altered states of consciousness here is best defined by Goodman.[51] According to Goodman "…religious experience can take place only if there are radical changes in the way they body functions, initiating the alterations in consciousness, in the perceptual state."[52] It is a consciousness in which participants invoke their mythic world. This altered state or subjunctive world in the ritual interpretation is made possible by the principle of metacommunication or shared experience which was already discussed in previous chapters.

The *boar* (shrine) is the symbolic representation of their founding parents. All members of the clan present are the transitional objects or symbolic representatives of the sons and daughters of the founding parents, some of whom are now themselves ancestors. The holistic nature or the interconnectedness of the healing ritual is understood best if we refer to the clan system described earlier. The Frafra refer to the common bond of all those within one clan as *duam* (offspring) or *biih* (children). So in *yaabnam kaaba,* the *duam* assembles, because they want new *duam* that is removal from contamination as in sin offering.

The *boar* serves as an icon of the wombs of the founding parents. Another term used to refer to this gathering is *dug duam* (born within the same room). *Dug* means a room that is the same word which the Frafra use for copulation of couples. Therefore, all *duam* of the *yir* have assembled before the room of copulation of the founding parents. The room is symbolic representation of the ritual rebirth. In a sense we call it a womb which is the basis of the physiological, psychological, spiritual, social and cultural interconnectedness.

This rebirth or renewal is experienced throughout the ritual acts of confession, or cleansing as are evident in the texts we have cited earlier. At the end there is also a dedication or commitment of the spiritual, physiological, psychological, social and cultural common ancestral ties: the ethical basis of "they belong therefore they are".

The Frafra symbols of *boar*

The various symbols are interrelated. They are attempts of the Frafra to make meaning out of their world as well as deal with the various undesirable circumstances such as sickness. *Boar* is one of the symbols around which their unity is expressed.

The *boar* is confined to a particiular spot which gives a sense of enclosure in a geo-political boundary. This particular spot, perhaps a graveyard becomes the sacred ground to that clan. This is the location of the external *boar* defined by Fortes as the shrine which symbolizes the identity and common ancestry of the entire maximal lineage."[53] Yet is spiritual, social, psychological, physiological, religious and cultural influence on the Frafra are both personal and communal as well as particular and universal. In other words, the ritual efficacy of *kaaba* pervades all Frafra experiences of life at all times and in all places.

Frafra notion of personality and society

This intricate complex multiple dynamic representation in *yaabnam kaaba* suggest some clues of the Frafra notion of personhood and society. the *boar* is an icon of Frafra society and suggests that society is not given. It is rather a historically constructed reality that encounters, interacts, mediates and manifests a specific tradition which shapes and identity. This society shapes that tradition as well as being shaped by it. the clan came into being through one person; the agnatic-founding ancestor. The analogy of Christ as head of the Church, and the rest of the members of the Christian Church as body is helpful in understanding the relationship between the Frafra notion of personhood, society, and the clan which each person embodies.

The Frafra notion of personality is symbolically expressed and reaffirmed in a ritual sharing of the meat. The head of the sacrificed animal goes to the most senior *kpeem* (elder) because he symbolizes the founding ancestor. The children of the women members get the neck which connects the head and the rest of the body. Hence they are called connectors. The children (*aheb*) are connectors of their paternal, maternal clans, and other clans.

The entire ritual and all the participants are symbolic icons of the ancestors, the cosmos and the society. This web of inner-personal and intra-personal relationships further suggests that the healing rituals are iconic representations of the clan system.[54]

The entire ritual and all the participants are symbolic icons of the ancestors, the cosmos and the society. This web of inter-personal and intra-personal relationships further suggests that the healing rituals are iconic representations of the clan system.[54]

The rules that govern the family is mediating and negotiating in the family life are internalized and are the same rules that the family uses at the macroscopic lineage or societal level based on genealogical connections (*duam*). "Social relations always have a genealogical coefficient".[57] Therefore, for the Frafra personality consists of the biological, sociological, psychological, spiritual and cultural entity. One aspect involves all, and all aspects are present in one aspect.

Meanings of other symbols in healing rituals

The climatic conditions, vegetation and general geography of Frafraland lends itself to the significance of rocks, caves and groves of trees in their healing rituals. Rocks, caves, groves of trees in Frafra society serve as nourishment for their bodies by providing food, water and shelter in a rough land. They also provide the Frafra protection from attacks by neighbours. We have already seen how trees, water and rocks are important aspects of Frafra mythic world. We have also seen the important roles they play in both Frafra etiology of sickness and healing rituals in previous chapters.

In discussing the relationship between humans and stones, Eliade offers some views that support our argument. For Eliade, humans have used stones as instruments of spiritual actions, as centres of energy designed to defend them or their dead.[58] Eliade makes another suggestion on the use of trees that also sheds light on the relation between the *boar* and the corporate family of the Frafra. According to Eliade, a vegetation cult may have emerged out of the use of trees. They serve as "images of the cosmos as repository of souls of man's ancestors symbols of resurrection of rebirth."[59]

The *boar* is a symbol of the great mother. The physical makeup of the *boar* supports this identification. The *boar* is a container filled with sand from the graveyard of the female founding ancestor, a couple of memorabilia which vary from clan to clan, but invariably denote the unique identity of the clan. The container is like a big funnel; it is the upper half of a clay pot.

It must also be noted that clay pots are important symbols of womanhood in the Frafra mythic world. The shrine is called *bupoam boar* which means *boar* through the uterine line. Therefore, they gather before the great womb that gave birth to them for another symbolical ritual rebirth. Therefore, the *boar* is an icon of Frafra personality, society, and spirituality. It symbolically represents their mythic world as well as portrays a unitary concept of person as consisting of the social, psychological, physical biological and spiritual. Therefore *yaabnam kaaba* help them to deal with the whole person and not only the bio-chemical or psychological as in Western medicine and psychotherapy. The also enable them to dynamically adjust themselves to new historical and social process.

The symbolic representation in *kaaba* is a process by means of which they use their mythic world to create life, nurture and renew life as well as shape Frafra identity. This process of nurture, renewal, and the emerging Frafra identity also shapes the Frafra mythic world. In short, *yaabnam kaaba* tell and make the Frafra story. They create and regulate society as well as being regulated and shaped by society.

The narrations of these rituals begin with who they are, and why they have assembled. The stories of their identities are retold. In order to understand the deeper meanings of the mythic world invoked by retelling their story, it is also important to note the Frafra myth of creation. According to the Frafra tradition, their founding ancestors sprang from the ground. It is a simple myth, but it has a direct bearing on understanding the image of womb and the theme of rebirth in these healing ritual systems. The myth is the source as well as the container of personal and collective archives contained in their mythic world. Myth provides the logic of the symbols in which there is "an ordering of symbolic experience in such a manner that it refers to the primordial immediate experience of the sacred and simultaneously expresses an intentionality toward action."[60]

The words such as *biih* (children) *duam* (offspring) are metaphors of themselves and very strongly suggests that *yaabnam kaaba* is experienced by the Frafra as a rebirth or spiritual metamorphosis in which the old contaminated body, person, and society are absorbed by the great womb and are ritually born anew with full protection. Here again, the themes of confession, cleansing, renewal and dedication pervade all aspects of the ritual through the symbols of earth, shrine, children, blood, water and incantations. We can conclude therefore with the words of Zuesse that the Frafra healing rituals as symbolic representation are

> ...spiritually more profound than any theology, it accomplishes more for those who participate in it than any number of rarified mystical treatises for faded anti-ritualistic modern connoisseurs of the occult. It deals with very specific realities that are not transportable into our living rooms for our casual inspection.[61]

The interpretative functions of the Frafra mythic world enables them to experience a unity of faith, praxis and reflection in *yaabnam kaaba.* The interpretative functions of the Frafra mythic world also enables the Frafra beliefs systems and *kaaba* to "...confront and mutually confirm one another; the ethos is made intellectually reasonable by being shown to represent a way of life implied by the actual state of affairs which the world view describes."[62]

The interpretative functions of their mythic world furthermore, reinforce their social values as well as provide the basis for the symbols of their mythic world "to formulate a world in which these values, as well as the forces opposing their realization ..."[63] Through metacommunication, the *kpeem* (ritual performer) creates a subjunctive world in which there is interpenetration of powers. In this inter-penetration, boundaries between physical and spiritual, sacred, and profane, sickness and health are broken. There is unconditional acceptance of *duam* as if *duam* has become a new creation of the biological, social, cultural, psychological and spiritual life by the founding of parents symbolized by *boar.*

In the subjunctive world, there is also inter-penetration of time. The boundaries between the past, present and future are broken. History is not linear but cyclical. The Frafra story is one of creation, chaos and recreation. The emerge from the subjunctive world with a strong sense of protection, dependence, interdependence and solidarity among themselves, between them and the ancestors and the entire creation.

The ethics of *duam* is to act justly towards all. They must walk in the ways of their ancestors to ensure their protective power which will prevent them from attacks. They must act justly to each other because an offense against a member of the clan is an offense against other members of the clan as well as the ancestors. They must also act justly towards the cosmos, trees, stones, rivers, and animals not only because their lives partially depend on them but more importantly because these trees and stones are symbolic presence of ancestral witnesses of how just or unjust they act.

In *yaabnam kaaba,* the whole community is called upon to deal with its wounds, brokenness, estrangements, negligence. Through *kaaba* there is reflection, restitution, confession, rebirth or renewal and solidarity. Through *kaaba* the proper boundaries are re-established and rights reasserted. Therefore, *kaaba* are symbolic representations in which the Frafra mythic world functions as interpretative mechanisms in order to interpret sickness to achieve well-being.

These insights raise important implications for a contextualized Frafra Christian ministry of healing. Such a contextualized Christian ministry of healing can utilize indigenous concepts as priest-healer, socio-psychoanalytical and religious insights of confession, cleansing, renewal, dedication, and Jesus as initiation of faith. *Kaaba* as a holistic healing models provide the Frafra Christian pastoral theologian a basis for an advocacy of better and holistic health care services in Frafraland. *Kaaba* can also provide important ecological insights for Frafra pastoral advocacy against the important of environmentally damaging industries and lifestyles to Frafraland.

References

1 Meyer Fortes, Dynamics of Clanship among the Tallensis (1945), p.30.

2 *Ibid.*

3. Mircea Eliade, Patterns in Comparative Religion (1988).

4. Meyer Fortes, (1945), p.42. Also see Geoffrey Lienhardt nDivinity and Experience : the Religion of the Dinka (Oxford : Clarendon Press 1961).

5. Meyer Fortes, Religion, morality and the person. Essays on Tallensireligion edited and with introduction by Jack Goody (Cambridge University Press 1987), p.27, 29, 30, 32-34.

6. *Ibid.*

8. *Ibid.*, p. 66.

8. *Ibid.*

9 *Ibid.* p. 67-69.

10. *Ibid.* p. 69.

112. *Ibid.*

12 Field, Religion and medicine of the Ga People (1937), p.93ff.

13. Fortes, Religion, morality and the Person (1987), p.69.

14. Ibid. p. 70.

15 Meyer Fortes, "Coping with destiny among the Tallensis" in R.H. Cook (ed) Fantasy and Symbol : Studies in Anthropological Interpretation, (London)\: Academic Press 1979), p.76.

16. J.B. Danquah, The Akan Doctrine of God : a fragment of Gold Coast ethics and Religion (London : Lutterworth Press 1944).

G.K. Nukunya, Kinship and Marriage among Anglo Ewe (New York :Humanities Press 1969).

Margaret J. Field, Religion and Medicine of the Ga People (London : Oxford University Press 1937)

17 M. Fortes, Religion, Morality and the Persons (1987), p.27.

18 *ibid.* p.28

19 *ibid.*

20 *ibid.*

21 *ibid.*

22 *ibid*

23 K.A. Dickson, "The meaning of Sacrifice" in The Ghana Bulletin of Theology vol. 2 Mo. 3 (December 1962). P.12.

24 Arnold Van Gennep, The rites of Passage (Chicago : The University of Chicago press 1960), p.10-11

25 *ibid.* p. 184.

26 Victor Turner, (1962), p.96.

27 Victor Turner, Forest of symbols (1967), p.89-99.

28. *ibid.* p. 15?

29. Turner, Drums of Afflictions (1968), p.49.

30. E. E. Evans-Pritchard, "The Meaning of Sacrifice among the Nuer" in Journal of the Royal Anthropological Society, vol. 84, (1954), p.21.

31 Victor Turner, Forest of Symbols (1967).

32 E. E. Evans-Pritchard, (1954), p.21.

33 Victor Turner, The Forest of Symbols (1967).

34 M. F. C. Bourdillon, "Introduction" in M. F. C. Bourdillon and M. Fortes (ed), Sacrifice (New York : Academic Press 1980), p.2.

35 *ibid.*

36 *ibid.* p.3.

37 Aidan Kavanagh, "Introduction" in James D. Shaughessy (ed) The Roots of Ritual (Grand Rapids, Michigan : Eerdmans 1973), p.7

38 Henri Hubert and Mariel Mauss (ed), Sacrifice : Its Nature and FunctionTranslated by W. D. Halls (Chicago : The University of Chicago Press, 1967), p.3.

39 *ibid.* p.9-10.

40 Rene Girard, Violence and the Sacred (Baltimore : John Hopkins University Press, 1977)

41 Gustaf Aulen, Christus Victor : An Historical Study of the Three Main Types of the idea of Atonement, translated by A. G. Herbert (New York : MacMillan Publishers 1975).

42 S. C. Gayford, Sacrifice and Priesthood (London : Methuen & Co Ltd., 1924), p.30-36. Also W. Robertson Smith, Religion of the Semites (Lecture VIII 3rd 1894). Also E. B. Taylor, Primitive Culture ed., (1891) and Herbert Spencer, Principles of Sociology No. 139 (1893).

43 S. C. Gayford, Sacrifice and Priesthood (1924), p.38.

44 ibid. p.35-36

45 ibid. p.39-40

46 ibid.

47. ibid. p.43
48. ibid. p.45

49. Robertson Smith, Religion of the Semites (1927), p.477.

50. ibid.

51. Felicitas D. Goodman, Ecstasy, Ritual and Alternate Reality : Religion in a Pluralist World (Bloomington : Indiana University 1988).

52 ibid. p.4

53 Meyer Fortes, The Dynamics of Clanship (1945), p.42.

54 Meyer Fortes, The web of kinship (1949), p.20.

55 ibid. p.12.

56 ibid.

57 ibid., p.13.

58 Eliade, Patterns in Comparative Religion translated by Rosemary Sheed (New York, 1958), p.216.

59 ibid. p.267.

60 ibid.

61 Evans M. Zuesse, Ritual Cosmos : the Sanctification of Life in African Religions (Athens, Ohio : Ohio University Press, 1982), p.238.

62 Clifford Geertz, The Interpretation of Cultures (New York : Basic Books Inc. 1973), p.127.

63 ibid.

CHAPTER SEVEN

Towards a Contextual Frafra Christian Ministry of *Kaaba*

Introduction

In this chapter we shall attempt to offer a model of contextualized Frafra Christian Ministry of healing with the help of the theological reflection method which is simultaneously contextualized, critical, and pastoral as outlined in Chapter One.

The purpose of this chapter is to suggest ways through which Christianity may become a native in Frafraland. Christianity can become a native if the Church draws upon some aspects of the Frafra rituals of *kaaba* to construct a Frafra Christian ministry of healing. We believe that our theological reflection method which is contextualized, critical, and pastoral is consistent with the principles of contextualization in the Bible itself. The evidence for such a belief will become clearer in the chapter. It must, however, be stressed that the purpose of this critical reflection is not to write a pastoral clinical manual on how to conduct a contextualized Frafra Christian ministry of healing. Instead, we are primarily concerned with proposing a Frafra Christian mythic world or a Frafra Christian anthropology and ecclessiology utilising the insights from the interpretative functions of the Frafra mythic world symbolically represented in *Kaaba.*

A contextualized Frafra Christian mythic would will be a prerequisite to the ability of a pastoral theologian to invoke the 'make believe' or subjunctive Christian Frafra mythic world to play the role of its interpretative mechanism in times of crises as its traditional counterpart. We agree with Song that it is not enough for missionary Churches to be repentant that they have, all these years after the white missionaries, not responded fully to the spiritual needs of their followers,[1] especially in the area of healing. Rather:

> ...there should be the will and courage to break away from the bondage to the missionary ecclessiology developed in the West and transplanted to the East [and in Africa]. They have shaped these Christian communities, moulded them and forced them to grow into 'white' churches in 'Black' Africa or 'Yellow' Asia.[2]

Some African theologians over the years have demonstrated the will and courage to free African Christians from inherited Western missionary Christianity. The various efforts by African theologians are best summarised by Fashole-Luke thus:

... the quest for African Christian theologies which has been vigorously pursued in the last decade, amounts to attempting to make clear the fact that conversion to Christianity must be coupled with cultural continuity. Furthermore, if Christianity is to change its status from that of resident alien to that of citizen, then it must become incarnate in the life and thought of Africa and its theologies must bear the distinctive shape of mature African thinking and reflection. What African theologians have been endeavouring to do is to draw together the various desperate sources which make the total religious experience of Christians in Africa into a coherent and meaningful pattern.[3]

In the genesis of the project, and in the brief history of Christian mission in Datuku, we raised some fundamental questions on the differences between the Frafra notion of sin and well-being in *kaaba*, and the missionaries' notion of sin and salvation. We asked whether it is possible to bridge the "epistemological distance" between the Frafra mythic world and its interpretative functions and the Christian gospel.

The pieces of evidence from the literature review, insights from *kaaba*, and the paradoxical role of culture in inherited Western models of theological education have clearly shown that the gap can be bridged. Hence, we shall use the insights accumulated thus far to engage in a contextual Frafra Christian pastoral theological hermeneutic of *kaaba*. The construction of a Frafra Christian anthropology and ecclessiology is a prerequisite to a contextualized Frafra Christian ministry of healing in view of our findings that the Frafra healing rituals do not operate in a vacuum. They operate within their mythic world.

Insights from *kaaba*

We shall recapitulate the insights from *kaaba* in our investigations which we shall use to construct a Frafra Christian ministry of healing.

There are some fundamental symbols in the Frafra mythic world which form the basis of their self-perception of themselves and their world, or what we call the totality of life. The power and therapeutic value of these rituals reside in their ability to invoke the entire Frafra mythic world and mobilise the symbols therein in order to engage in an interpretative mechanism for purposes of achieving well-being in all aspects of their life. These symbols include *yir,* blood, *boar*, *yaabnam,* and people.

The Frafra self perception of themselves is that they are the extensions of the ancestors as well as embodying these ancestors who are the founders and guardians of *yir*. Therefore there is an inseparable role of the *yir* and *kaaba* in their mythic world.

Our investigations have also shown that *kaaba* maintain and express the physiological, psychological, social, spiritual and cultural unity among the Frafra. The Frafra notions of sickness, healing rituals and health are based on their belief in their common ties in the *yir*. The *yir* is the source of life, strength, identity, protection, healing and hope. It is also the source of sin and sickness. The *yir* consists of humans, plants and rivers, indeed the entire cosmos.

Towards a construction of a Frafra Christian anthropology and ecclessiology

As already indicated, our primary task is to construct a Frafra Christian anthropology and ecclessiology that includes some aspects of Frafra mythic world in order to mobilise the symbols from the mythic world in the Christian liturgies of healing. So we shall begin with a Frafra Christian reading of the Genesis myths of creation.

Comparison of the Frafra and Genesis creation myths

The Frafra anthropology, *yir*, and *kaaba* and the traditional Judaeo-Christian anthropology, ecclessiology, and ministry are based on their myths of creation and primary redemptive acts respectively. In the case of the Frafra their primary redemptive act is *kaaba*, while for Judaeo-Christianity it is the Christ-event.

Therefore it is imperative that any attempt to construct a Frafra Christian anthropology and ecclessiology begins with a contextual critical pastoral theological reflection between the two myths of creation and primary redemptive acts from both traditions.

There is an important incentive to our chosen method that begins with Judaeo-Christian myth of creation and the redemptive act of the Christ-event. The incentive is that the creation myth in the Hebrew Bible and the Christ-event in the New Testament respectively are themselves "paradigms of" and "paradigms for" indigenization. Hence they are incentives to this project.

By definition "paradigms of" means the process through which the faith was indigenized. "Paradigms for" means that in the process of indigenization consciously and unconsciously is produced. In other words a method of indigenization has come out of the process.

For purposes of easier comparison and clarity of issues in the comparison, we shall begin a comparison between the two creation myths in order to determine their implications for a Frafra Christian anthropology and ecclessiology. According to Westermann:

> It is a fact that the creation belief long ago faded into the background of the Church's preaching and theology. The creation narratives of the Bible were accepted for a long time without question as accounts of an actual event. These stories, together with the first sentence of the creed, 'Creator of heaven and earth', formed the reliable, unshakable foundations which supported all thought and talk about the beginning of the world and of man.[6]

The above quote clearly offers an inspiration and the imperative to a Christian pastoral theologian who seeks to appropriately incorporate both the Frafra and the Judaeo-Christian myths of creation into Frafra Christian anthropology and ecclessiology.

James, a renowned scholar in the Hebrew Bible, makes some important observations on the Judaeo-Christian myth of creation:

Though no serious attempt was made at first to formulate a Christian cosmology along the lines of current Gnosticism and the Graeco-Roman world, the doctrine of creation in the early Church was inherited from Judaism largely under the influence of St. Paul.[7]

He further states that:
In the Hebrew background lay the Canaanite cosmogonic tradition, and so far as is discernible from the fragmentary ugartic texts their god El, probably the counterpart of the Mesopotamian Ela and prototype of Yahweh, seems to have

been regarded as the creator of the world and mankind.[8]
Stadelmann's view is similar to James when he says one can "... discover traces either of borrowings or of parallels to the cosmogonic traditions of the Ancient Near East".[9] According to Heidel, the Genesis story of creation consists of two sources:

> Genesis 1:1-2:4a Priestly sources which can be dated back to post exilic period and 2:4b-25 Yahwistic source that dates back to the 9th century BC. In Heidel's view the Yahwistic tradition was not interested in tracing the origin of the world. It was instead a description of creation.[10]

He also observes that the:
etymological derivation of the terms [paradise, river, ground flow] suggests Mesopotamian background for the Yahwistic account. Furthermore, the topographical features of the Yahwistic creation narrative portray the Mesopotamian valley dependent upon rain and artificial irrigation.[11]

The Priestly sources "... paint a vivid picture of the way in which an ancient Hebrew imagined the primeval state and what he thought might have been the first acts in the process of divine creation".[12]

Heidel further suggests:
... narratives of the creation are the product of that peculiar Hebrew interest in the past which finds expression in the attempt to contemplate history in a typological way. As in 'the days of old' Yahweh succeeded in subduing the primordial deep and proceeded to create the world, so he will perform once more his wonderful deeds in a specific historical setting on behalf of Israel and in punishment of foreign oppressors.[13]

The intention of this typological interpretation is to show that the "... current cosmogonic tradition should be shaped to form a consequential narrative of redemptive activity in accordance with the monotheistic outlook that have been established as the faith of Israel".[14]
The creation narratives, he suggests:

... testify to a profound conviction that nature is created by God and, as such, is visible evidence of his reality and his omnipotence, and of his participation in the affairs of the world. Their attitude towards it is revealed in the routine of daily life as much as in moments of crisis.[15]

He concludes:

... Therefore, the Yahwistic conceptions of creation was a syncretic inheritance from a variety of sources in middle Eastern cosmology before in post-exilic Judaism. It came under Iranian and Hellenistic influences, with its own unique conception of ethical monotheism and its doctrine of creation.[16]

it is not our intention to agree or disagree with these authors on whether or not God has created out of nothing or that the creation myth was taken from Babylonian myths of creation. Our position is simply to infer from the above pieces of evidence from various scholars that the creation narratives in the Hebrew Bible were attempts at indigenization of Judaism. In our view these observations can be regarded as "paradigms of" and "paradigms for" indigenization. We now offer a summary of a Frafra Christian reading of the Genesis myth of creation.

The Frafra Christian now read one source of creation that God used some already existing material and gave it a different form of existence in relation to God than before. (Psalm 74:13-17). For example God took sand, modelled it into a form he wanted and gave breath or life. In other words God imparted God-self to the sand in order that it became human. (Genesis 2:4b-8; 15-22).

In another source God spoke out words and these words had the efficacy of producing their intentions: separating water from land, giving form to earth, and giving plants and rivers existence in relation to God. (Genesis 1:1-2:4a; 6-23; Job 37:11b-12; 38:8-11; Isaiah 40:28; 43:1; 45:1; Proverbs 8:22-31).

From the perspective of the Frafra mythic world, the Hebraic myths of creation narratives reinforce their belief that the earth (teng), the trees, stones, sand, rivers embody some aspects of the spirit of God. (Proverbs 8:22-31). Psalm CAPut!':1 reads: "The heavens declare the glory of God. The skies proclaim the work of his hands." The creation and all therein are agents of God's spirit and can mediate the power of God's spirit. To the Frafra, therefore, the whole of creation is symbolic representation of God. The physical, psychological, social, environmental, and cultural relationships are connected by spiritual unity by virtue of the very act of creation by God.

There is, therefore, an inseparability in the relationship among humans and between humans and the rest of creation. The Frafra myth of creation in which their first ancestors sprang from the ground, is affirmation of this unity between the Creator and the created. (Isaiah 40:28; 43:1).

The call of the prophets, and the appointment of kings and judges in the history of Israel according to the Frafra reading of them can be surmised as moments of becoming agents of divine power, in order to mediate this power or induce a situation in which there can be acts of justice.

When they also construct the *boar* of the *yir* they perceive the sand and trees from the grave of the ancestors as symbolic representation of the spirit of their ancestors. The herbs, or the trees from the graves of their ancestors are physical, medical, and spiritual by virtue of the very act of creation by God.

The Frafra myth of creation, the basis of the Frafra anthropology, *yir,* and *kaaba* can fulfil similar theological functions as the Jewish myth of creation and the Christ-event. Both myths and redemptive acts are also the basis of the Judaeo-Christian anthropology and *yir* ecclessiology respectively. Therefore, the Frafra myth of creation, their concept of *yir* and *kaaba* can become the basis of the Frafra Christian anthropology and ecclessiology *mutatis mutandis*.

Yir ecclessiology can offer the Frafra Christians a more holistic reading of the creation myth in Genesis than those offered them by the "pasta" and "fada". The Biblical myth of creation can reinforce the interconnectedness of humans, the spiritual world, and the entire inhabited world. God created the world including humans through God's spirit. Therefore the world including humans to some extent reflect and embody God's spirit.

The Frafra Christians can infer that there is physiological, psychological, pharmacological, social, spiritual, cultural and ecological interconnectedness between God's creation and God on the one hand and among humans, and between humans, and the entire world on the other hand.

The *yir* ecclessiology also implies that every human symbolic interaction is a transitional phenomenon between God and God's creation. It further implies that human beings are agents of God's spirit and can mediate the power of that Spirit in creating harmony or healing by following the divine law of the love of God, neighbour and creation.

Comparison of the Frafra and Judaeo-Christian Acts of Redemption

We shall next consider a comparison of the two redemptive acts from the two traditions and their implications for a contextual Frafra Christian anthropology and ecclessiology.

According to Cullmann "the Christological utilisation of kyrios 'logos' and 'son of God" has already shown that on the basis of the Christological views connected with these titles the New Testament could designate Jesus as 'God'."[17]

Cullmann offers the following theological explanations of the titles designated to Jesus Christ. He writes:

> kyrios is the present divine ruler who since his exaltation rules the Church, the world, and the life of each individual; the 'logos' is the eternal revealer, who communicates himself since the very beginning; the 'son of God' is the one who wills and works in complete oneness with the father, from whom he goes forth and to whom he returns.[18]

He further states:
... the concept Son of Man ultimately led us to Jesus 'deity' since it shows Jesus as the only true 'image of God'. ... Jesus Christ is God only in his revelation of himself. This is the only dimension which the Old and New Testaments consider, but it does not exhaust the nature of God the Father.[19]

For Cullmann "... The passages which confer upon Jesus the title kyrios, the name of God, are at least as important as those in which he is directly addressed as 'God."[20]

Another relevant example of contextualization in the New Testament is the typological interpretation of the role of Jesus as high priest in early Christianity. Cullmann further suggests that in Hebrews :... Jesus the high priest stands in the foreground, and the whole letter deals with him in this role ...."[21] For the writer of Hebrews Jesus was not the messiah. Rather, he " ... fulfils absolutely the high priestly function of the Jews."[22]

The typological method of interpretation of Old Testament in our view is a form of indigenization of the Christ-event to Jewish Christians. For the writer, the priesthood of the Old Covenant. He sees this new priesthood as realised in Jesus Christ, who is the priest in an absolute final sense, the fulfillment of all priesthood".[23]

The writer also employs the Jewish notion or belief in ancestry. For example the Jewish priesthood begins with Levi, who they believed existed in the

“’lions’ of Abraham so that what happened to Abraham therefore happened also to him.”[24]

Cullmann concludes that although there are exegetical problems with the logic of reason, “… behind it lies the deep theological thought that as the true high priest, Jesus Christ not only sets aside the Old Testament priesthood, but also fulfills it.”[25] Therefore, Jesus is the sacrifice, sacrificer and sacrificed. (Hebrew 7:27; 9:28 is direct reference to Isaiah 53:12).

For Cullmann:

It is precisely in offering himself and taking the greatest humiliation upon himself that Jesus exercises the most divine function conceivable in Israel, that of the high priestly mediator. In the light of the high priest concept the atoning death of Jesus demonstrates the true New Testament dialectic between the deepest humiliation and highest majesty.[26]

Verse 10:1 of the letter to the Hebrew Church says the blood of bulls and goats cannot take away sin, “because he himself is ‘priest’. Jesus as high priest brings humanity to its ‘perfection’. The covenant with God is renewed in such a way that humanity is made ‘perfect”[27]. God made Christ perfect (Hebrew 2:10; 5:9; 7:29) and Christ made his brothers perfect (Hebrew 2:10ff; 10:14). In order to present humans perfect before God, Hebrew 2:17-3:1, clearly suggests that Jesus the high priest participated in all human predicaments. Christ, leader of the new community, is the source of salvation by virtue of sharing human life and death. (*refer to Romans 5:12ff Old Adam and New Adam Hebrews 13:8)*.

Cullmann is also of the new that Protestants are incorrect in describing the Catholic mass as ‘repetition’ of the sacrificial act of Jesus. For him Catholic theologians have always rejected this interpretation. They speak rather of ‘making present’ Christ’s act:

…It is the saving consequences of that atoning act, not the act itself, which become a present event in our worship. The Lord present in worship is the exalted kyrios of the Church and world, raised to the right hand of God. He is the risen Lord who continues his mediating work on the basis of his unique, completed work of atonement. The words … (in remembrance of me) describe the connection between his crucifixion and celebration of the Lord’s supper. This means ‘in remembrance of that which I have completed, on the basis of which I now dwell among you as the resurrected Lord”.[28]

These additional pieces of evidence have shown beyond doubt that the Biblical writers were proto-types of contextualizers. They sought to make the Judaeo-Christian faith incarnate in its host culture and become a native. Hence, our project is indeed justified within the Judaeo-Christian tradition itself.

In the section on the genesis of this project we posed the questions who is Jesus and what is the Western Christian concept of the Church to the Frafra Christian? The answers to these questions have been unfolding and have become clear in the comparisons between the Frafra ancestors and Jesus Christ.

Comparison of the Frafra Ancestors and Jesus Christ

We shall summarise here Nyamiti's comparison between the notion of Brother-Ancestor in Africa and Christ's relationship to Christians. In Africa ancestorship is founded on consanguineous ties. The Christ relationship is also consanguineous with humans through Adam. The supernatural status of the ancestors attained by death make them closer to God. So they are able to intercede on behalf of their living kinship. In Christianity, the supernatural status of Christians is attained through the death, and resurrection of Christ who mediates between his human brethren[29], and God.

The model of behaviour of the ancestor is the source of tradition and harmony in society. The behaviour of Christ is also the model of Christian conduct. The living communicate with their ancestor through ritual and prayer.[30]

The failure to do so constitutes an offence which may result in bodily harm. Christians also communicate to Christ through ritual and prayer. The failure to do so also results in spiritual calamities.[31] the ancestors visit the living in the form of other beings as well as trees, stones, graveyards. Christ visits the Christians through priests and fellow Christians with whom Christ "mystically identifies himself".[32] It is also believed that he contacts believers through the sacraments. Finally, the relationship between the living and the ancestor is through common parents. In Christianity God "the first person of the Trinity is the common and immediate Father and Mother of Christ and His earthly members."[33]

Nyamiti however points our some very important differences between the African Brother-Ancestor relationship and that of Christ and humanity. In our view only one difference is so obvious. Although both Brother-Ancestor and Christ relationship are based on consanguinity[34], Nyamiti suggests that there are differences between the consanguineous relationship between the ancestors and their kinsfolk and Christ's and his followers.

According to Nyamiti, "... The difference lies in the fact that being Adamite in character Christ's brotherhood transcends all family, clan, tribal or racial limitations."[35] In our view if Nyamiti had based the similarities on the Adamite origin in the creation myth as we are doing rather than on consanguinity, the difference between the relationship of ancestors and their living kinsfolk, and that of Christ and Christians would hardly exist as we have argued in the case of the Frafra.

In our approach Christ is not just a proto-type ancestor, he is indeed the founding ancestor to all humanity by virtue of both the creation myth as well as His symbolical act of *kaaba* by His death, resurrection, and in the active presence of the Holy Spirit. If we locate our ancestorship with Christ in the creation myth and the Christ-event, then every human being in every land is our kinsfolk by virtue of creation and the Christ-event. The definition of ancestor here takes on a more inclusive meaning. The human race is looked at as an extended family.

The question is whether or not Christianity is reduced to Frafra religion by using ancestors and Christ interchangeably. In our opinion, it is difficult if not practically impossible to make a clear distinction between their ancestors and Jesus, at the level of symbolic functions and representations in ritual, among most adult Ghanaians who become Christians without trying to play God. So we cannot repeat that naiveté of Western missionaries, that people have to be extracted from their mythic worlds when they become Christians. Therefore, Jesus Christ to the Frafra Christian is the first *yaab* who has come to assemble all before God, the founding spirit of all there is, who is I am *(M be)*. Jesus is the first yaab by definition. As their *yaab* they share the spiritual, physical, social, cultural, biological, and psychological relationship with him. As such they embody him and consequently are symbolic representatives of him to each other. We are all members of his *yir*.

A question can be legitimately raised thus: If Christ is just one of the *yaabnam* of the Frafra, is there a need for the role of Jesus Christ in their lives? In other words is Jesus Christ not theologically redundant, an unnecessary theological and perhaps cultural inconvenience?

We shall use an illustration from the extended family system among the Frafra as the basis for a theological response. Among the frafra it is a common practice for a child born into a large family not to be able to identify his/her real biological father. There is no malice intended. Instead, every uncle sincerely wants to demonstrate that he cares and loves him/her as his/her real father.

At the opportune time the child is publicly introduced to his/her father through a ritual. There is joy and celebration. The child now has a feeling of security because knowing the father means he/she rightly belongs to that *yir*. S/He is a true heir to all the rights, privileges, and responsibilities of belonging to that *yir*. He/she also knows he/she now has the first direct person to ask questions of identity and complex issues of life, seek support, and care from. The biological and spiritual relationship with the uncles is not denied, rather it is subsumed in his/her relationship with the father.

In the same way, Jesus Christ as the first *yaab* plays a similar role among the Frafra Christians as the real father plays in the life of his child. The child has become aware of a relationship that has always existed. But that awareness has inexplicable existential consequences for the totality of life, throughout life, and beyond life. So is the relationship between Christ and the Frafra Christians.
We can, therefore, conclude with certainty that the Christian ministry in general and the ministry of healing in particular will only be relevant and effective if the Frafra Christians can articulate for themselves and others their new identity; their Christian anthropology, *yir*, and *kaaba* using aspects of their parent mythic world.

The interpretation of the Western Christian notion of the Church as the Frafra Christian *yir* is not imposed from without. *Yir* is presently used to describe the Western Christian notion of the "Church" by Frafra Christians. For example, on Sundays when you ask Frafra Christians going to Church where they are going they will say *to y la Fada yir* (we are going to Father's house). Therefore for the Frafra Christians the Church is *yir mutatis mutandis*.

We are aware that for some Christians, the mere mention of the word "ecclessiology" invokes sentiments, debates and even theological positions of traditional credal formulations. Others may even be afraid or concerned that we shall betray our Western missionary heritage or the common ties with founding missionary Churches. Notwithstanding these sentiments it is imperative that Frafra Christians redefine for themselves what Western

Christianity calls the "Church". By redefining the "Church" as *yir* based on their mythic world the Frafra Christians can claim the Christian faith in one of the phrases in the Apostles' creed "maker of heaven and earth and in our Lord Jesus Christ" as coming out of their experience and not imposed from without.

This interpretation has two advantages. The first advantage is that the Frafra Christians will have no cause to approach the Church's creeds with a high degree of ideological suspicion. The second advantage is that it frees the Church's creed from ideologies that form the basis of their formulations that are often socio-politically, and socio-economically exploitative as well as psycho-spiritually and socio-culturally impoverishing for Frafra Christians. Jesus Christ as Co-creator and Sustainer of all in the world makes Him the source and resource in the Frafra Christians' experiences of life and their expectations of Jesus the Christ to help them experience well-being.

We have thus far attempted to show that the Frafra Christians can truly confess that *Yesu Krista a te Yaab ka te a u yir biih* (Jesus Christ is our ancestor and we are children of his house) based on their Christian anthropology and *yir* ecclessiology. We shall in the rest of this chapter attempt to construct a contextual Frafra Christian ministry of *kaaba* based on the Frafra Christian anthropology and *yir* ecclessiology utilising the insights from *nya, tiim* and *baanaam,* and *yaabnam kaaba.*

Implications of *kaaba* to the concept of holistic healing

In *nya* healing, the roots or herbs are agents of the spiritual powers which they share with their ancestors by the very act of creation and passed on to them biologically, and spiritually. So in the Frafra understanding pharmacology does not only heal because of chemical properties alone but also spiritually by the very act of creation.

They embody the ancestral spirit which is the same Spirit from which the herbs come from by the very act of creation. Such a belief, however, does not contradict the fact that the healer also need training in identifying the herbs and the technique of mixing them. There is an inherent inseparability between the physical, spiritual, pharmacological, as well as the social in the Frafra mythic world. One involves all and all involves one. Consequently, all humans are qualified to offer one type of healing or the other by the very fact that humans trace their origin to God. The definition of sickness and healing then is in terms of invoking the Spirit of God to heal directly, or through drugs, hands and other created substances.

Implications of insights from *kaaba* to the Dialogue with Western scientific medicine and religion

The emphases of Western scientific medicine and psychotherapies are on the individual body or psyche. The Frafra healing rituals on the contrary are based on what Lartey calls "relational holism".[36] The notion of holistic healing in kaaba raises fundamental questions of the relationship between religion and Western scientific medicine in Western hospitals imported into Ghana. We can appreciate the impact on the clinical theological project founded by Lake[37] in the United Kingdom and the clinical pastoral education movement are making in an effort to offer some notion of holistic healing to patients in the West. In our experience of the clinical education movement in North America and the findings from *kaaba*, we are beginning to critically question whether we can truly and theologically call these models holistic healing or partnership healing.

In *Nya kaaba* medicine and religion are inseparable. This holistic inseparable relationship between medicine and healing is different form that of the partnership approach in Western medicine. In *nya* healing, medicine implies religion and religion implies medicine. The two are not competitors.

Therefore, in *yir* ecclessiology *mutatis mutandis* the unity between medicine and religion is clearly established in the myth of creation. In such an understanding scientific medicine is not intended to disprove religious beliefs. Rather, the very substances of scientific discovery and research have some dimensions of some sacredness by virtue of the myth of creation.
The medical practitioner by virtue of the creation myth consists of biology and spirit. For s/he is the embodiment of the great Spirit of creation. Hence, to remove cancer by surgery, to take an x-ray of a part of the body, to take antibiotics against viruses are all physiological, medical and spiritual actions. For at creation God imparted God's Spirit to all creation including all the substances used to make the x-ray machines, the antibiotics, and the body that diagnoses, administers, and takes the antibiotics.

In this contextual *yir* ecclessiology all the Frafra Christians are healers by virtue of the myth of creation. For they embody the Spirit of God and Jesus Christ. Consequently, every action is both secular and sacred.

The physical acts like laying hands, sharing food with the hungry, visiting the sick, speaking against injustice, washing a wound, and using a Western psychological insight to revitalise life are all acts of both physical and spiritual healing. Perhaps that may be what Jesus meant when he said "Whatever you did for one of the least of these brothers [and sisters] of mine, you did for me" (Matt. 25"40b).

In *kaaba* there is an inseparable holism between the spiritual, physiological, pharmacological, social and cultural. The holism is the reason why the aetiology and healing of both the personal and community healing ritual are also inseparable and interdependent. One is incomplete without the other. The presence of the family members is not just to give support but vitally necessary for both the causes and healing of the sickness. The point is clearly demonstrated in *yaabnam kaaba* in which all members of the family need to be present for confession and rebirth of the *yir*.

In the light of insights from *kaaba*, the medical doctors, nurses, x-ray technicians, cooks, domestic assistants, pastoral care givers both ordained and lay, and other members of the Christian *Yir* who pray for the sick are all healers. The basis of healing for all and by all is the one Spirit of God also the Spirit of Jesus Christ and the same Spirit they embody. That Spirit is also the Object of their worship as well as inspires all their actions.

Implications of *kaaba for holistic health education*

The healing model that operates in Western hospitals is different from *kaaba*. In Western scientific medicine the surgeon does his/her operation. The religious leader either prays before or after the operation. The social worker is later called if necessary to arrange where the patient will go, and what benefits he or she can apply for form the state of insurance. The physio-therapist will also give the necessary instructions for recovery. All these services are necessary but it is difficult to call them holistic healing from the perspective of the Frafra *kaaba*. They are for all intents and purposes a partnership. Therefore, the importation of such partnership into Ghana in our view denies the Ghanaian Christians the holistic priest-healer" experience they expect from the Church.

In other words, in the Frafra mythic world the interconnectedness of sickness, healing and health are not either medical or spiritual, but they are physiological, psychological, pharmacological, social, medical, spiritual and cultural. Hence, sickness healing rituals, and health are approached with an attitude of one in all, all in one.

In the light of *yir* ecclessiology, sickness may be likened to an ecclessiological virus, caused by an act or acts which lead to estrangement from God, the centre; the source and resource of life for all connected to God. In other words, sickness results from failure to act justly to the members of the household, and/or ecosystem. Therefore, sickness, healing, and health involve persons and the community. Paul wants the Christians in Thessalonica to "avoid every kind of evil" (1 The. 5:22) and to those in Colossia, that "whatever you do, whether in word or deed, do it all in the name of the Lord Jesus, giving thanks to God the father through him" (Colo. 3:17). These pieces of advice of Paul to young Christians from the perspective of kaaba are both medical and spiritual.

The above evidences suggest that to act justly in *Kaaba* can be reinforced by Biblical Christianity. Hence, the prophetic role of crying for justice, equal access to health facilities are both medical and spiritual in the understanding of a contextualized Frafra Christian ministry of healing.

Our present knowledge of eating a proper balanced diet, exercise, maintaining a clean environment also clearly point to the need to act justly if we are to avoid sickness. Therefore a contextualized Frafra Christian ministry of healing can also offer a contribution in Christian pastoral ecological ethics and primary health campaigns.

Implications of *Tiim* and *Baanaam* healing for *Yir* ecclessiology

There are both differences and similarities between the Christian teaching on the Holy Spirit and the Christian call, preparation and ordination (and in some traditions the process of confirmation), and the Frafra belief in *Tiim* and *Baanaam* healing, and the process of becoming a *Baanaab*.

One important difference is that most orthodox Christian traditions do not believe that Christians can control the Holy Spirit by contracting with the Holy Spirit to perform tasks for believers for rewards. However, Scripture teaches that the Holy Spirit can be grieved by some acts such as bitterness, rage, anger, slander, and malice (Eph. 4:30). Whether we can interpret making the Spirit grieve by doing these acts and pleasing the Spirit by not doing them as rewards is uncertain.

Another important difference is the sexist nature of *Tiim* and *Baanaam* healing. Since all embody the Spirit who has endowed all with gifts, the Frafra Christian *yir* cannot limit healing to only men without running into serious contradiction with its pastoral theological anthropology thus far constructed.

Notwithstanding these important differences there are also important similarities that can be used as insights for a contextual Frafra Christian ministry of healing.

The phenomena of *Tiim* and *Baanaam* healing are similar to the Moses, and Solomonic traditions, the "priest-exorcist" tradition and soothing of evil spirits (1 Sam 1:14-23) in Judaism as well as Nolan's concept of "Jesus as initiator of faith" in the New Testament, as we have already seen in Chapter Five.

Some of the Biblical healing narratives point to the view that sickness is caused by demonic forces. Hence, healing is not acting justly but exorcising the demonic forces. For example, the man possessed by evil spirit (Mk 1:23; Matt 12:22; Lk 8:26; Matt 9:32), and Mary Magdalene and others (Luke 8:2).

These similarities suggest that the act of healing by exorcism as in *tiim* and *baanaab* healing can also be enforced by Biblical accounts of healing. The Frafra pastoral care giver may have to deconstruct and reconstruct the inherited missionaries' dispensational theologies in order to conduct a contextual ministry of healing which includes exorcism.

Some of Paul's teaching on the contrast between sinful nature and the fruit of the Holy Spirit are similar to the Frafra belief in *Tiim* and *Baanaam* healing. (Galatians 5:16-25). However, it does not mean that we deny the fact that sickness can be caused by viruses and bacteria and healed through antibiotics, nor can we deny the fact that psychological, socio-economic and socio-political factors have significant impact on sickness and well-being, if these factors are removed.

The position of a Frafra Christian anthropology is that the spiritual is not compartmentalised from the medical, and the socio-political and economical. Rather, the spiritual interacts with humans for good and evil at the social, psychological, medical, cultural, and political.

This kind of Christian anthropology is one in which persons are identified as having the necessary ability to use the powers of Spirits to fight evil spirits for the sake of well-being of humans and indeed the entire creation. It also implies a belief that the evil spirits can influence political leaders to become dictators, to be greedy, as well as to implement exploitative economic policies. These spirits can also influence a medical doctor to perform a surgery, or administer the wrong drugs. They can also influence some workers to steal drugs from Government hospital, as well as not care for the sick members of the community. Here again one involves all. This belief does not deny human responsibility or irresponsibility and competence or incompetence. Rather, all these are simultaneously implied in the belief. The moral, spiritual, intellectual, technological, medical, and religious, and socio-political actions are interconnected.

In other words, Western psychological counselling, medical social services, and drugs and be used provided they are not seen to be competitors but instead are inspired by one and the same Spirit of God, who was in Christ by virtue of creation and redemption. Therefore in *Yir* ecclessiology, all are endowed with gifts of healing in a holistic sense and are encouraged to offer their gifts to the community. This kind of Frafra Christian anthropology and *yir* ecclessiology is also powerfully reinforced by scriptures; for example, Paul's teaching on One Spirit but different gifts: "There are different kinds of gifts, but the same Spirit. There are different kinds of services, but the same Lord. There are different kinds of working, but the same God works all of them in all men" (1 Cor. 12:4).

Elsewhere he writes: "The body is a unit, though it is made up of many parts; and though all its parts are many, they form one body. So it is with Christ. For we were all baptised by one Spirit into one body whether Jews or Greeks, slave or free we were all given one Spirit to drink." (1 Cor. 12:12-13). Paul emphases that "all these are the work of one and the same Spirit and He gives them to each other, just as he determines" (1 Cor. 12:11).

Implications of *yaabnam kaaba*

We have established that Jesus can be justifiably called *Yaab* among the Frafra Christians. As such Jesus (the sacrificer) is the one who presides in any gathering for worship (*kaaba*) of the Frafra Christians (*yir*). He is also the *kaaba* (sacrifice) as well as the founding ancestor (*Yaab*) to whom the sacrifice is made to their *yaab Yesu Krista*. Hence, he is the one who receives their confessions, also sanctifies or renews their lives as well as receives their pledge to act justly towards all. The efficacy of *Kaaba* is in the active presence of the ancestors who they also embody and symbolically represent. Such a belief revitalises the traditional Christian theological belief in the active presence of the Holy Spirit in the lives of Christians. Hence, every human encounter is a transitional phenomenon of spiritual encounters.

The Frafra Christians can easily understand Pauline's notion of the body as the temple of God (1 Cor. 3:16; 1 Cor. 6:CAPut!'; 2 Cor. 6:16; Acts 17:24) in which the Spirit of God lives. Therefore, the Frafra Christians know the efficacy of their actions in healing are based on the active presence of God's Holy Spirit.

In this approach, a pastoral theologian can improvise a contextualized Frafra Christian liturgical resource of healing that is free from Western theological inhibitions, categories of division, dichotomising, and symbols of impoverishment. The inherited Western liturgical resources reflect Western historico-political and religious circumstances that are mostly not relevant to Frafra Christian pastoral needs.

The adaptation of the Frafra concept of *Yaar* as models of house Churches in *yir* ecclessiology

It seems there has been little or no attempt to question whether the common Christian practice of meeting once a week usually on Sunday in a rectangular building is suitable to the nurture and growth of the Frafra Christians in their new found faith. There are occasions when the Frafra come together once or twice a year for rituals. These are usually the various first fruits rituals associated with harvests. Other occasions include political rallies. Besides these occasions the Frafra usually stay and interact, and share with each other closely at the clan level.

We have already described the Frafra clan system in Chapters Three and Six. The groups of houses of one clan location of the village are referred as *yaar*. *Yaar* comes from *ya* which means houses or a group of houses located at one area. *Yaar* connotes the idea of base communities in Latin America. It is best translated as neighbouring community. The spirit of sharing and supporting each other in these communities is best defined by Jesus' parable of the good Samaritan in Luke 10:33-37.

In daily life the members of each *yaar* are responsible for giving support, and care to each other. The kind of situations in which they offer support and care include deaths, and sickness. They share food with each other. It is common to eat in neighbours' houses without appointments and even take some home for the children. It is also common practice to go for salt, pepper, and sugar from neighbours if one runs out of supply. They also borrow each other's cloths, bicycles, shoes, as well as accompany each other to places.

From what we know about Frafra culture and spirituality the Christian practice inherited from Judaism, of going for worship on Sundays in these rectangular buildings is strange to the Frafra Christians. More importantly, it is unconducive to their Christian nurture and growth. We shall offer some alternatives based on the Frafra anthropology and *yir* ecclessiology we have proposed.

If the Christian Church is to be expressed as a truly caring and healing community, it seems better to organise the Frafra Christian congregations along the forms of *yaar*. Indeed the Frafra situation calls for *yaar* Churches or house Churches. The idea of house churches is not new in Ghana. It is commonly called "Christian fellowships" in Ghana. The rise of these Christian Fellowships in our opinion was due to the inability or unwillingness of the missionary founded Churches to provide the kind of context for sharing of their faith, the nurturing and caring for each other, the freedom of worship, the simple but by no means simplistic theologies and the voluntary style of leadership.

For Frafra Christians the notion of house Churches is also similar to the Hebraic covenantal notion of the house or household of God. The house church concept offers the Frafra Christians the contexts in which there is dynamic relationship between faith and praxis based on a direct encounter between their mythic world and Biblical Christianity. However, the Frafra house churches can learn from some of the mistakes of the Christian Fellowships. Some of these mistakes include their tendencies to be intolerant to those who have different experiences of their faith, and views of the Bible, and some negative "God-against-culture" attitudes. By definition a Frafra Christian *yaar* (community) is where there is holistic ministry of healing and all are heard and respected. The fundamental ethical codes are love God and neighbour and act justly.

Implications for architectural design of chapels

Our findings on the sitting configuration during *yaabnam kaaba* also have some important applications for designing chapels in Frafraland. Most chapels are rectangular buildings. The pews or benches are in straight rows parallel to each other. Those in front do not see those at the back. Those at the back only see the backs of those sitting in front. At times even those people sitting on the same row cannot see each other. All eyes are focused on the leader who is in front.

This kind of sitting arrangement clearly demonstrates the vertical relationship between Christians and Christ. The Christians are seen as individuals related to Christ by the individual confession of faith in Christ. By implication this symbolically suggests to the Frafra Christians that the Church consists of individuals.

In a contextual Frafra Christian chapel which utilises insights from *kaaba*, the chapel must be round. The pews or benches must also be arranged in semi-circle. Such a sitting arrangement reflects the sitting arrangements in *kaaba*. But more importantly, it symbolises theologically that the Frafra Christians at worship are truly the *biih* (children) of the *yir* (household) of Christ. All have different functions and roles but all are interdependent on each other for well-being. They are the embodiment of the Spirit of God and they also embody each other.

The round chapel can then replace the traditional Frafra *boar*. Indeed there is a close similarity between the symbols of the sanctuary of the Christian chapel and the traditional Frafra *boar*.

These symbols include semi-circle platform, a lectern, altar, pulpit, water, wine, blood of Christ and animals, presiders who invoke the respective mythic worlds, and a gathering of kinsfolk. All these symbols are the iconic representations of creation and redemption in both ritual systems.

They enable the participants to use their mythic worlds as interpretative mechanisms in the ritual system. The term ritual system is used here as Fernandez defines it. According to him:

the ritual system is in essence, a system of enacted correspondences. A metaphor (and related tropes) is the statement, explicit or implied, of a correspondence between some subject of thought in need of clarification and an object that brings some clarity to it.[38]

In our view the subject of thought that needs clarification is the experience of sickness. The objects that clarify the experiences of sickness are the creation myths and redemptive acts of both mythic worlds. Therefore, because these traditional symbols serve as enacted correspondences in both ritual systems they can be reinterpreted in the light of the Christ-event for the Frafra Christians.

In the Frafra Christian anthropology based on *yir* ecclessiology the traditional Frafra *boar* can serve as a Frafra Christian equivalent of the Western Christian chapel. Therefore, we can call the traditional Frafra *boar* the Frafra Christian *boar mutatis mutandis.* These indigenized architectural designs and sitting arrangements will make a liturgy of worship a symbolic representation. The most important benefit of this contextualization for the Frafra Christians is that it helps them to maximise the use of Christian faith through their mythic world as an important source and resource for healing in times of sickness.

A prospective Frafra Christian *Kaaba* (worship/healing service)

As stated earlier, we are not writing a liturgy of healing here. However, we shall attempt to make a theological eschatological leap into what might happen when a Frafra Christian *yaar* meet in its Christian *boar.*

In the Frafra Christian *boar* the entire Christian *kaaba* and all the participants are symbolic representations of God, Christ, their founding *yaab*, clouds of witness of the saints, and the cosmos. This web of inter-personal and intra-personal relationships further suggests that the Frafra Christians assembled are the iconic representations of the *Yir* of Jesus Christ. Through metacommunication, the Christian leader creates a subjunctive world in which there is interpenetrating of powers. In this interpenetration, boundaries between physical and spiritual, sacred, profane, sickness and health are broken. There is unconditional acceptance of *Yesu Yir*. The Frafra Christian *kaaba* become a renewing process of the biological, social, cultural, psychological and spiritual life in Christ.

In their subjunctive world, there is also interpenetrating of time. The boundaries between the past, present and future are broken. The Frafra Christian salvation history is not linear but cyclical. The Frafra story is one of creation, chaos and recreation.

In Frafra Christian *Kaaba*, the whole community is called upon to deal with its wounds, brokenness, estrangements, and negligence. Through Christian *kaaba* there is reflection, restitution, confession, rebirth or renewal and solidarity. The Frafra Christian *kaaba* are both spiritual as well as medical. Through Christian *kaaba,* the proper boundaries are re-established and rights reasserted. In Frafra Christian *kaaba* in Christian *boar* a Frafra Christian can truly feel Jesus Christ is their *yaab*. Some Biblical verses such as the following examples will reinforce their Christian experience: "For we are

God's workmanship, created in Christ Jesus to do good works, which God prepared in advance for us to do" (Eph. 2:10). And,

In him the whole building is joined together and rises to become a holy temple in the Lord. And in him you too are being built together to become a dwelling in which God lives by his Spirit (Eph. 2:21-22).

The God who made the world and everything in it is the Lord of heaven and earth and does not live in temples built in hands. And he is not served by human hands, as if he needed anything, because he himself gives all men life and breath and everything else. From one man he made every nation of men, that they should inhabit the whole earth; and he determined the times set for them and the exact places where they should live. God did this so that men would seek him and find him though he is not far from each one of us. For in him we live and move and have our being. As some of your own poets have said 'we are his offspring' (Acts 17:24-28).

Conclusion

We hope that the contextual Frafra Christian anthropology and *Yir* ecclessiology that we have proposed can offer resources for a contextualized Frafra Christian ministry of *kaaba*. In *yir* ecclessiology, we can invoke a Frafra Christian mythic world which allows the Frafra Christians to appropriate the Biblical accounts of healing. This approach will offer a holistic Frafra Christian conversion experience to the Frafra. This kind of conversion is best defined by James, thus:

… a conversion has taken place when a system of ideas that has become a religion is moved from the periphery of consciousness to its centre and becomes permanent there a self hitherto divided and consciously wrong, inferior and unhappy becomes unified."[39]

A *yir* ecclessiology can mobilise and incorporate into the Christian mythic world the Frafra mythic world. In this Frafra Christian mythic world the Frafra Christians can invoke the theological themes of confession, cleansing, dedication, and grace which are already native to their mythic world.

Consequently, *yir* ecclessiology can help the Frafra Christians bridge the gap between the faith and praxis within the debate of Christ and culture. The *yir* ecclessiology will make Christianity a native in Frafraland and operate with some important aspect of the Frafra mythic world.

Therefore, the Frafra Christians can enjoy Jesus Christ through a contextualized Frafra Christian ministry of healing that is transformative, liberative and holistic. Such a ministry utilises aspects of their mythic world which is their source and resource in dealing with sickness to achieve the Western concept of well-being or the Judaeo-Christian concept of *Shalom*. We also hope that this approach may also become a contextualized "theological paradigm of" and "paradigm for" transcultural pastoral theology of healing in the Church of Jesus Christ world-wide.

References

1. Choan-Sing Song, Christian Mission in Reconstruction An Asian Attempt

2. (Madras: the Christian Literature Society 1975), p.7.

3. Ibid.

4. *Ibid.*

5. E. W. Fashole-Luke, "The Quest for an African Christian theology" in The Ecumenical Review vol. 27, No. 3, (July 1975), p. 267-268.

6. Lamin Sanneh, Translating the Message : The Missionary Impact on Culture (Maryknoll, New York: Orbis Books 1991)

7. A. Krass, "Towards a more Indigenous Liturgy" in The Ghana Bulletin of Theology vol. 3; no. 7; (December 1979), p.20-23

8. Also see A. Nickles, "The Offertory Processions" in The Ghana Bulletin Theology vol.3; no. 7 (December 1979), p.29-32.

9. Claus Westermann, Creation Translated by John J. Scullion (London:SPCK 1971), p.1.

10. E. O. James, Creation and Cosmoslogy (Leiden: E.J. Bril 1969), p.92.
11. *Ibid.,* P.130.

12. Luis I. J. Stadelmann, The Hebrew Conception of the World (Romeo : Pontifical Institute, 1970), p.11.

13. A. Heidel, The Babylonian Genesis (2nd Phoenix Ed. Chicago: University of Chicago Press, 1965), p.10.

14. *Ibid.,* P.11.

15. *Ibid.*

16. *Ibid.,* p. 27.

17. *Ibid.*

18. *Ibid.,* P.183.

19. *Ibid.*

20. Oscar Cullmann, The Christology of the New Testament (London: SCM Press, 1959), p.306.

21. *Ibid.*

22. *Ibid.*

23. *Ibid.,* P.307.

24. *Ibid.,* P.89.

25. *Ibid.*

26. *Ibid.,* P.90.

27. *Ibid.*

28. *Ibid.,* P.90-91.

29 *Ibid.,* P.91-92.

30 *Ibid.,* P.92.

31 Oscar Cullmann, Christ and Time (London: S.C.M 1951), p.169.

32 Charles Nyamiti, Christ As our Ancestor (Gweru, Zimbabwe; Mambo Press 1984), p.20.

33 *Ibid.*

34. *Ibid.*

35. *Ibid.*

36. *Ibid.*

37 *Ibid.* chapter two, p.10-20, 20-24.

38. *Ibid.* P.20.

39. E. Y. Lartey, "African Perspectives in Pastoral Theology : a contribution to the quest for more encompassing models of pastoral care" in Contact, Vol. 112,, (1993), p.7.

40 Frank Lake, Clinical Theology (London : Darton, Longman and Todd, 1966.

41 James W. Fernandez, "Analysis of Ritual : Metaphor Correspondences as Elementary Forms" in Science, vol. 182 (1973), p.1366.

42. W. James, Varieties of Religious Experience (New York : The American Literature Library, 1958), p.196.

BIBLIOGRAPHY

Achebe, China, A man of the people (London: Heinemann 1966). Achebe, Chinua, Arrow of God (London: Heinemann 1964). Achebe, Chinua, Things fall apart (London: Heinemann 1959) Ackernecht, H., A Short History of Medicine (New York: The Roland Press 1955).

Adegbola, A., "Theological Educators in Africa Today and Tomorrow" in Ministerial Formation, January 1980, Vol.9,

Ademuwagun, Z.A., "Problem and Prospect of Legitimatizing and Integrating Aspects of Traditional Health Care systems and Methods with Modern Medical therapy: The Igbo-Ora Experience" in Z.A. Ademuwagun et al (eds) African Therapeutic Systems (Massachussetts: Crossroads, 1979).

Ademuwagun, A Z, Ayoade, JAA, Harrison, IE, Warren, DW (eds), African Therapeutic Systems (Massachusetts: Crossroads Press for African Studies Association 1979).

Agbeti, J.K., "Theological Education in Ghana" in The Ghana Bulletin of Theology June 1971, Vol.3.

Amirtham, Samuel, "A Vision for Theological Education in African" in Ministerial Formation Vol.35 Sept 1986.

Ampofo, O., "The traditional Concept of Disease, Health and Healing in The Ghana Bulletin of Theology June 1967, Vol.3 No.2 .

African Medicine in the Modern World Seminar Proceedings No. 27. Proceedings of a Seminar of Centre of African Studies, University of Edinburgh 10 & 17 Dec. 1986.

Anafu, Moses, " The Impact of British rule on Tallensi Polotical Institutions 1898-1967" in Transactions of the Historical Society of Ghana Vol. 14 no. 1 June 1973.

Anderson, Ephraim, Churches at the Grass roots : A study in Zongo-Brazzaville. World Studies of Churches in Mission WCC (London: Lutterworth Press 1968).

Ansre, Gilbert, "Some Language Problems in Theological Training in West Africa" in The Ghana Bulletin of Theology Dec 1962, Vol. 2. No.3.

Appiah-Kubi, Kofi, "Jesus Christ: Some Christological Aspects from Africa perspectives" in J.S.Mbiti (ed) African and Asia Contributions to Contemporary Theology (Report of a Consultation held at the Ecumenical Institute, Bossey. June, 1976), Geneva W.C.C. 1977.

Appiah-Kubi, Kofi, Man Cures, God Heals (New York: Free Press, 1981).

Appiah-Kubi, Kofi, "The Church's Healing Ministry in Afica" in Contact W.C.C. 1985, Vol.29, 2-6.

Appiah-Kubi, Kofi, "Religion and Healing in an African Community: the Akan of Ghana" in Lawrence E. Sullivan (ed) Healing and Restoring (New York: Macmillan Publishing Co., 1989).

Appiah-Kubi and Torries, S. (eds), African Theology Enroute (Mary Knoll NY: Orbis Books 1979).

Armah, Kwei A., The Beautiful Once are not yet Born (London: Heimann 1969).

Assemblies of God, Ghana 1931-1981.

Awoonor, Kofi, This earth, my brother: An allegorical tale of Africa (New York: Doubleday & Co. 1971).

Axtine, V. M., Play Therapy: The Inner Dynamics of Childhood (Boston: Houghton Mifflin Co. 1947).

Baaren, Van P Th, and Drijvers, h.J.W. (eds), Religion, Culture and Methodology: Papers of the Groningen Working-group for the Study of Fundamental problems and methods of Science and Religion (The Hague: Mouton and Co., 1973).

Baeta, C. G., Prophetism in Ghana, A study of some 'spiritual' Churches (London: SCM Press1962).

Baeta, C.G., "Christianity and Healing" in Orita , 1965, Vol.1.

Banana, C. S., "The case fro a new Bible"in l. Mukonyora, J.L. Cox and F.J.Verstraelem (coordinator) (eds) Rewriting the Bible the real issues (Gweru, Zimbabwe: Mambo Press 1993.

Banton, M. (ed), Anthropological Approaches to the Study of Religion (London: Tavistock Publication 1966).

Barbour, Iain G., Issues in Science and Religion (New York : Harper and Row Publishers, 1971).

Barker, Peter, People, Languages, and Religion in Northern Ghana: A preliminary report (Accra: Ghana Evangelism Committee in association with Asempa Publishers, 1986).
Barret, D.B., Schism and Renewal in Africa: An analysis of six Thousand contemporary religious movements (Nairobi : Oxford University Press 1968).
Bartels, F. L., Roots of Ghana Methodism (Cambridge: The University Press in Association with Methodist Book Depot, Ghana 1965)
Beattie, John, and Other cultures: Aims, methods and achievements in Social anthropology (New York, The Free Press, 1964).
Beecham, John, Ashantee and the Gold Coast with introduction and notes by G.E.Metcalfe (London: Dawson of Pall Mall, 1968).
Bell, J., Doing your Research (Milton Keynes: Open University Press, 1987).
Bellah, Robert N., "Theology and Symbolic Realism" in Gill, R (ed) Theology and Society. A Reader (London : Paulist Press 1987).
Berinyuu, Abraham A., Pastoral Care the Sick : An Approach to Transcultural Pastoral Theology (Frankfurt: Peter Lang 1987).
Berinyuu, Abraham A., Towards Theory and Practice of Pastoral Counselling in Africa, (Frankfurt), Peter Lang, 1989
Berinyuu, Abraham A., History of the Presbyterian Church of Ghana in Northern Ghana: Memories and Reflections 1945-1972, in Press (Asempa Publishers Church Council of Ghana)
Berinyuu, Abraham A., "Change, Ritual and Grief : Continuity and Discontinuity of Pastoral Theology in Ghana" in Journal of Pastoral Care, Summer Vol.46 no.2 1992.
Berinyuu, Abraham A., "The Encounter of Western Christianity and Civilization and Islam on Ghanaian Culture & Implication for the Ministry of Pastoral Care and Counseling" in Africa Theological Journal, Vol. 17, No.11, November 1988.

Berinyuu, Abraham A., Hunger and Poverty and the Church's Responses as Model of Redemption." In The Month: A Review of Christian Thought and World Affairs, Vol. 21, No. 11, October London, 1988.
Berinyuu, Abraham A., "Dialogue Between African Traditional Religion and the Christian Faith via the Principle of Corporate Dialogue." In African Christian Studies (A Journal of the Faculty of Theology of the Catholic Higher Institute of Easter Africa.) Vol. 4, No. 1, March, 1988.
Berinyuu, Abraham A., "The practice of Divination in Christian Pastoral Care and Counselling in Ghana" in African Christian Studies: Vol. 3, No. 3, September 1988.
Berinyuu, Abraham A., "A Transcultural Approach to Pastoral Care to the Sick in Ghana." In Africa Theological Journal, Vol. 16, No. 1, 1987.
Bibeau, Gilles, "The World Health Oraganization in the Encounter with African Traditional Medicine: Theoretical Conceptions and Practical Strategies" translated by Sandra Mahaniah in Z.A. Ademuwagun et al (eds) African therapeutic Systems (Massachussetts: Crossroads, 1979).
Birk, L., Biofeedback: Behavioural Medicine (New York : Grune and Stratton, 1974).
Blumer, H., Symbolic Interactionism : Perspective and Method (Englewood, New Jersey: Prentice Hall, 1969).
Boesak, Allan, Farewell to innocence : A socio-ethical study of black theology and black power. (Maryknoll, New York: Orbis Books 1977)
Boulaga, E., Christianity without Fetishes : An African Critique And Recapture of Christianity (Maryknoll : Orbis Books 1981).
Bourdillon, M.F.C., "Introduction" in M.F.C. Bourdillon and Meyer Fortes (eds) Sacrifice (New York : Academic Press 1980).
Bradbuty, R..E., review of "Oedious and Job in Man, 1959, Vol.59,
Bretherton, I., "Representing the Social World in Symbolic Play :

Reality and Fantasy" in Inge Bretherton (ed) Symbolic play (Orlando : Academic Press 1984).
Browning D. S., (ed) Practical Theology: The Emerging Field in Theology, Church and World (New York: Harper & Row 1983).
Browning D. S., Pluralism and Personality: William James and Some Contemporary Cultures (London: Associated University Press 1981).
Busia Kofi A., The Challenge of Africa (New York : Frederick Prarger 1962).
Busia Kofi A., "The Ashanti of the Gold Coast" in Fortes M and Dierterlen G (eds) African Systems of Thought (London: Oxford University Press 1965).
Campbell, Alastir V., "The Nature of Practical Theology" in Forrester B. Forrester (ed) Theology and Practice (1990).
Cardinal, A. W., The natives of the Northern Ghana of the Gold Coast (London: MacMlllan & Co 1921).
Carmody, B. P., "Conversion to Roman Catholics in Zambia. Shifting pedagogies" in African Christian Studies Vol. 4, No. 2, June, 1988.
Carothers, J. C., The African Mind in Health and Disease : A Study in Ethnospsychiatry (New York : Negro University Press 1990).
Christaller, J.G., Erinnerungen aus sein Leben (Stuttgart, 1929).
Capra, F., The Turning Point: Science, Society and the Rising Culture (London: Fontana 1983)
Cox, James L., Expressing the Sacred: An Introduction to the Phenomenolgy of Religion (Harare, Zimbabwe: University of Zimbabwe Publishing, 1992).
Cox, James L., "Not a New Bible but a New Hermeneutics: An Approach from within the Science of Religion" in I. Mukonyora, J.I.Cox and F.J.Verstraelen (Co-ordinator) (eds) "Rewriting" the Bible: the real issues (Gweru, Zimbabwe: Mambo Press, 1993.
Cornin, B., "Religious and Christian Conversion in an African Context" in African Christian Studies Vol. 3, No. 2. June 1987.

Cullmann, Oscar, The Christology of the New Testament (London: SCM Press 1959)
Cullmann, Oscar, Christ and Time the primitive Christian concept Of time and history trans. Floyd V. Filson (S.C.M. Press Ltd 1951)
Capra, F., The Turning Point: Science, Society and the Rising Culutre (London: Fontana 1983),
Daneel. M. L., Old and New in Southern Shona Independent Churches (The Hague: Mouton & Co 1971).
Danquah, J.B., The Akan doctine of God (London: Lutterwoth Press 1968 2nd ed.)
Debrunner, Hans W., A History of Christianity in Ghana (Accra: Waterville Publishing House, 1967).
Der, Benedict, "Church-State Relations in Northern Ghana, 1906-1940" in Transactions of Historical Society of Ghana, Vol. 15, June 1974.
Dickson, Kwesi A., "The Meaning of Sacrifice" in The Ghana Bulletin of Theology Vol.2 No.3 Dec 1962.
Dickson, Kwesi A., "The Minister Then and Now" in J.S. Pobee (ed) Religion in a Pluralistic Society: Essays Presented to C. G. Baeta (E.J.Brill,Leiden: 1976).
Dickson, Kwesi A., Aspects of Religion and Life in Africa, J.B.Danquah Memorial Lecutres Series ID, 1977 (Accra: Ghana Academy of Arts and Sciences, 1977)
Dickson, Kwesi A., Theology in Africa (Mary Knoll, New York: Orbis Books, 1984).
Douglas, Mary, "The Lele of Kasai" in Forde D (ed) African Worlds (Published by International African Institute. London: Oxford University Press 1954).
Douglas, Mary, Purity and analysis of Concept of Pollution and Taboo (London: Ark Paperbacks 1989).
Douglas, Mary, Natural Symbols (London: Barriet Nad Jenkins Ltd 1973).
Duncan, Dennis, Pastoral care and Ethical Issues: Health and Healing: A Ministry of Wholeness (Edinburgh: The Saint

Andrew Press, 1988).
Durkheim, Emile, The Elementary Forms of Religious Life translated by Joseph Ward Swain (London : George Allen & Unwin Ltd. 1964).
Durkheim, Emile, and Mauss, M. The Elementary Forms of Religions translated and introduction by Rodney Needham (Chicago : The University of Chicago Press 1963).
Dupre, Wilhelm, Religion in Primitive Cultures: a Study in Ethnophilosophy (The Hague: Nouton and Co., 1975).
Edge, H. L., Morris, R. L., Rush, J.H., and Palmer, J . (eds), Foundations of Parapsychology McConnell, R.A. An Introduction to Parapsychology in contexts of Science, London : Routledge and Kegan Paul 1986, R.A. McConnel (1983).
Eliade, Mircea, Cosmos and History; The myth of the eternal return translated by W.R. Trask (New York: Harper Torch Books, 1954).
Eliade, Mircea, Rites and Symbols of Initiation: the mysteries of birth and re-birth translated by W.R. Trask (New York: Harper Torch Books, 1958).
Eliade, Mircea, The Sacred and Profane: the Nature of Religions: Significance of Religious myths, symbolism, and ritual within life and nature translated W.R.Trask (New York: Harcourt, Brace and World Inc., 1959).
Eliade Mircea, Myth and Reality translated by Trask WR (New York: Harper Torch Books 1963).
Eliade, Mircea, Shamanism : Archaic Techniques of Ecstasy translated by W.R. Trask (Princeton : Princeton University Press 1966)
Eliade, Mircea, The Quest (Chicago : University of Chicago Press1969).
Eliade, Mircea, Myth and Reality translated by Willard R. Trask (New York: Harper Torch Books, 1975).
Eliade, Mircea, and Kitagawa J. M. The History of Religions : Essays in Methodology (Chicago : University of Chicago Press 1959)
Eliade, Mircea, and Tracy David, (eds), What is Religion : An Enquiry for Christian Theology (Edinburgh: T & T Clark 1980).

Eliade, Mircea, "Homo faber and homo religious" in Kitagawa J. M. The History of Religions: Retrospect and Prospect (New York: Macmillan Pub. 1985).
Evans-Pritchard, E. E., Witchcraft, oracle and magic among the Azande (Oxford: Oxford University Press, 1937).
Evans-Pritchard, E. E., "The meaning of Sacrifice among the Nuer" in Journal of Royal Anthropological Society Vol. 84, 1954,
Evans-Pritchard, E. E., Nuer Religion (Oxford: Clarendon Press, 1956).
Evans-Pritchard, E. E., Theories of Primitive Religion (Oxford : Clarendon Press, 1977).
Fashole-Luke, E. Gray, R. Hasting, A., and Tasie, G., (eds), Christianity in Independent Africa (London : Rex College, 1978).
Fashole-Luke, E. W., "The Quest for an African Christian theology" In The Ecumenical review vol.27 no.3 July 1975 P267-268
Fernandez, James W., " Analysis of Ritual : Metaphor Corres-Pondences as Elementary Forms" in Science vol.
Field, Margaret, Religion and Medicine of the Ga People (London: Oxford University Press, 1937).
Field, Margaret, Social Organization of the Ga People (Accra: Governments Printing depot, 1940).
Field, Margaret, Search for Security (London : Faber & Faber 1960).
Field, Margaret, Angels and Ministers of Grace (Longman Group Ltd. 1971)
Forde, Daryll, edited with introduction African Worlds : studies in the cosmological ideas and social values of African People (London : Oxford University Press 1954)
Forrester, Duncan B., "Divinity in Use and Practice" in Duncan B. Forrester Theology and Practice (London : Epworth Press 1990)
Fortes, Meyer, The Web of Kinship Among the Tallensis (London :Oxford University Press 1949)
Fortes, Meyer, "Culture Contact as Dynamic Process" in International African Institute Methods of Study of Culture Contact in Africa with an introductory Essay by B.Malinowski (London: Oxford University Press for International

African Institute, 1965).

Fortes, Meyer, "The Political System of the Tallensis of the Northern Territories of the Gold Coast" in M.Fortes and E.E. Evans-Pritchard (eds) African Political Systems (London:Oxford University Press, 1966. Reprinted for International African Institute).

Fortes Meyer, " Informants" in L'Uomo vol. Iv no.2 1980.

Fortes, Meyer, Oedipus and Job in West African Religion with an essay by Robin Horton (Cambridge: Cambridge University Press 1983).

Fortes, Meyer, Religion, Mortality, and the Person : Essays on Tallensi Religion edited with Introduction by Jack Goody (Cambridge : Cambridge University Press, 1987).

Fortes, Meyer, and Dieterlen G., eds. African Systems of Thought : studies presented and iscussed at the third International African seminar in Salisbury, December, 1960 (London :Published for the International African Institute by Oxford University Press 1965).

Foster, George M., "Diseases Etiologies in Non-Western Medical Systems" in American Anthropologist 1976, 775 Vol. 78,

Frank, Jerome, Persuasion and Healing : A Comparative Study of Psychotherapy. (Baltimore : Johns Hopkins Press, 1963).

Frank, Jerome, Therapeutic components of psychotherapy. Journal of Nervous and Mental Disease 1974 Vol. 159.

Frank, Jerome, Physiotherapy of bodily disease : An overview. Psychotherapy and Psychosomatics 1975 Vol. 26:

Frank, Jerome, Mind-body relationships in illness and healing. Journal of the International Academy of Preventive Medicine 1975 2(3):

Frazer, James, The Golden Bough (London : MacMillan Publishing Co. 1922), the 1976 edition.

Freire, Paul. Pedagogy of the Oppressed (New York : Continuum 1981) translated by Myra Bergman Rands and Education for Critical Consciousness (New York : Continuum1981).

Freud, Sigmund, Normality and Pathology in Childhood (London : Hogarth Press and the Institute of Psychoanalysis, 1965).

Freud, Sigmund, Collected Psychological Works (1955).

Frion, G.J., "Current Knowledge and concepts of the relationship of malignancy, Autoimmunity and immunologic disease" in Annals of the New

York Academy of Sciences, , 1974, Vol. 230

Fuchs, S., "Magic Healing Techniques among the Bahahis in Central India" in Ari Kiev (ed) Magic, Faith and Healing (New York The Free Press 1964).

Gaba, C.R., "Sacrifice in Anlo Religion: Part I" in The Ghana Bulletin of Theology Vol.3. No.5 Dec 1968.

Gaba, C.R., "Sacrifice in Anlo Religion Part II" in The Ghana Bulletin of Theology Vol.3 No.7 Dec 1969.

Gastel, Val L., "Teaching the Healing Ministry in Theological Centre" in The Ghana Bulletin of Theology Vol.3 No.3 Dec 1967.

Geertz, Clifford, The Interpretation of Cultures (New York : Basic Books 1973).

Gehman, Richard, African Traditional Religion in Biblical Perspective (Kijabe, Kenya: Kesho Publications, 1989).

Gennep, Arnold van, The Rites of Passage translated by Monika B.Vizedom and Solom T.Kimbell (Chichage: University of Chichage Press, 1960.

Gifford, Pual, "Ghana's Charismatic Churches" in Journal of Religion in Africa vol. xxiv Fasc 3, (August, 1994).

Gill, Robin, (edited and introduced) Theology and Sociology: A Reader (London: Chapman, 1987).

Gluckman, Max., "The Rites of Passage" in C.D. Fordes, M. Fortes, V.M. Turner Essays on the Ritual of Social Relations (Manchester : Manchester University Press 1962).

Gluckman, Max., Custom and Conflict in Africa (Oxford : Basil Blackwell 1955)

Gluckman, Max., Order and Rebellion in Tribal Africa (Oxford : Basil Blackwell 1955)

Goody, Jack, Death, Property and the Ancestor (London: Tavistock, 1962).

Goollig, F. X., and Haley, H. B. (ed) Medical Anthropology (The Hague : Moulton publishers (1976).

Gray, Richard, Black Christians, White Missionaries (New Haven : Yale University Press 1990).

Grottanelli, V. L., "Witchcraft : An Allegory?" in Francis X Grollig and Harold B. Haley (eds) Medical Anthropology (The Hague : Mouton Publisher 1976).

Growe, F., Son of God, Holy Spirit and World Religions. The contribution of

Bernard Lonergan to the Wider Ecumenism (Toronto : Regis College Press, 1985).
Haar, Gerrie Ter, Spirit of Africa : the healing ministry of Archbishop Milingo of Zambia (London : Hurst & Co 1992).
Halebrian, Krikor, "The Problem of Contexualization" in Missiology 1983, XI.
Healing and Wholeness: The Churches' Role in Health A Report of aStudy by the Christian Medical Commission, W.C.C., 1990.
The Healing Church. The Tubigen Consultation 1964 (Geneva: W.C.C., 1965)
Healing in the Church Today (Accra: Asempa Publishers, 1985).
Helman, Cecil. Culture, Health and IIlness (London : Wright PSG 1984).
Heidel, A., The Babylonian Genesis (2nd Phoenix Ed. Chicago:University of Chicago Press 1965)
Hiebert, Pual G., "Critical Contextualization" in Missiology, XII 1984.
Hiltner, Seward, Preface to Pastoral Theology (Nashville: Abidgon Press, 1958).
Hilton T. E., "Notes on the History of the Kusasi" in Transactions Of the Historical Society of Ghana Vol vl, 1962.
Hofstadter, D. R., Godel, Escher, Back : An eternal golden braid (New York : Basic Books, 1979).
Hollenweger Walter J., "African and Western Medicine in Dialogue" in Abraham A. Berinyuu Pastoral Care to the Sick in Africa. (Frankfurt: Peter Lang 1987).
Hollenweger, Walter J., The Pentecostals (London : SCM Press Ltd. 1972).
Horton, Robin, "Ritual Man in Africa" in Africa April 1964, Vol.34 No.2.
Horton, Robin, "African Traditional Thought and Western Science" Part 1 from Tradition to Science in Africa 1975, Vol.45,No.3.
Horton Robin, "African Traditional thought and Western Science" Part II the 'Closed' and 'Open' Predicaments in Africa 1875.

Horton, Robin, "On the Rationality of Conversion" in Africa Vol. 45, No. 3, 1975, Vol.45 No.3.
Horton, Robin, "African Conversion" in Africa April 1981 vol. 4, No. 2,.
Hours, Bernard, "Africa Medicine as 'Alibi' and as a reality" in African Medicine in the Modern World (Seminar held in the Center of African Studies,

University of Edinburgh, 10,11, Dec. 1986)

Howell, Allison M., Resolving Conflict When People of Different Cultures Work Together (Accra: SIM Ghana, 1990).

Huppenbauer, H.W., "The Healing Ministry in Theological Training" in The Ghana Bulletin of Theology Dec 1967, Vol.3.

Huppenbauer, H.W., and Verstraelen, F.J., "The Healing Ministry of the Church" in The Ghana Bulletin of Theology June 1967, Vol.3 No.2.

Idowu, E. B., African Traditional Religion : A definition (London : SCM 1973).

Idowu, E. B., Olodumare : God in Yoruba Belief (London : Longmans 1962).

Ilogu, Edmund, "Theology as an Academic Discipline in Relation to Culture" in The Ghana Bulletin of Theology Dec 1962, Vol.2 No.3.

James, E. O., Creation and Cosmology (Leiden: E.J. Brill 1969)

James, William, Varieties of religious Experience (New York: The American Literature Library, 1958).

Janzen, J. M., "Health, Religion and Medicine in Central and Southern African Traditions" in Lawrence E. Sullivan Healing and Restoring (1989)

Janzen, J. M., The Quest for Therapy in Lower Zaire (Berkeley : University of California 1978).

Jenkins, Paul, "The Anglican Church in Ghana, 1905-1934 in Transactions of Historical Society, Vol. 15, No. 1, June 1974.

Jules-Rosette, B., African Apostles.. Ritual and Conversion in the Church of John Maranke(lthaca : Cornell University Press 1975).

Kane, E., Doing your own Research. How to do Basic Descriptive Research in Social Science and Humanities (London : Marian Boyars, 1985).

Karp, Ivan and Bird., Charles S., (eds), Explorations in African Systems of Thought (Washington: Smithsonian Institute Press, 1980).

Kato, Byang, Theological Pitfalls in Africa (Kisumu, Kenya:Evangel Publishing House, 1975).

Kee, Howard Clark, Medicine, Miracle and Magic in the New Testament Times (Cambridge: Cambridge University Press,1986).

Keen, Sam, To a Dancing God (New York, Colins Fontana Books 1971).

Kegan, Robert, The Evolving Self : Problem and Process in Human Development (Cambridge Mass, Harvard University Press, 1982).

Kelsey, Morton T. , Healing and Christianity (New York: Harper and Row

Publishers, 1973).
Kiev, A (ed) Magic Faith and Healing (Glencoe : The Free Press 1964).
Kilson, Marion, African Urban Kinsman: The Ga of Central Accra (London: G.Hurst and Co., 1974).
Kimble, David, A Political History of Ghana (Oxford: Oxford University Press, 1963).
Kirby, Jon P., God, Shrines and Problem-solving among the Anufo of Northern Ghana (Berlin: Dietrich Reimer Verlag, 1986)
Kirwen, Michael C., The Missionary and the Diviner (Mary Knoll, N.Y., Orbis Books, 1987).
Kitagawa, Joseph M., (ed) The History of Religions: Retrospect and Prospect (New York: MacMillan Publshing Co., 1985).
Kluckhohn, C., Navaho witchcraft (Boston : Beacon Press, 1967).
Kpobi, David Nii Anum, Mission in Chains: The Life, Theology and Ministry of the Ex-slave Jacobus E.J.Capitein (1717-1747) with a translation of his major publications (Zoeterneer: Uitgeverij Boeken centrum)
Kraft, Charles H., Christianity in Culture: A Study in Dynamic Biblical Theologizing in Cross-Cultural Prespective.Forward by Bernard Ramm (Maryknoll, New York: Orbis Books, 1987).

Krass, A., "Toward a More Indigenous Literurgy" in The Ghana Bulletin of Theology, 1969, Vol.3 no.7 Dec.
Krass, A., "Our Mission to the North" in The Ghana Bulletin of Theology Dec1970, Vol.3 No.9.
Kretschmar, L., The voice of black theology in South Africa. (Johannesburg : Raven Press 1986).
Landy, D., (ed), Culture, Disease and Healing Studies in Medical Anthropology (New York : MacMillan Publishing Co. Inc.1977).
Lartey, Emmanuel Yartekwei, "Healing: Tradition and Pentecostalism in Africa Today" in International review of Mission, Vol. LXXV No.297 January 1986.
Lartey, Emmanuel Yartekwei, "Some Contextual Implications for Pastoral Counselling in Ghana" in Jean Masamba ma Mpolo and Diasy Nkwachuku (eds) Pastoral care and Counselling in Africa Today (Frankfurt: Peter Lang 1991. Published for African Pastoral Studies).

Lartey, Emmanuel Yartekwei, Pastoral Counselling Intercultural Perspective (Frankfurt Peterlang 1987).
Lartey, Emmanuel Yartekwei, "African Perspectives in Pastoral Theology: A contribution to the quest for more Encompassing models of pastoral care" in Contact, Vol.112, 1993
Laye, C., A dream of Africa trans. James Kirkup (New York : Collier MacMillan 1971).
Lennox, J.A., "The Role of the Church in Preventative Medicine" in The Ghana Bulletin of Theology Dec 1967, Vol.3 No.3.
Lerner, Daniel, The Passing of Transitional Society (Glencoe, III. The Free Press 1958).
Leonard, Christine A Giant in Ghana (Chichester: Newwine Press 1989)
Lienhardt, Geoffrey, Divinity & Experience : The Religion of the Dinka (Oxford : Clarendon Press 1987).
Lloyed, P. C., Africa in Social Change : Changing Traditional Societies into the Modern World (Middlesex : Penguin Books 1967).
Lobowicz, Nicholas, Theory and Praxis: History of Concept from Aristotle to Marx (New York: University Press of America, 1967).
Long, Charles, Significations: signs, Symbols and Images in the Interpretation of Religion (Philadelphia Fortress Press 1986).
Longergan, Bernard, Method in Theology (London : Darton. Longman And Todd 1971)
Longergan. Bernard, A Second Collection (London : Darton Longman, and Todd 1971) and The Third Collection (London : Darton, Longman, Todd, 1985).
Maclean, Una, Magical Medicine : A Nigerian Case Study (London : Allen Lane, The Penguin Press 1971).
Mbillah, Johnson Apenad, Islam and Culture with Special reference to the role of the Mallamai of Northern Ghana (M. Phil Thesis University of Birmingham, Dept of Theology 1990)
McGilvary, James, The Quest for Healing and Wholeness (Tubingen: German Institute for Medical missions, 1981).
Maier, D.J.E., Priest and Power: The case of the Dente Shrine in the nineteenth century Ghana (Bloomington: Indiana University Press, 1983).
Malinowski, B., "Introduction Essay : The Anthropology of changing African

cultures" in Methods of Study of Culture Contact in Africa with an introductory essay by B. Malinowski, (Oxford : Oxford University Press for International African Inst. 1965).
Malinowski, B., Sex, Culture and Myth, (London : Hart Davies 1963).
Malinowski, B., Magic, Science and Religion and Other Essays (London : Souvenir Press1974 Edition).
Martin, Soskice Janet. Metaphor and Religious Language (Oxford: Clarendon Press, 1989).
Marty, Marty E., and Vaux, Kenneth L., (eds), Health/Medicine and the Faith Tradition : An inquiry into religion and medicine (Philadelphia : Fortress Press, 1982).
Mbiti, John S., " The Encounter of Christianity and African Religion" in Dean William Ferm Third World Liberation Theologies : A reader (Maryknoll, New York : Orbis Books 1986).
Mbiti, John S., Concepts of God in Africa (London : SPCK 1970).
Mbiti, John S. New Testament Eschatology in an African background: A Study of the Encounter between New Testament Theology and African Traditional Concepts (London: Oxford University Press, 1971).
Mbiti, John S., "Christianity and African Culture" in Journal of Southern Africa Theology Vol. 20 (1977).
Mbiti, John S., Bible and Theology in African Christianity (Nairobi: Oxford University Press, 1986).
Mendonsa, Eugene L., The Politics of Divination (Berkeley: University of California, 1982).
Mensah-Dappa, W.S., "Observations on Traditional Healing Methods in Ghana" in Z.A. Ademuwagun et al (eds) African Therapeutic Systems (Massachusetts: Crossraods, 1979).
Metuh, Emefie Ikenga, God and Man in African Religion (London:Geoffrey Chapman, 1981).
Middleton, John, (ed), Myth and Cosmos: Readings in Mythology and Symbolism (Austin: University of Texas Press, 1967).
Milingo, E., The World in between : Christian healing and the struggle for spiritual survival (London : Hurst & Co. 1984).
Monter, W., Ritual, Myth and Magic in Early Modern Europe (Brighton, Sussex : The Harvester Press 1983).

Morris, Brian, Anthropological Studies of Religion: An Introductory Text (Cambridge: Cambridge University Press, Reprinted 1988).
Mphahlele, E., The Wanderer (New York : Macmillan, 1976).
Mpolo, Ma Masamba., and Kalu, Wilmeim, (eds), The Risk of Growth, Pastoral Counselling in Context (Geneva : WCC 1985).
Mudge, Lewis S., and Poling, James N., (eds), The Promise of Practical Theology: Formation and Reflection (Philadelphia: Fortress Press, 1987).
Mullings, Leith, "Religious change and social stratification in Labadi, Ghana, the Church of the Messiah" in George Bond, Walton Johnston and Sheil S. Walker (eds) African Christianity : Patterns of Religious Continuity (New York : Academic Press 1979).
Mullings, Leith, Therapy, ideology and social change: Mental healing in Ghana (Berkeley: University of California Press, 1984).
Nabilah, John Sebiyan, The Migration of the Frafra of Northern Ghana A Case study of Cyclical Labour Migration in West Africa (Unpublished Ph.D. of Michigan State University, 1974)
Nadel, S. F., "A study of shamanism in Nuba Mountain" in Lessa L. William and Vogt Z. Evon (eds), Reader in Comparative Religion : An Anthropological Approach (New York : Harper & Row 1965) p.18-29.
Nadel, S. F., "Witchcraft in four African societies : An essay in comparisons in American Anthropologist, Vol. 54, 1952.
Ngubane, Harriet, Body and Mind in Zulu Medicine (London :Academic Press 1977).
Nickels, A., " The Offertory Processions" in The Ghana Bulletin Theology Dec, 1979, vol.3 no. 7.
Nida, Eugene A., Message and Mission (New York : Harper & Row. (Reprinted 1972 by Wm Carey Library, South Pasadena).
Nida, Eugene A., God's Word in Man's Language (New York: William Carey Library, Harper and Row Pub. Inc., 1973).
Nida, Eugene A., Componential Analysis of Meaning (The Hague: Mouton, 1975).
Nida, Eugene A., Signs, Sense Translation (Cape Town: Bible Societies of South Africa, 1984).
Nida, Eugene A., and Taber, Charles R., The Theory and Practice of Translation, (published for the United Bible Societies by E.J.Brill, Leiden,

1974).
Niebuhr, Richard H., Christ and Culture (New York : Harper & Row. Publisher 1951).
Nkrumah, Kwame, Dark days in Ghana (New York : International Publishers 1968).
Nkwetia, J. H. Kwabena, "Prayers at Kple Worship Part I" in The Ghana Bulletin of Theology Vol.2 No.4 June 1963, 19-29.
Nkwetia, J. H., "Prayers at Kple Worship Part II" in The Ghana Bulletin of Theology Vol.2 No.5 Dec 1963.
Nolan, Albert, Jesus before Christianity : The Gospel of liberation (London : Darton, Lonscmar and Todd 1976).
Northcott, Michael, How to Start a Dissertation A guide for Practical theology, Christian Ethics Dept. (unpublished)
Nothcott, Michael, Research Methods in Practical Theology : The Vocation of Research in Practical Theology. A manual of research for students of practical theology and Christian Ethics Dept. (unpublished)
Nothcott, Michael, "New Age Rites : The Recovery of Ritual" in The Way vol. 33, No. 3, 1993.
Numbers, R. L., and Amundsen, D. W., (eds), Caring and Curing : Health and Medicine in the Western Religion Traditons. (London : MacMillan Publishing Co. 1986).
Nyamiti, Charles, Christ As our Ancestor (Gweru, Zimbabwe: Mambo Press 1984)
Nyamiti, Charles, "Christ's Ministry in the light of African tribal initiation Ritual" in African Christian Srudies Vol.3 No. 1. March 1987.
Nyamiti, Charles, "The Initiatic Aspect of th4e Church: An Essay on Africa Ecclesiology" in African Christian Studies, June 1987, Vol.3 No.2.
Nygren, A., Meaning and Method : Prolegomena to a Scientific Philosophy of Religion and a Scientific Theology translated By Philip S. Watson (London : Epworth Press 1972).
Obechina, E., Culture, tradition and society in the West African novel (Cambridge : Cambridge University Press 1975).
Odudyoye, Mercy amba, Hearing and Knowing: Theological Reflections on Christianity in Africa (Maryknoll, New York: Orbis Books, 1986).
Odudyoye, Mercy Amba, "The Value of African Religious Beliefs and

Practices for Christian Theology" in Dean William Ferm Third World Liberation Theologies : A reader (Mryknoll, New York : Orbis Books 1986)
Official Records of the WHO No.299 Geneva 1976.
Okorocha, Cyril C., The Meaning of Religious Conversion in Africa (Aldershot: Gower Publishing Co. Ltd, 1987).
Ollennu, Nii Ama, "How Society looks at the Churches ministry of Healing" in The Ghana Bulletin of Theology Vol.3 No.2 June 1967.
Olney, J., Tell me Africa : An approach to African literature (Princeton : Princeton University 1973).
ong, W.J., Oraility and Literacy : The Technologizing of the the Word (London : Methuen 1982).
Opoku, Kofi A., "Traditional religious beliefs and the spiritual Churches in Ghana : A preliminary statement" Research Review, Legon, 1968, Vol.5,
Opoku, Kofi A., "The University Prayer Group" Impae bokow" The call of the Prophet in Research Review, Legon, 1967. Vol. 5,
Opoku, K. A., "Changes with Christian: the Case of the Musama Disco Christo Church" in Fashole-Luke et al Christianity in independent African (1978).
Otoo, S., "The Actual Need for Christian Healing Ministry in Ghana" In The Ghana Bulletin of Theology June 1967, Vol.3 No.2.
Otoo, s., "Teaching the Healing Ministry in Medical training Programme" in The Ghana Bulletin of Theology Dec 1967, Vol.3 No.3.
Ouoleguem, Y., The Bond to Violence trans. Ralph Manheim (New York : Harcourt Brace Jovanovich 1971).
Parratt, John, Papuan Belief and Ritual (New York: Vantage Press, 1976).
Parratt, John, (ed), A Reader in African Christian Theology (London: SPCK, 1987).
Parrinder, Geoffrey, West African Religion (London : Epworth Press 1949).
Parson, Talcott, Social Structure and Personality (New York : Free Press : Cooier-MacMillan Ltd. 1970).
Peel, J. D. Y., Aladura : A religious movement among the Yoruba (London : Oxford University Press, 1968).
Penoukou, E. J., "Realite africiane et salut en Jesus Christ" in Spiritus No.88, Dec 1982, Vol.23.
Pobee, John S., "Contextuality and University in Theological Education" in

John S. Pobee and Carl H. Hallencreutz (ed) Variations in Christian Theology in Africa (Nairobi: Un=zima Press, 1986).

Pobee, John, "Why are we Here? and Quo Vadimus?" in Ministerial Formation Spet 1986, Vol. 35.

Price-Willaims, R., "A Case Study of Ideas Concering disease among the Tiv" in Z.A. Ademuwagun et al (eds), African Therapeutic Systems (Massachusetts: Crossraods, 1979).

Produfoot, W., Religious Experience (Berkeley : University of California Press 1985)

Radcliffe, Timothy, "Relativizing the relativizers : A theological assessment of the role of sociological explanation of religious phenomena and theology today in David Martin, John B. Mills and W.S.F. Pickering (eds), Sociology and Theology : Alliance and conflict (Brighton, Sussex : The Harvester Press, 1980).

Rattray, R. S., Religion and Art among the Ashanti (London : Oxford University Press 1927, rep. 1969).

Rattray, R. S., The Tribes of the Ashanti Hinterland with a chapter by Professor D. Westermenn Vol. 1 and Vol. 2.

Riesman, D., The Lonely Crowd (London, 1964).

Roston, Holmes III, Religious Inquiry Participation and Detachment (New York: Philosophical Library, 1985).

Ruel, Malcolm, "Non-sacrificial ritual killing" in Man 1990, Vol.25.

Sanneh, Laminah, Translating the Message : The Missionary Impact on Culture (Mary Knoll, NY, Orbis Books 1991).

Sanneh, Laminah, " Reciprocal Influences : African Traditional Religions and Christianity" in Dean William Ferm Third World Liberation Theologies : A reader (Mryknoll, New York : Orbis Books 1986).

Sarpong, Peter, The Sacred Tools of the Akan (Tema: Ghana Pub. Co., 1971).

Sarpong, Peter, "Spiritual Formation and Theological Education: and African Perspective" in Ministerial Formation Vol. 46, July 1989.

Sawyer, Harry, God : Ancestor or Creator? : Aspects of Traditional Belief in Ghana, Nigeria and Sierra Leone (London : Longman Group Ltd. 1970).

Scharfenberg, Joachim, Sigmund Freud and His Critique of religion translated by O.C. Dean Jr. (Philadelphia: Fortress Press, 1988).

Schlater, W., Geschichte der Basler Mission 1815- 1915, 3 Vols. (Basel,

1916).
Schelgel, J. B., Schlussel zur Ewe Sprache (Bremen, 1857).
Schmidt, W., The Origin and Growth of Religion: Facts and Theories translated by H.J.Rose (London: Methuen and Co.Ltd, 1931).
Schreiber, A. W., Bausteine Zur Geschichte der Norddentschen Missionsgellschaft (Bremen: Norddentshen Missions-Gellschaft, 1936).
Schreiter, Robert, "Culture, Society and Contextual Theologies" Missiology 1984, XII.
Schreiter, Robert, L., (ed.), Faces of Jesus in Africa (Mary Knoll, New York : Orbis Books. 1991).
Segal, Robert A., Religion and the Social Sciences: Essays on the Confrontation (Atlanta, Georgia: Scholars Press, 1989).
Segundo, Juan Luis, Our idea of God : A theology for a New Humanity (1980 : Gill & Macmillan Ltd).
Segundo, Juan Luis, The Liberation of Theology (Mary Knoll, New York: Orbis Books, 1976).
Shaughnessy, James, D., The Root of Ritual (Grand Rapids: Erdmans, 1973).
Shinne, P.L., and Ozanne, P.C., "Excavations at Yendi Dabari" in Transactions of the Historical Society of Ghana 1962, Vol.VI, 87-118.
Shorter, Aylward, African Culture and the Christian Church (Mary Knoll, New York: Orbis Books, 1974).
Shorter, Aylward, Prayer in the Religious Traditions of Africa (Nairobi: Oxford University Press, 1975).
Shoter, Aylward, African Christian Theology (Mary Knoll, N.Y. :Orbis Books 1977).
Shoter, Aylward, Jesus the Witch Doctor: An Approach to Healing and Wholeness (Maryknoll, N. Y. : Orbis Books 1985).
Shoter Alyward, "Christian Healing and Traditional Medicine" in Africa Kergyma 1986, Vol.20.
Sintim, Misa G.K., "Healing the Sick and Preaching Salvation" in The Ghana Bulletin of Theology June 1967, Vol.3 No.2.
Smart, Ninian, Concepts of Empathy: Essays in the Study of Religion edited by Donald Wiebe (London: The MacMillan Press, 1986).
Smith, Noel, The Presbyterian Church of Ghana 1835-1960 (Accra: Ghana University Press, 1966)

Smith, Robertson, W., Lectures on the Religions of the Semites (London: Adam and Charles Black, 1927).

Song, Choan-Sing, Christian Mission in reconstruction An Asian Attempt (Madras : The Christian Literature Society, 1975).

Spradley, J., Participant Observation (New York: Rinehart & Winston , 1979)

Spradley, J., The Ethnograpic Interview (New York : Holt, Rinehart & Winston 1979)

Stadelmann, Lusi, I. J., The Hebrew conception of the world (Romeo: Pontifical Institute 1970) Strenski, Ivan, Four Theories of Myth in Twenthieth-century History: Cassirer, Eliade, Levi-Strauss and Malinowski (London: The MacMillan Press Ltd Reprinted 1989).

Sundkler, Bengt, "Worship and Spirituality" in Fashiole-Luke et al Christianity in Independent Africa (Bloomington: Indiana University Press, 1978).

Sundkler, Bengt, The Christian Ministry in Africa (London : SCM Press Ltd. 1960).

Tait, David. The kokomba of Ghana (Oxford: Oxford University Press, 1961).

Taylor, John, V., The Primal Vision (London : SCM Press 1963).

Thiongo, Ngugi, Decolonising the mind : Politics of Language in African Literature. (Nairobi: Heinemann 1991).

Thiongo, Ngugi Wa. Homecoming : Essays on African and Caribbean Literature, Culture and Politics (London : Heinemann).

Tooth, G., Studies in Mental IIlness in the Gold Coast (Ghana), (London : His Majesty's Stationary Office, 1950).

Tracy, David, Blessed rage for Order: The New Pluralism (New York: Seabury Press, 1975)

Tracy, David. "Practical Theology in Pluralism in the Situation of Global Pluralism" in Lewis S. Mudge & James N. Polling (eds), The Promise of Practical Theology : Formation and Religion (Philadelphia : Fortress Press 1987).

Turner, Bryn, S., The Body and Society (London: Basil Blackwell, 1984).

Turner, Harold, W., African Independent Church (Oxford : Oford University Press 1967).

Turner, Victor, Ndembu Divination (Manchester : Manchester University Press 1961)

Turner, Victor, W., Schism & Continuity in Africa Society : A Study of Ndembu Village Life (Manchester University Press 1957)

Turner, Victor, W., The Drums of Affliction (Oxford : Clarendon Press 1968)

Turner, Victor, W., The Forest of symbols : Aspects of Ndembu Ritual (Ithaca : Cornel University Press 1967

Turner, Victor, W., The Ritual Process : Structure and Anti- Structure (Chicago University Press 1969)

Turner, Victor, W., "Ritual Symbolism, Morality and Social Structure among Ndembu", Meyer Fortes and G. Dietarien (eds), African Systems and Thought (London : Oxford university Press 1965.

Tutu, Desmond, "Whither African Theology" in Fashole-Luke et al Christianity in Independent Africa (Bloomington: Indiana University Press, 1978).

Twumasi, Patrick, A., Medical Systems in Ghana : A Study of Medical Sociology (Tema: Ghana Publishing Corporation 1975).

Twumasi, Patrick, A., "Ashanti Traditional Medicine and its relations to Present-day Psychiatry" in Z.A. Ademuwagun et al (eds), African Therapeutic Systems (Massachusetts: Crossroads, 1979).

Tylor, E. B., Primitive Culture (London : Murray 1891).

Tylor, E. B., Theories of Primitive religion (oxford: Oxford University Press/Clarendon Press, 1965).

Ukpong, Justins., "Contextualizating Theological Education in Western Africa: Focus on Subjects" in Africa Christian Studies Sept 1987, Vol.3 No.3.

Van de Castle, R. L., "Parapsychology and Anthropology" relying on R.G. Trilles Les pygmes de la foret equatorials Paris (1932) in Benjamin B. Wolman (ed). Hand Book of Parapsychology (1977).

Warren, Dennis, M., "The Interpretation of Change in a Ghanaian Ethnomedical study" in Z.A. Ademuwagun et al (eds), African Therapeutic Systems (Massachusetts: Crossroads, 1979) 247-250.

Warren, Dennis, M., "The role of Emic Analyses in medical Anthropology: the Case of the Bono of Ghana" in Z.A.Ademuwagun et al (eds), African Therapeutic Systems (Massachusetts: Crossroads, 1979).

Warren, Dennis, M., "Bono Traditional Healers" in Z.A.Ademuwagun (eds),

African Therapeutic Systems (Massachusetts: Crossroads, 1979).
Weber, Max, The Sociology of Religion translated by Ephraim Fischoff. Introduction by Talcott Parsons. (London: Methuen and Co. Ltd, 1965).
Westerman, Claus, Creation Translated by John J. Scullion (London: SPCK 1971)
Williamson, S. G., The Akan Religion and the Christian faith (Accra: Ghana University Press, 1965).
Wilson, B. R., Religious Sects (London Weidenffeld and Nicholson 1970).
Wilson, Monica, Religion and the Transformation of Society (Cambridge : Cambridge University Press 1971).
Wilson, Monica, "Cooperation and Conflictive Eastern Cape Frontier" in M Wilson and Leonard Thompson (eds), South Africa to 1970 Vol. 1 of the Oxford History of South Africa Series (Oxford : Clarendon Press 1969).
Wingern, G., Theology in Conflict Nygren,: Barth, Bultmann, translated by Eric H. Wahlstrom (Edinburgh : Tweedale Court 1958).
Wink, Walter, Naming the Powers: the Language of Power in the New Testament (Philadelphia: Fortress, 1986 2nd edition).
Winnicott, D. M., Collected Papers (London : Tavistock, Pub. 1958).
Winnicott, D. W., Playing and Reality (London: Routledge 1989).
Wolff, Hanna, Jesus the Therapist. Forward by John A. Sanford. Translated by Robert A. Barr (Oak Park, IIlinois: Meyer- Stones Books, 1987).
Wolman, B. B., (ed), Handbook of Parapsychology, Jefferson, North Carolina : McFarland and Co. Inc. Publisher (1977).
Worsley, Peter, "Non-Western Medical Systens" in Annual Review Anthropology Vol.2, 1982..
Wyllie, Robert, W., Spiritism in Ghana : A study of new religious Movements AAR Studies in religion 21 (Misoula, Montana :Scholar press 1980).
Yawkey, Thomas, D., and Pellegrini, Child's Play: developmental and Applied (London: Lawrence Erlbaum Associates, Publishers, 1984).
Zuesse, E. M., Ritual Cosmos : The Sanctification of Life in African Religions (Athens : Ohio University Press 198

Religionsethnologie

Abraham Berinyuu
Healing Rituals as Theological Drama
Insights from Kaaba Healing Rituals Among the Frafra in Ghana
Bd. 1, Herbst 2007, ca. 232 S., ca. 24,90 €, br., ISBN 978-3-8258-9940-0

Wissenschaftliche Paperbacks
Ethnologie

Michael J. Rainer (Red.)
"Dominus Iesus" – Anstößige Wahrheit oder anstößige Kirche?
Dokumente, Hintergründe, Standpunkte und Folgerungen
Die römische Erklärung "Dominus Iesus" berührt den Nerv der aktuellen Diskussion über den Stellenwert der Religionen in der heutigen Gesellschaft. Angesichts der Pluralität der Bekenntnisse soll der Anspruch der Wahrheit festgehalten werden. Mit Beiträgen von Hans-Martin Barth, Ingolf U. Dalferth, Albert Franz, Ottmar Fuchs, Hermann Häring, Bernd Jochen Hilberath, Helmut Hoping, Wolfgang Huber, Peter Hünermann, Maria Jepsen, Eberhard Jüngel, Hans Küng, Karl Lehmann, Robert Leicht, John D'Arcy May, Peter Neuner, Konrad Raiser, Joseph Ratzinger, Johann Reikerstorfer, Theodor Schneider, Clemens Thoma, Jürgen Werbick, Siegfried Wiedenhofer u. a.
Bd. 9, 2. Aufl. 2001, 350 S., 20,90 €, br., ISBN 3-8258-5203-2

Rainer Bendel (Hg.)
Die katholische Schuld?
Katholizismus im Dritten Reich zwischen Arrangement und Widerstand
Die Frage nach der „Katholischen Schuld" ist spätestens seit Hochhuths „Stellvertreter" ein öffentliches Thema. Nun wird es von Goldhagen neu aufgeworfen, aufgeworfen als moralische Frage – ohne fundierte Antwort. Wer sich über den Zusammenhang von Katholizismus und Nationalsozialismus fundiert informieren will, wird zu diesem Band greifen müssen: mit Beiträgen u. a. von Gerhard Besier, E. W. Böckenförde, Heinz Hürten, Joachim Köhler, Johann Baptist Metz, Rudolf Morsey, Ludwig Volk, Ottmar Fuchs und Stephan Leimgruber.
Bd. 14, 2., durchges. Aufl. 2004, 400 S., 19,90 €, br., ISBN 3-8258-6334-4

Wissenschaft aktuell
Ethnologie

Hans-Georg Ziebertz (Hg.)
Erosion des christlichen Glaubens?
Umfragen, Hintergründe und Stellungnahmen zum „Kulturverlust des Religiösen"
In regelmäßigen Abständen bringen die Medien Schlagzeilen über die Erosion des christlichen Glaubens, der Religion insgesamt. Woher stammen die Prognosen? Was messen die Studien wirklich? Was lassen sie außer Acht? Neben der kritischen Sichtung liefern die Autoren ein differenziertes Bild und fragen: Welche Konsequenzen ergeben sich für Theologie, Kirche und Gesellschaft?
Bd. 4, 2004, 152 S., 14,90 €, br., ISBN 3-8258-7092-8

Detlev Dormeyer, Friedhelm Munzel (Hg.)
Faszination „Harry Potter": Was steckt dahinter?
Harry Potter wird von unzähligen Menschen leidenschaftlich verschlungen und umjubelt, von manchen dagegen verschmäht und lieber verbrannt als gelesen. Viele finden ihn von seinem Werteangebot her banal und akzeptieren ihn allenfalls als Lesespaß, andere entdecken in ihm Tiefendimensionen und stufen ihn als religiöse, ja christliche Literatur ein. Wie immer die Einstellung dazu ist, es lohnt sich, dieses populärkulturelle Phänomen genauer zu betrachten. Die Beiträge des Buches stammen aus der Fakultät Human-

wissenschaften und Theologie der Universität Dortmund und von Linus Hauser, Gießen.
Bd. 5, 2005, 128 S., 14,90 €, br., ISBN 3-8258-7644-6

Kölner ethnologische Studien

hrsg. von Prof. Dr. Ulla Johansen und Prof. Dr. Martin Rössler

Michael Bollig
Die Krieger der gelben Gewehre
Intra- und interethnische Konfliktaustragung bei den Pokot Nordwestkenias
Bd. 20, 1992, 400 S., 35,90 €, br., ISBN 3-89473-364-0

Barbara Jacobs
Kleidung als Symbol
Das Beispiel der Altgläubigen Südsibiriens im 19. und beginnenden 20. Jahrhundert
Bd. 21, 1993, 220 S., 24,90 €, br., ISBN 3-89473-571-6

Susanne Knödel
Die matrilinearen Mosuo von Yongning
Eine quellenkritische Auswertung moderner chinesischer Ethnographien
Die matrilinearen Mosuo, eine tibetobirmanische Ethnie Südwestchinas, haben eine außergewöhnliche Form der sozialen Organisation. Formelle Ehen sind bei ihnen zwar bekannt, aber selten. Die sozial erwünschte Form der Mann-Frau-Bindung ist die "Azhu-Beziehung", die ohne Mitwirken Dritter aufgenommen und beendet wird. Der Mann besucht die Frau nur über Nacht, beide bleiben Vollmitglieder ihres mütterlichen Haushalts. Kinder aus einer solchen Beziehung gehören ausschließlich der Mutterseite an. Trotz großen Drucks von Seiten der kommunistischen Partei haben die Mosuo ihre Lebensform auch nach Gründung der Volksrepublik bewahrt. Die vorliegende Arbeit beschreibt die sozialen Institutionen der Mosuo sowie das wirtschaftliche und ethnische Umfeld, in dem ihre Gesellschaft sich befindet.
Bd. 22, 1995, 370 S., 30,90 €, br., ISBN 3-89473-805-7

Castulus Kolo
Computersimulationen als Instrument der Prozeßanalyse in der Ethnologie
In fast allen wirtschaftlichen Disziplinen werden heute zunehmend Computersimulationen zur Untersuchung komplexer Prozesse eingesetzt; insbesondere dann, wenn deren Ablauf nicht auf experimentelle Weise erfaßt werden kann. Auch für den Forschungsgegenstand der Ethnologie legen verschiedene Aspekte der Komplexität, wie etwa die starke Vernetzung kultureller, demographischer und ökologischer Zusammenhänge sowie die Vielzahl möglicher Entwicklungspfade, ein Nachdenken über neue Hilfsmittel des Prozeßverstehens nahe. Neben einer allgemeinen Einführung in die Methodik und Terminologie von Computersimulationen werden anhand konkreter Anwendungsbeispiele die fachspezifischen Möglichkeiten bzw. Grenzen diskutiert. Auch dem mathematischen Laien werden dabei Kriterien vermittelt, um den eigenen Einsatz von Simulationsmodellen planen bzw. die Ergebnisse fremder Simulationsstudien besser beurteilen zu können.
Bd. 23, 1997, 232 S., 24,90 €, br., ISBN 3-8258-3321-6

Susanne Spülbeck
Biographie-Forschung in der Ethnologie
Im Mittelpunkt der ethnologischen Methode steht die Begegnung zwischen einem Ethnologen und seinem Gegenüber, dessen Lebenswelt es zu verstehen gilt. Nicht zuletzt deshalb hört der Ethnologe immer wieder biographische Erzählungen, zeichnet sie auf und kann im Forschungsprozeß häufig noch nicht genau absehen, welche Rolle sie in der Auswertung spielen werden. Genau hier setzt der vorliegende Überblick an: wie kann biographisches Material interpretiert werden, um etwas über soziale Prozesse zu sagen? Welche Rolle spielen die Entstehungsbedingungen

der biographischen Erzählung dabei? Wie kann ein biographischer Text sinnvoll in einer ethnologischen Studie dargestellt werden? Dabei geht es vor allem um das Verhältnis von biographischer Erzählung, ethnologischer Begegnung und Wirklichkeit.

Bd. 25, 1998, 176 S., 12,90 €, br.,
ISBN 3-8258-3401-8

Christoph Brumann
Die Kunst des Teilens
Eine vergleichende Untersuchung zu den Überlebensbedingungen kommunitärer Gruppen

Kommunitäre Gruppen – Gemeinschaften, die freiwillig alles gemeinsam haben – treiben das Teilen ins Extrem. Wie alle Formen der Kooperation, in denen Zwang (Staat) und individuelle materielle Anreize (Markt) ausgeschlossen sind, macht sie dies anfällig für den Egoismus ihrer Mitglieder. Die meisten dieser Experimente scheitern denn auch schnell, doch einige blühen über Jahrzehnte oder gar Jahrhunderte und unternehmen mutige, oft utopische kulturelle Experimente. Anhand eines Vergleichs von 43 Gruppen aus den letzten drei Jahrhunderten – darunter so bekannte wie die Hutterer, die Kibbutzim, Oneidea, die Shakers und die Bruderhof-Gemeinschaften – klärt Christoph Brumann die Gründe für die seltenen Erfolge. In Bereichen wie Größe, Zweigstrukturen, Ehe und Familie, charismatischer Führung und Überzeugung entdeckt er überlebensförderliche und -hemmende Bedingungen, die er in integrierten Modellen zusammenfaßt. Statt der in Kulturvergleichen sonst üblichen statistischen Verfahren nutzt er dazu intensive Fallanalysen und die Möglichkeiten der Implikationslogik. Es zeigt sich, daß es eine Reihe von Gesetzmäßigkeiten gibt, die sich unabhängig von den offiziellen Überzeugungen der Gruppen auswirken, mitunter ohne diesen überhaupt bewußt zu sein. Diese Studie ist ein Plädoyer für die empirisch orientierte, vergleichende Erforschung von Kooperation. Oft scheitert Kooperation nicht am mangelnden Idealismus, sondern am falschen Design. Wer Menschen dazu bringen möchte, zu teilen – ob nun Güter, Arbeitsplätze oder Aufmerksamkeit –, sollte daher die bereits gemachten Erfahrungen nicht ignorieren. Kultur- und Sozialwissenschaftler aller Disziplinen sind mit diesem Thema angesprochen. Umschlagphoto: Die Mitglieder der amerikanischen Kommune Twin Oaks (mit freundlicher Genehmigung von Jonathan Roth)

Bd. 26, 1998, 368 S., 30,90 €, br.,
ISBN 3-8258-3732-7

Julia Pauli
Das geplante Kind
Demographischer, wirtschaftlicher und sozialer Wandel in einer mexikanischen Gemeinde

Demographische Phänomene werden heute zunehmend in der Ethnologie in ihrer elementaren Bedeutung für die Erklärung kulturellen Wandels berücksichtigt. Die Studie untersucht den Zusammenhang von demographischen, wirtschaftlichen und sozialen Transformationen am Beispiel einer ländlichen Gemeinde in Zentralmexiko. Der Rückgang der Sterbeziffern und der Geburtenziffern sowie eine starke Zunahme der nationalen und internationalen Migration haben die Familie, die Haushaltsstruktur und die Haushaltsökonomie grundlegend verändert. Durch die Analyse qualitativer und quantitativer Daten gleichermaßen gelingt es der Autorin, eine Typologie der unterschiedlichen, sehr heterogenen, Lebensstrategien zu entwickeln, die in den letzten 50 Jahren in der Gemeinde entstanden sind.

Bd. 27, 2001, 392 S., 35,90 €, br.,
ISBN 3-8258-5120-6